Faulkner and
Yoknapatawpha
Conference 2003 :
University of
Mississippi)
 Faulkner and the
ecology of the South

Faulkner and the Ecology of the South

FAULKNER AND YOKNAPATAWPHA,
2003

Faulkner and the Ecology of the South

FAULKNER AND YOKNAPATAWPHA, 2003

EDITED BY
JOSEPH R. URGO
AND
ANN J. ABADIE

UNIVERSITY PRESS OF MISSISSIPPI
JACKSON

www.upress.state.ms.us

The University Press of Mississippi is a member of the Association of
American University Presses

First edition 2005

∞

Library of Congress Cataloging-in-Publication Data

Faulkner and Yoknapatawpha Conference (30th : 2003 : University of Mississippi)
    Faulkner and the ecology of the South / Faulkner and Yoknapatawpha, 2003;
edited by Joseph R. Urgo and Ann J. Abadie.
      v. cm.
    Includes bibliographical references and index.
    Contents: "Old man" : shackles, chains, and water water everywhere / Cecelia
Tichi—The land's turn / Philip Weinstein—Environed blood : ecology and violence
in The sound and the fury and Sanctuary / Eric Gary Anderson—William Faulkner,
Peter Matthiessen, and the environmental imagination / Ann Fisher-Wirth—The
enemy within : Faulkner's Snopes trilogy / Michael Wainwright—Is Faulkner
green? the wilderness as aporia / François Pitavy—The ecology of Uncle Ike :
teaching Go down, Moses with Janisse Ray's Ecology of a cracker childhood /
Thomas L. McHaney—Visceral Faulkner : fiction and the tug of the organic world /
Scott Slovic—McCrady's La-fay-ette County / Jeanne de la Houssaye—Collecting
Faulkner / Seth Berner.
    ISBN 1-57806-782-0 (cloth : alk. paper)
    1. Faulkner, William, 1897–1962—Knowledge—Southern States—Congresses.
2. Faulkner, William, 1897–1962—Knowledge—Natural history—Congresses.
3. Yoknapatawpha County (Imaginary place)—Congresses. 4. Southern States—In
literature—Congresses. 5. Human ecology—Southern States—Congresses.
6. Human ecology in literature—Congresses. 7. Nature in literature—Congresses.
I. Urgo, Joseph R. II. Abadie, Ann J. III. Title.
    PS3511.A86Z78321175   2005
    813'.52—dc22   2005002380

British Library Cataloging-in-Publication Data available

In Memoriam,
Murry Cuthbert "Chooky" Falkner II
November 22, 1928–April 23, 2004

Contents

Introduction

It was the way he dried out—he took it out on bitterweeds. I think he had an obsession about bitterweeds—he always kept a hoe or two leaning against the side of the house, and when he had a hangover, or when things weren't going well with his writing, he'd go out into the pasture and attack them.

—*Malcolm Franklin*
Bitterweeds: Life with William Faulkner at Rowan Oak

I'm interested primarily in people, in man in conflict with himself, with his fellow man, or with his time and place, his environment.
—*William Faulkner, 1957*

1

By ecology we do not exclude the natural world, though what we have in mind is more akin to the idea of a human ecology, the interaction of humans with their environment—made and found, communities as well as habitats. While Faulkner would often discount the importance or the centrality of the South because it was simply what he knew best, the fact remains that he did know it and the way he knew it is inextricable from the world he imagined in his fiction. To the terminologically weary, the nominative, ecocriticism, may be no more than theoretical dressing on what we've always known as setting, time and place, or environment. However, the recent school of criticism which calls itself ecocriticism (and which has an association and a journal[1]) has led to a renewed interest among literary scholars for what in this volume Cecelia Tichi calls "humanness within congeries of habitats and environments." Faulkner scholars, such as Philip Weinstein, locate within Yoknapatawpha County "a precarious ecosystem" which may be illuminated in fresh ways through the application of ecocritical theory. The essays collected in *Faulkner and the Ecological South* probe Faulkner's environmental imagination, seeking what Ann Fisher-Wirth calls the "ecological countermelody" of his texts.

The term *environment* seems to have held deep meaning for Faulkner; at least, that is, it was a word he relied on in public. Among the more resonant formulations upon which Faulkner relied while writer in residence at the University of Virginia in the late 1950s was his statement of primary interest in "man in conflict with himself, with his fellow man, or with his time and place, his environment."[2] Faulkner may have acquired the phrase, a common dramatic trope, during his experience in the theatre in the 1950s, collaborating on stage productions of *Requiem for a Nun*. He repeated the statement often, with variations such as "man in conflict with his heart, or with his fellows, or with his environment" (59) and "man in his constant struggle with his own heart, with the hearts of others, or with his environment" (239). The statement served Faulkner well in successive classroom meetings and interviews. It is both an intriguingly succinct encapsulation of an aesthetic, and it is remarkably applicable to nearly everything Faulkner wrote. Apparent universality may well be the function of a sweeping generalization, of course, but a close reading of Faulkner's deployment of the statement suggests a more precise significance. At the same time, the formulation served equally well as a kind of fallback response to questions that otherwise would demand far greater exposition. When asked about the function of the race horse segment in *A Fable*, for example, Faulkner responded, "That was simply another struggle between man and his conscience and his environment" (63). Nonetheless, the formula would come to Faulkner's mind as a response to specific questions about form and structure in his work. Upon close examination, the trope takes on a consistent significance revealing an attitude which we might call the human ecological structure of Faulkner's imagination.

Conflict within the self and with others is self-evident in Faulkner because it is clear who occupies these thematic positions of protagonist and antagonist. Exactly what Faulkner meant by environment is less transparent, but discernable. In Japan in 1955, Faulkner gave the idea its fullest treatment, and elaborated in relatively extended detail on what he meant by environment:

> As I see it, the writer has imagined a story of human beings that was so moving, so important to him, that he wants to make a record of it for his own satisfaction or, perhaps, for others to read, that story is a very old story, it's the story of human beings in conflict with their nature, their character, their souls, with others, or with their environment. He's got to tell that story in the only terms he knows, the familiar terms, which would be colored, shaped, by his environment. He's not really writing about his environment, he's simply telling a story about human beings in the terms of environment. . . . The novelist is talking about people, about man in conflict with himself, his fellows, or his environment.[3]

As was often the case in interviews, Faulkner would explain an idea only so much before escaping from the talking by reverting to a formulation. The *environment* Faulkner seems most concerned with is not the ecological one of the natural world, but the social ecology, situations of race and class and gender, as we might characterize these matters today.

The 1950s interviews and public statements reveal that Faulkner possessed a philosophical sensibility which may be understood as Platonic: there exists an eternal world of universal stories, accessible through the imagination (Faulkner would say, the *spirit*), and these ideal forms take shape momentarily in the local, or materially real experience (Faulkner would say the *avatars*) of individual human beings—for this phenomenon Faulkner used the term *environment*. When the writer first imagines the story, his mind is filled with a kind of ideal, perfect narrative. It may be "a very old story" and it may be an eternal story of human conflict. To make the story intelligible and recognizable to other minds, the writer must "tell that story in the only terms he knows, the familiar terms, which would be colored, shaped, by his environment." In much the same way, the Platonic ideal of Justice is told in local, familiar terms in the courts; the ideal of the Good is revealed in human benevolent relations; the ideal of Beauty is approached through aesthetic norms. Once we recognize the source of Faulkner's thought process, we can see the perfectly logical explanation contained in the claim that the writer is "not really writing about his environment, he's simply telling a story about human beings in the terms of environment."

Significantly, in Faulkner's mind the artist's ecology extended to and embraced the critic and the reader as well. "The writer has got to write in terms of his environment," he explained at the University of Virginia, "and his environment consists not only in the immediate scene, but his readers are part of that environment too" (41). Through the texts, the reader enters and participates in an ecosystem which includes Faulkner's work, his materials, and his imagination. The conception that the reader occupies a formal position in such a network of interdependence may account for the demands on readers characteristic of Faulkner's writing, demands which never abated, and for which he never seemed especially concerned. Generations of readers for whom an initial taking up of Faulkner means disorientation, confusion, and the feeling of "not getting it" may well be experiencing a carefully crafted intellectual experience, as if standing on the borders of a self-sustaining ecosystem that demands more than passive consumption if it is to allow one to gain entrance and place.

The formula, then, assumes an almost all-purpose applicability. When asked whether his writing was based in, or motivated by, revolt, Faulkner responded that it was, "in that it is the condition of the environment" (57). When asked about the level of social criticism in his writing, he explained that "[t]he writer uses his environment—what he knows" (58). To explain Nancy Mannigoe's radically destructive conduct in *Requiem for a Nun*, Faulkner said that "she was compelled by her environment, her circumstances" when she killed Temple's child (196). In each instance, the aspect which has caught the eye of Faulkner's interlocutor—rebelliousness, social criticism, irrational action—is accounted for by the incarnation of an old story of human conflict within a local environment, or human ecology. One questioner at Virginia got the matter reversed and asked whether the Southern materials had universal relevance. "People are the same," Faulkner replied, "but the differences in their background, the milieu they function in, which is different, not their behavior," thus stressing once again the Platonic formula. The act, the story, partakes in an eternal struggle; the local ecology determines the relative value of the behavior and the meaning of the events. What is heroic in one environment may be criminal in another, but the act itself does not alter. Faulkner continued: "But of course the milieu, the background, the environment will change the terms of their behavior not the act itself, and so the writer simply uses the background he knows just as the carpenter uses the tools he has at his hand" (168). Faulkner's retreat to the trope of the "carpenter's tools" indicates that he had engaged in about as much philosophical explication of his work as he cared to do at that moment. Nonetheless, the comments clarify further Faulkner's equation of the environment with what in this collection we're calling "the ecology of the South."

At Virginia and in other comments in the 1950s, Faulkner provided obscure but sustained and consistent evidence for the writer's systematic acknowledgment of the function of environment in his fiction. To my knowledge, Faulkner never used the term *ecology* or if he did, it never came to play an important much less formulaic function in any of his lexicons—public, literary, or epistolary. The word *environment*, on the other hand, was an important word for Faulkner, as it explained the dialectic between "universal" or transcendent themes in his work, and the clearly significant use of regional, local, and even immediate materials from Oxford and Lafayette County, Mississippi. The term, as Faulkner employed it, contained within it all that is involved in the sociological idea of nurture, the philosophical notion of interlocutors (readers and writers), and the political conception of human negotiation. It contains as well the natural world, including the world of hunting and of agriculture. It contains, that is to say, everything we now mean by the term *ecology*—the sum total of the found and built worlds of human existence, as well as the inherited nature of the human subject which is constructed into and out of that environment.

In 1952, Faulkner noted the exceptional nature of the Southern environment when he characterized the South as "the only really authentic region in the United States, because a deep indestructible bond still exists between man and his environment." He continued, explaining: "In the South, above all, there is still a common acceptance of the world, a common view of life, and a common morality"(*Lion in the Garden* 72).

Juxtaposed with other uses of the term, one might conclude that Faulkner found in the South a situation wherein the trinity of conflicts ("man in conflict with himself, with his fellow man, or with his time and place, his environment") was dominated by its last: *man in conflict with his time and place, his environment*. How often do we encounter in Faulkner a protagonist whose fate is determined in some small part by self-conflict and conflict with others, but determined to a much larger degree by a sense of being trapped by circumstances neither made nor foreseen by the character. Against whose will is Quentin Compson struggling? Or Joe Christmas, Isaac McCaslin, Harry Wilbourne? These characters struggle in part with others, to be sure, and they struggle in part with their inner conflicts; but their main and constant antagonist is best understood as their time and place, the social and intellectual environment which has produced them and their alienation. Anse Bundren, for one, thought Darl was perfectly fine until his time and place erupted and the human ecology was fatally disturbed: "I says to them, he was alright at first, with his eyes full of the land, because the land laid up-and-down ways then; it wasn't till that ere road come and switched the land around longways and his eyes still full of the land, and they began to threaten me out of him, trying to short-hand me with the law."[4] The other Bundrens adapt; Darl does not, and he is removed from the environment which, throughout Faulkner, is more powerful than the will of any human singular.

The ecology of the South is thus characterized by what Faulkner termed a persistent and "common acceptance of the world, a common view of life, and a common morality." The sense of commonality is fertile ground for conflict, when one person's will, acting on something perhaps far deeper than community standards or practices, comes up against an orthodox or entrenched view held in common and enforced universally. One thinks of Isaac McCaslin's struggle not so much with his cousin, Cass Edmonds, but with generations of social and familial injustice. Cass is simply the one in the room at the time the conversation unfolds. Or consider Temple Drake's insistence that Popeye alone is not to blame for the events that transpired at the Old Frenchman Place, but rather that it was a more generic "him," the men as a community, which oppressed her and killed one of their own. In court she simply agrees that Goodwin was as culpable as any individual avatar of that common morality. And Darl Bundren is unquestionably the most sympathetic figure in *As I Lay Dying*; he is the artist figure without whose alienation we would perhaps have no entry into the world Faulkner created. Faulkner's most extended and sustained treatment of this ecology is the Snopes trilogy, where the very idea of human ambition (perhaps the supreme expression of nonacceptance of circumstance) encounters a very Southern "common acceptance of the world" and results in an epochal encounter encompassing the town and county's history. And at his most audacious, Faulkner inserts the idea of Jesus (without naming and thus displacing the orthodox figure) into the environment of Western militarism, in *A Fable*, where military culture outdistances the South in terms of possessing a "common acceptance of the world, a common view of life, and a common morality."

A common acceptance, a common view, and a common morality are very different things from a tradition of incorporation, progressive change, or adaptation. By the term *environment* Faulkner envisions something as orthodox and as unyielding as a military hierarchy, or what social scientists call a closed society, characterized throughout Faulkner's work as a vital and unyielding community will against which the individual struggles. Seldom in Faulkner is the individual confronted with an environment that compels him or her toward progressive change or alteration. This is not to say that the social world in Faulkner is static, only that it is not readily malleable. It is this sensibility that earned Faulkner the opprobrium of leftist critics in the 1930s, who found him apolitical, or worse, reactionary. Even in the tremendously modernistic world of *Pylon*, the rules of flight competition are fixed and demand conformity, even sacrifice. What the Reporter cannot fathom is that this environment is the one against which the fliers struggle, whereas he, at first, confuses them with their time and place and labels them inhuman. And in *Absalom, Absalom!*, where human creative freedom seems to reign supreme, historical facts are manufactured and manipulated in order that history conform to the common view of life which has created Quentin Compson and which so mesmerizes Shreve McCannon. Quentin and Shreve are not free to create what they will; they are imprisoned by the intellectual ecology of their time and place so that in the end their final word is not "see what we have done" but "see how our efforts have fared in the struggle with this intransigent, inherited set of ideas about human action and behavior." Faulkner saw such struggle as endemic to life, so much so that it forms a keystone in his understanding of human existence—man in conflict with self and others and "with his time and place, his environment."

In 1977, Malcolm Franklin, Faulkner's stepson (Estelle's son by her marriage to Cornell Franklin), published a memoir entitled *Bitterweeds: Life with William Faulkner at Rowan Oak*. The title of the book comes from Franklin's recollection of Faulkner's relationship with a particular plant that grew wild on the grounds of the family home in Oxford, Mississippi. In the heat of June and July, according to Franklin, was "when Pappy did a great deal of his writing. He would sit at his typewriter for long stretches at a time, there before the window that looked out across the pasture.

Quite suddenly he would get up, open the door to his office, reach for his hoe placed conveniently just outside the door beneath the porte-cochere, and head for the pasture. There he would stay for an hour or more furiously chopping bitterweed. The hot sun beat down on his bare back, for he rarely wore a shirt when chopping away at his enemy. Then he would return to his typewriter and begin work."[5] Not only did chopping bitterweed interrupt (or more likely provide respite from) his writing, but Franklin also observed that the activity served as a distraction from the discomforts of sobriety and writing both. "It was the way he dried out—he took it out on bitterweeds," Franklin explains in the epigraph to his memoir. "I think he had an obsession about bitterweeds—he always kept a hoe or two leaning against the side of the house, and when he had a hangover, or when things weren't going well with his writing, he'd go out into the pasture and attack them" (9).

Bitterweed, or *Helenium amarum*, is a common north Mississippi annual. Beating it back with a hoe would remove it from sight, but not from the ecology of Rowan Oak. The image is emblematic of Faulkner's ecological sensibility. Faulkner's understanding of the human predicament, gleaned from the statements he would repeat publicly, was that it was characterized by perpetual conflict. The formula of "man in conflict" contains no sense of progression—man is not conflicted in order to reach an advanced state of being. His conflict with himself reaches no resolution; his conflict with others leads to no political program or institutional change. And his conflict with his time and place, his environment, improves neither himself nor makes the environment more hospitable. Like Faulkner's battle with the bitterweeds of Rowan Oak, these conflicts are *sui generis*, they characterize the nature of existence itself. What William Faulkner does is beat back the encroaching *Helenium amarum*; what the plant does is to reproduce itself annually. The conflict both defines each of them integrally and defines their relationship; the conflict, in short, is ecological.

Franklin seemed to be most aware of Faulkner's struggle with bitterweed adjunct to his writing and drinking. Faulkner's relationship with alcohol, as with anyone suffering an addiction, marked his struggle with himself more than any single factor in his life. As far as conflict with his fellows, the estate of Rowan Oak, the large property on the outskirts of town, with its driveway dug up to discourage visitors and its signs warning away trespassers, is emblematic of Faulkner's preference to remove himself from material contact. The tales of encounters, conflict, and occasional hospitality along this pathway are legendary, as are Faulkner's solitariness and sense of himself as someone who preferred solitude to society. Faulkner's participation in the ecological conflicts of the South, however, was lifelong, vocational, and epic. The world he created in his writing is nothing less than a sustained squaring off with his time and place. The cosmos of his own, the postage stamp of native soil, and the imagined, mapped world that included himself as sole owner and proprietor are each a means of articulating a Faulknerian sense of the environed subject. Furthermore, by calling himself a farmer, a country boy, and anything but a literary man, Faulkner acknowledged that, in his view, a human being struggles throughout the span of a lifetime with "time and place, environment" despite his accomplishments and despite the illusion of distance traveled from intellectual origins.

At the center of this articulation, we find the image of "Pappy" Faulkner abandoning his writing for a few minutes or an hour to beat back the bitterweeds on his property. Maybe the writing was not going well, and it was his conflict with his environment, his quarrel with time and place that manifested itself in a struggle against the bitterweeds. Faulkner did not want to see the plant moving close to the house, and he took it upon himself to resist and fight back. The weed's victory would mean the end of Faulkner's influence with hoe or pencil, so when the writing slowed, the bitterweed was targeted. Or perhaps it was a particularly tough hangover, the persistent symptom of his struggle with himself. The hangover was interfering with the writing, and had to be sweated out, in which case the bitterweeds provided the opportunity for sublimation—what looked like gardening in this environment was in fact Faulkner prevailing in conflict with himself. Or maybe it wasn't the writing going poorly but the reader's obtuseness, the hoeing a displacement of anger towards his fellow man, the publisher who expected the manuscript, the magazine editor who refused the first draft. These readers were also part of the environment with which the writer struggled. In any case, the hoe was kept outside the door, itself symbolic neither of husbandry nor of fruitful farming but of conflict. In Faulkner's imagination, I would suggest, the ecology of the South was one that pitted the Southerner against himself, against his fellows, and against the very environment that nurtured the distinctive regional identity. It is an ecology of intellectual ambivalence, moreover, of minds (to paraphrase Faulkner) that love their homes not because, but despite, of the heirs of Quentin Compson whose midnight calls of *"I dont hate it"* are perhaps all too common, too shared, to be claimed by anyone as a private nightmare.

2

That's the one trouble with this country: everything, weather, all, hangs on too long. Like our rivers, our land: opaque, slow, violent; shaping and creating the life of man in its implacable and brooding image.

—As I Lay Dying

Even the most casual of Faulkner readers knows that the writing is deeply inflected by the Mississippi climate. Vardaman's epiphany in *As I Lay Dying*, equating the experience of his mother's death with the experience of catching, preparing, and ingesting a fish ("My mother is a fish" [84]), signals that he is ready to join a community of characters who incessantly equate or locate parallels to their experiences within the Southern ecology. The trials afflicting the Bundren family on its funereal journey are successively ecological: the flooding tributaries of the Mississippi River, the rotting corpse, the private struggles with mortality and physical predicament. Much critical attention has been arrested by Faulkner's language and with the human situations he created; too little has sought to understand his conception of the peculiar salience of Mississippi's climate as the setting, the ecology, of these situations and of this language, "shaping and creating the life of man in its implacable and brooding image" (45). The scholarly essays in the present volume attempt to trace the outlines of that shaping and creating, by attending to the ecological Faulkner.

We open this collection with Cecelia Tichi, "'Old Man': Shackles, Chains, and Water Water Everywhere," a reconsideration of the question of Faulkner and social realism. Any suggestion of a Faulkner engaged in the political ecology of his time and place, unless it proceeds ahistorically, must confront the first generation of Faulkner critics who sought canonical status for Faulkner based on what appeared, in the late 1940s, to be the pitch of his fiction in a transcendent world removed from material existence. Presently, we have come to understand both terms, *social* and *realism*, in refined ways. "As ecological criticism formulates humanness within congeries of habitats and environments," Cecelia Tichi suggests, "Faulkner's texts necessarily become repositioned." Focusing on the detachable "Old Man" segment of *The Wild Palms*, and treating it as a discrete text (one that was marketed as an independent novella, moreover), Tichi places Faulkner's narrative squarely within its social and historical context: the great Mississippi River flood of 1927 and contemporary penal conditions at Parchman Penitentiary. Working from archival materials, Tichi finds Faulkner to be deeply engaged with the time and place of this epic struggle with the environment. A range of meanings emerges, including the cross-gendering of the river and the rich significance of waterways and escape in American literary tradition. And embedded in the myth and symbol of the river called Old Man is a detailed representation of American incarceration and Faulkner's critique of it, "his engagement in civic values and material conditions" and his "outrage at social injustice in America."

Turning next to an encompassing theoretical consideration of Faulkner's ecological imagination, Phil Weinstein, "The Land's Turn," reads a number of Faulkner scenes, characterizations, and themes through Pierre Bourdieu's notion of *habitus*, the "prediscursive shaping of behavior" which operates so strongly in Faulkner's work. According to Weinstein, "Bourdieu's notion of habitus dissolves the oppositions between individual motive and social limitation" by involving "recurring objective conditions which, over time, individuals have unthinkingly absorbed into their own reckoning, turning such reckoning into active disposition." Quoting Bourdieu's aphorism, "in each of us . . . there is part of yesterday's man," Weinstein carefully distinguishes Bourdieu's thought from Freudian individualism and aligns it fruitfully with the ecological. As a result, we find in Yoknapatawpha County "a precarious ecosystem itself established only by the inveigling and uprooting of a native population," and yet subject to the menace of subsequent and repeated crises "driven by long-inculcated convictions and practices of opposing races, classes, and regions." With a holistic scope, Weinstein finds examples and illustrations from *The Sound and the Fury* through *The Hamlet*. "Habitus enters [Faulkner's] fictional world as a rebuke, as resistance to change, as prejudice, but rarely as visible norm. Habitus does not prosper: Faulkner's protagonists typically shatter, and are shattered by, habitus." The shattering is brought about through collision, "when events of break-neck speed burst upon traditional practices," a collision which Weinstein finds to be "virtually the hallmark of Faulknerian narrative." Faulknerian ecology, then, emerges from this recurrent moment of collision, from Faulkner's "sense for the inertial, for impersonal forces immune to individual will and likely at any moment to torpedo the progressive reach of individual projects."

The title phrase in Eric Gary Anderson, "Environed Blood: Ecology and Violence in *The Sound and the Fury* and *Sanctuary*," comes from *Light in August*, when Gail Hightower is listening to church music in the distance and "seems to hear within it the apotheosis of his own history, his own land, his own environed blood." The idea is tied to spilling blood in the land, especially as the result of violent encounters. "After the grandson excitedly settles in Jefferson, acts of violence involving his wife, himself, his house, and his acquaintances continue to bind him to this particular place, rather than wrench him away from it." As a result, for Hightower "violence begets something like rootedness in place and a commitment to his own particular, peculiar strain of participatory and rather bloody regionalism." While admitting difficulty placing Faulkner "within conventional ecocritical confines," Anderson argues that "it is also clear that Faulkner's fiction has much to do with ecology, that he is very interested in the functioning and the 'careers' of particular socially constructed human communities as they interact with the natural world and with other built communities." Anderson notes that in Faulkner "there is a powerful, underestimated relationship between the traumas or other violent experiences of particular characters and the ways those characters articulate and reflect upon their traumas ecologically." The essay juxtaposes *Sanctuary*'s "criminal narrative" with *The Sound and the Fury*'s "family romance" in order to demonstrate "the compulsive if not nightmarish elements of interrelatedness, that crucial—and often romanticized—ecocritical concept."

The application of contemporary ecocritical thought to Faulkner continues with Ann Fisher-Wirth, "William Faulkner, Peter Matthiessen, and the Environmental Imagination," by way of a dual focus: first, to pair *Absalom, Absalom!* with Matthiessen's Watson trilogy; and second, to read *Absalom, Absalom!* by centering the environmental imagination embedded within it. Matthiessen, unlike Faulkner, is an internationally known environmental activist and writer. Although Matthiessen admits to having read all of Faulkner in his youth, he claims never to have gone back to these books and that Faulkner's influence on him is, as a result (and in his own words), "little to be seen." Nonetheless, Fisher-Wirth's analysis demonstrates that Faulkner worked hard on Matthiessen's subconscious, as themes, characterizations, and significance may be traced to at least one Faulkner text. And then, after reading Matthiessen through Faulkner, Fisher-Wirth goes back to *Absalom, Absalom!* to find in this novel a deeply embedded ecological presence, more than a subtext, what Fisher-Wirth calls "an ecological countermelody" to the novel's overt obsession with racism, violence, miscegenation, incest, and betrayal. Focusing on passages in *Absalom, Absalom!* which neither advance plot nor reveal character, Fisher-Wirth plays the countermelody on a clear scale and finds a common link between Matthiessen and Faulkner in these "novels of struggles and loss" within a "world [that] is ecological."

Michael Wainwright, "The Enemy Within: Faulkner's Snopes Trilogy," intriguingly argues that "[f]or Faulkner, Mississippi remained a Darwinian country" in his lifetime; the Mississippi of his experience was very much a frontier region. As a result, Faulkner "links [the] impulse to establish communal stability to the aesthetic sense" in human beings. Wainwright proceeds to interpret major events in the Snopes trilogy through the employment of "a Darwinian hermeneutic," specifically applying three categories of analysis: the foreigner, the outlander, and the extrinsic stranger. As community stability is crafted, these categories of human subspecies are negotiated politically and assigned relative value. The apocryphal Snopes chronicle was conceived around 1925, "a seminal year" in Faulkner's intellectual development, according to Wainwright, one that included a visit to Europe, an encounter with the work of Hippolyte Taine, and the unfolding drama of the Scopes Monkey Trial in Tennessee.

All of these influences converge in Snopes, where "Faulkner figures genetic mutation in addition to environmental suitability, a combination that brings success to this emergent clan as they pervade and therefore undermine the evolutionary stability of the Bend." The extended treatment of this phenomenon allowed Faulkner to fully explore an "aesthetic of conflict between biological heredity and cultural inheritance."

After all is said and done, the question may remain, as asked by François Pitavy, "Is Faulkner Green? The Wilderness as Aporia." Starting with the bold thesis that despite Faulkner's turn late in his career to "Arcadian nostalgia" through meditations on the wilderness, "there is in the last analysis no real man-nature interrelationship in his fiction: it is an ontological impossibility." Pitavy traces "the history of American colonization of the new world" as one that belongs not to the ecologist but "to the humanist, [and the] imperialist tradition." Historically, in the United States, "a bountiful nature was itself proof that it was meant to provide for man's dominion." Faulkner, however, "goes counter to the American grain" in his work, which casts the idea of progress, imperial or otherwise, as a delusion. As a result, Faulkner "must believe in man's capacity to endure rather than to change the world, or even himself." To answer the question in his title, Pitavy finds that in the subject matter of his later fiction, such as in *Go Down, Moses* and *Requiem for a Nun*, Faulkner is apparently green; in what he does with his materials, however, Faulkner is profoundly *not* green, at least not according to our current conception of the term. Faulkner's wilderness is *unnatural*, in Pitavy's understanding of it, because it is less a real space than "the object of a quest, the reflection of man's longing and frustrations." The wilderness has no apparent reason for existence except to assist a character like Ike McCaslin to work out the terms of his existential predicament, to escape history for a while, or to provide a smooth canvas against which history may commence. "Faulkner's reflection on progress, nature, and wilderness in *Go Down, Moses* and *Requiem for a Nun* leaves him in a territory of impossibilities," according to Pitavy; the wilderness is "his *locus solus*, the cosmos of his own, where he must fail splendidly."

Thomas G. McHaney has his eye on much of the same material as Pitavy, but sees Faulkner in a countertradition of nature writing carried on today by writers such as Wendell Berry and Janisse Ray. In "The Ecology of Uncle Ike: Teaching *Go Down, Moses* with Janisse Ray's *Ecology of a Cracker Childhood*," McHaney argues that Ray's work "helps us unpack from *Go Down, Moses* drama that encompasses ecologies of family, farm, community, and region, not merely the ecology of the hunter's woods." Critics have worked for over half a century to see Faulkner's novel as a cohesive unit, and it may be that current ecocritical sensibilities provide the surest method for doing so. Reading Faulkner through the lens of Ray's popular and influential memoir, McHaney has found that his students easily see "the plight of nature in terms of the plight of an individual [and also] see the plight of culture in terms of the plight of nature." By carefully juxtaposing scenes and imagery from *Ecology of a Cracker Childhood* with familiar episodes in Faulkner's novel, McHaney has us consider familiar tropes from the novel with fresh eyes and in revealingly distinctive contexts. There is no effort here to rehabilitate Isaac McCaslin; on the contrary, what we learn of Faulkner's aesthetic we learn through a finer understanding of Ike's grand failure. "Ray's memoir," McHaney claims, "dramatizes an initiation into the 'wilderness' that offers a relevant standard about the conduct of everyday life, an ecologically oriented drama that helps show readers of *Go Down, Moses* exactly how, in T. S. Eliot's words, Ike McCaslin 'had the experience but missed the meaning.'"

Scott Slovic, "Visceral Faulkner: Fiction and the Tug of the Organic World," focuses primarily on the *idea* of ecocriticism, including an engagement with current critical debates, recent criticism by Robert Taylor Ensign, a reading of *Deliverance*, and a review of contemporary writing in the South about the natural world. Slovic's "tug of the organic world" refers to Edward Hoagland's ingenious connection between walking one's dog and going fishing, "to feel the tug of another life," the tug, as Slovic says, implying organic connection. Such connectivity informs the purpose of much ecocriticism today, including Slovic's essay, which has as its stated purpose "the role of literature to help readers use their sensory faculties and thus achieve a greater awareness of their animal selves and their presence in particular places on earth." Slovic agrees with Ensign and finds Faulkner's work marked by "highly subjectivized descriptions of sensory experience." Moreover, the realm of physical experience in Faulkner "is often a realm of disappointment." For this reason Ensign, and perhaps Slovic, endorses a reassessment of Thomas Wolfe's place "as a protoecological author," a designation which may resuscitate a literary reputation that suffered at the hands of modernist critics.

The visual artist of Lafayette County, Mississippi, is the subject of Jeanne de la Houssaye, "McCrady's La-FAY-ette County." William Faulkner and John McCrady were rough contemporaries (Faulkner was fourteen years older), and for a while the two artists lived in Oxford at the same time. They met at least once, at the University of Mississippi, where they both attended college and worked on student publications. In 1937, *Time* magazine compared the two artists, claiming that McCrady was doing for painting in the South what Faulkner had done for literature. McCrady and Faulkner spent careers turning what seemed to be a fairly common place, northern Mississippi's Lafayette County, into the subject of art.

Jeanne de la Hussaye has gathered eighteen examples of McCrady's work in an essay that successfully draws the two artists into the same orbit of representations.

Seth Berner has attended the Faulkner and Yoknapatawpha Conference for years, accompanied by a catalog of Faulkner collectibles, driving his car, with its Maine license plate, filled with books and other Faulkneriana. He's a sought-after registrant, not only by those ready to buy, but by readers asking advice about collecting Faulkner and sometimes about the value of this or that "find" from a garage or estate sale. We asked Mr. Berner to organize a lunch-time presentation on collecting Faulkner materials, and it was a great success. He's written up his comments and advice, and we are happy to conclude this volume with Seth Berner, "Collecting Faulkner."

Joseph R. Urgo
The University of Mississippi
Oxford, Mississippi

NOTES

1. The organization is the Association for the Study of Literature and the Environment (ASLE); its journal, *Interdisciplinary Studies of Literature and the Environment*, or *ISLE*.

2. Frederick L. Gwynn and Joseph L. Blotner, eds., *Faulkner in the University: Class Conferences at the University of Virginia, 1957–1958* (New York: Vintage, 1959), 19. Subsequent citations are made parenthetically.

3. *Lion in the Garden: Interviews with William Faulkner, 1926–1962*, ed. James B. Meriwether and Michael Millgate (New York: Random House, 1968), 177. Subsequent citations are made parenthetically.

4. William Faulkner, *As I Lay Dying* (1930; New York: Vintage International, 1990), 36–37. Subsequent citations are made parenthetically.

5. Malcolm Franklin, *Bitterweeds: Life with William Faulkner at Rowan Oak* (Irving, Tex.: Society for the Study of Traditional Culture, 1977), 84. Subsequent citations are made parenthetically.

A Note on the Conference

The Thirtieth Annual Faulkner and Yoknapatawpha Conference sponsored by the University of Mississippi in Oxford took place July 20–24, 2003, with more than two hundred of the author's admirers from around the world in attendance. Ten presentations at the conference are collected as essays in this volume. Brief mention is made here of other conference activities.

Oxford Mayor Richard Howorth and Joseph R. Urgo, chair of the University English Department, welcomed participants to the conference, and Charles Reagan Wilson, director of the Center for the Study of Southern Culture, presented the seventeenth annual Eudora Welty Awards in Creative Writing. Ke Ji, a student at Jackson Academy, first prize, $500, for her poem "Wuhan Marketplace 1990." Josh Swan, a student at the Mississippi School for Math and Science in Columbus, won second prize, $250, for his short story "Days Inn." Frances Patterson of Tupelo, a member of the Center Advisory Committee, established and endowed the awards, which are selected through a competition held in high schools throughout Mississippi. Donald M. Kartiganer, director of the conference, introduced Michael Egan, who read the winning entry—"The Sound and the Furry"—of the fourteenth annual Faux Faulkner Contest, sponsored by *Hemispheres* magazine of United Airlines, the University of Mississippi, and Yoknapatawpha Press. Local actors presented Voices from Yoknapatawpha, readings from Faulkner's fiction selected and arranged by actor George Kehoe and Betty Harrington, wife of former conference director Evans Harrington. Following a buffet supper, at historic Isom Place, Scott Slovic gave the first lecture of the conference.

Monday's program included two lectures, Jeanne de la Houssaye's slide presentation about Faulkner and artist John McCrady, Seth Berner's talk on collecting Faulkner, and "Teaching Faulkner" sessions conducted by James B. Carothers, Robert W. Hamblin, Charles A. Peek, and Theresa Towner. Laurel E. Eason, Emily Hogan, Mikko Saikku, Lindsey Claire Smith, Matthew Sutton, and Bart H. Welling were panelists for two sessions sponsored by an anonymous gift made in honor of Joseph Blotner, Faulkner biographer and longtime friend of the University of Mississippi and the Faulkner and Yoknapatawpha Conference. Colby Kullman moderated the fourth Faulkner Fringe Festival, an open-mike evening at Southside Gallery on the Oxford Square.

Guided tours of North Mississippi and the Delta took place on Tuesday, as did an afternoon party at Tyler Place, hosted by Charles Noyes, Sarah and Allie Smith, and Colby Kullman. The day ended with Cecelia Tichi's lecture. In addition to three lectures and author Tom Franklin's reading on Wednesday, "Faulkner in Oxford" assembled local residents Will Lewis Jr. and Meg Faulkner DuChane as panelists for a discussion moderated by M. C. "Chooky" Falkner, the writer's nephew. Among the events that took place on Thursday were a lecture, two discussion sessions, and a closing party at the home of Dr. and Mrs. Beckett Howorth Jr.

Receptions for two exhibitions took place during the conference, with *Tom Allen: American Illustrator*, at the University Museums, and *Red Hills to Gulf Shores: Autographics,* photographs by Todd Bertolaet, in the Gammill Gallery at Barnard Observatory. The University's John Davis Williams Library displayed Faulkner books, manuscripts, photographs, and memorabilia; and the University Press of Mississippi exhibited Faulkner books published by university presses throughout the United States. Films relating to the author's life and work were available for viewing during the week. Other events included a walk through Bailey's Woods before the annual picnic at Faulkner's home, Rowan Oak, and at the home of Dr. and Mrs. M. D. Howorth Jr.

The conference planners are grateful to all the individuals and organizations who support the Faulkner and Yoknapatawpha Conference annually. In addition to those mentioned above, we wish to thank Square Books, St. Peter's Episcopal Church, the City of Oxford, and the Oxford Tourism Council.

Faulkner and the Ecology of the South

FAULKNER AND YOKNAPATAWPHA,
2003

"Old Man":
Shackles, Chains, and Water Water Everywhere

CECELIA TICHI

The ecological Faulkner occupies the very world from which his postwar "rescuers" thought they had extricated him—a world of social realism and sociocultural critique, which is to say, an ecological world. To locate this Faulkner, one begins with a critical study that has been insufficiently appreciated by many Faulknerians. It is Lawrence Schwartz's *Creating Faulkner's Reputation* (1988), which shows that in the postwar moment, an alliance of Southern Agrarians, notably Robert Penn Warren and Allan Tate, together with northeastern critics, deliberately redeemed Faulkner from his pre-World War II reputation as a writer mired in obscurantism, violence, and incoherence.[1]

The recovery of Faulkner was motivated largely from political considerations, his literary rescue and repositioning crucial in a postwar moment of American Democracy Triumphant. The need for a national nonideological American genius was self-evident in those years. He—surely a *he*—was required to embody the values of democracy, the values that won the world war and pointed naturally to a postwar democratic American hegemony. This American writer could not, by definition, exhibit politically leftist views nor a literary record of caustic critique of the shortcomings of democratic America. Such writers as John Dos Passos and John Steinbeck were thus ineligible to be nominated as America's modern Literatus (just as Theodore Dreiser, Frank Norris, and Stephen Crane were ineligible predecessors). All these were discredited for stylistic crudity, superficiality, and didacticism, as *Creating Faulkner's Reputation* reveals. The agrarians and northeastern intelligentsia, Malcolm Cowley key among them, found in Faulkner the writer who was arguably severed from traditions of American social realism. As Schwartz shows, Faulkner won out because he could be recreated as a writer focused on the world within, his art henceforth regarded as universal and transcendent of politics.

Faulkner, however, engages the very world denied to him by his postwar sponsors—the world of sociopolitical realism identified with Dos Passos, Steinbeck, *et al*. Theirs is a realm of human ecology. As the era of U.S.

3

Cold War literature and criticism delineates itself in retrospect, it becomes both possible and necessary to reconceive Faulkner amid these cohorts and to do so from the perspective of a twenty-first-century contemporary moment. The recognition of this Faulkner (and his cohorts) is additionally crucial in a related "post" moment—less postwar than posttheory. This is to say a radical rereading of high canonical figures is imperative in a perilous early twenty-first-century moment, and that Faulknerian socially realist ecology is accordingly an urgent undertaking.[2] As ecological criticism formulates humanness within congeries of habitats and environments, Faulkner's texts necessarily become repositioned. Within Faulkner's *oeuvre*, moreover, texts heretofore regarded as ancillary come to the fore because they speak particularly to the contemporary sociopolitical critical moment.

One such text is surely "Old Man" (1939), a novella comprising one-half of the alternating chapters in *The Wild Palms*.[3] "Old Man" must be regarded as a text that situates itself shoulder to shoulder with narratives of Dreiser, Frank Norris, Steinbeck, and others in trenchant social critique of human ecological conditions.

To begin with self-evident ecological issues, we turn to the Viking *Portable Faulkner* (1946) in which Malcolm Cowley prefaced "Old Man" with this note: that during the Great Mississippi Flood of 1927, the worst flood in the history of the river, 20,000 square miles including the entire Delta were inundated, and the entire population of the state prison farm at Parchman, Mississippi, was set to work on a threatened levee.[4] During the six weeks of that spring, over 600,000 persons were driven from their homes, Cowley wrote, and hundreds were drowned, as were 25,000 horses, 50,000 cattle, 148,000 hogs, 1.3 million chickens. Some 400,000 acres of crops were destroyed, as were hundreds of miles of levees. (A recent comprehensive history of the flood is John Barry's *Rising Tide: The Great Mississippi Flood of 1927 and How It Changed America* [1997]).[5]

Cowley provided the factual basis of Faulkner's narrative: "one tall convict was ordered out on a rowboat to look for a woman in a cypress snag and a man on the ridgepole of a cottonhouse. . . . A few weeks later after the river—the Old Man of the story—after the river had returned to its bed, the tall convict rowed back to the state prison farm. 'Yonder's your boat,' he said, 'and here's the woman. But I never did find that bastard on the cottonhouse.' "[6] Here was a bare bones comedic plot intact, a tale not of the attempted escape effort but volitional return—no Ulysses to Penelope, but a convict to Parchman.

In "Old Man," Faulkner visualized that convict as a "hill-billy" of "about twenty-five, tall, lean, flat-stomached, with a sunburned face and Indian black hair and pale, china-colored, outraged eyes."[7] The outrage, we learn, is directed neither at the law enforcement officers nor prosecutors, nor judge nor jury—but at the paperback writers whose Wild West pulp adventure stories he, the convict, had mistaken for actual primers on train robbing. His motive to rob a train had not been mere money but pride: "to show that he too was the best at his chosen gambit in the living fluid world of his time." In Faulkner's term, the pen-named pulp writers are "not actual men but merely designations of shades who had written about shades" (22). At age nineteen, the aspirant Jesse James was sentenced to serve fifteen years at the farm, Parchman, for an attempted (hilariously botched) train robbery executed with a dud of a pistol, a malfunctioning lantern, and a handkerchief disguise purchased through subscription sales of a detective magazine (surely Faulkner's pulping of the pulps). Six years have been served by the time of the flood.

Yet in "Old Man," the "fluid world of his time" becomes ecologically literally fluid in the Great Flood of '27. The convict, like his fellows, had "plowed and planted and eaten and slept beneath the shadow of the levee," hearing the "whistles of steamboats" but experiencing the river at best as "hearsay"—that is, until prison rumors and accounts in Memphis newspapers told of "conscripted levee gangs, mixed blacks and whites working in double shifts against the steadily rising waters" (24–25).[8] A breech in a nearby levee—at Mound's Landing (twelve miles above Greenville)—prompts the nighttime arousal and transport of the convicts to the levees.

"Old Man" is episodic, in fact arguably picaresque. The convict tacitly acknowledges to prison officials the ability to paddle a boat and accepts the assignment to paddle a light skiff to a designated bayou and to retrieve, first, a woman on a cypress snag, and then a man on a cottonhouse roof. Initially, he is accompanied by a second, plump and pale, convict who professes ignorance of any watercraft skill. The two set out.

Almost immediately, the plump, pale convict returns on a rescue steamer in the company of a penitentiary deputy warden to describe the water's whirling gyre into which the skiff has spun, with the tall convict sucked to his death—"drowned"—and thus automatically to be pardoned (65, 66).

The tall convict, of course, actually survives, and Faulkner's narrative charge is to propel the story with varied descriptions of the floodwaters and with the episodic experiences of the paddling convict. Faulkner's challenge is a rudimentary narrative one. What might the tall convict eat? Where sleep? How manoeuver the boat in the roiling currents? Above all, how is he to cope with the travelling companion whom he indeed retrieves from the cypress snag, the woman in calico—and very pregnant—who greets him, à la Lena Grove, with the words, "It's taken you awhile" (125).

In enforced domesticity (heightened by her imminent childbirth), the two set forth, and readers familiar with "Old Man" know the sequence of events—the encounter with a "shanty boat trio" who donate canned milk and a hardtacklike bread; the landing platform episode when, trying his best to surrender, the convict instead is shot at and wounded (146). Next is the landfall on an Indian mound, where he makes a fire as the woman gives birth while the skiff and campsite are infested by moccasins (a sort of poor man's peaceable kingdom). Hoping to sight Vicksburg or Yazoo City, the convict instead finds himself driven into French-speaking Cajun country, riding for a span on a steamboat bound for New Orleans, though with the skiff leashed to his wrist by a grapevine painter. Later on, he spends days partnered with a Cajun river rat, an alligator hunter who lives in a stilt house shack on the water. Finally, on the day the levee is to be dynamited (by a Federal permit wrangled by New Orleans city fathers to spare their city at the cost of inundating tens of thousands of acres downstream), he is captured and handcuffed for failure to obey the evacuation order. Taken to an armory shelter in New Orleans, he manages to surrender to a deputy with the words, "Yonder's your boat, and here's the woman. But I never did find that bastard on the cottonhouse" (233).

Ecologically, Faulkner works consistently to gender the flood male. The Mississippi is Old Man River and explicitly the "Father of Waters." He speaks in "a deep faint subaqueous rumble . . . like a subway train" and moves as forcefully as an "avalanche." It has "fangs" and a will to "do what it likes to do," and "its voice is the sound of deliberate and irresistable and monstrously disturbed water." The flood itself is the Old Man in a week-long "debauch" (53, 61, 127, 132, 134, 143, 144).

The convict's struggle—in fact, the text, "Old Man"—takes its place within a gendered aquatic ecology in American literature. One thinks of the male-identified oceans and the "rivers of empire," as Donald Worster titles his study of the history of water in the American West.[9] One thinks of the oceans in Richard Henry Dana Jr.'s *Two Years before the Mast* (1840, 1869), or Melville's *Moby-Dick* (1851), or of Henry David Thoreau's wilderness-identified *Walden* (1854) or Longfellow's Great Lakes epic, *Hiawatha*, and especially of Twain's Mississippi in *The Adventures of Huckleberry Finn* (1884) or *Life on the Mississippi* (1883). In the traditional canonical texts, males embark upon treacherous waters to face tests of physical and metaphysical courage. (Of course, Faulkner also anticipates Hemingway's *Old Man and the Sea* [1952].)

Crucial issues in these texts range from the initiation rites of a civilizing Native American hero (Hiawatha), to attempted flight from stifling civility to wild woodland (Thoreau), to survival and morality in a slaveholding America (Huck), to youth-unto-adult self-fashioning (the cub pilot Clemens), to spiritual-psychological restoration of health within a revenge plot (Dana and Melville's Ishmael). Whatever the thematic crux, the "Big-Sea Waters," the planet's open oceans, and the mighty Mississippi are represented as commensurate in importance with the trials of the American males for whom these waters comprise both staging area and *metier* of heroic struggle. One tends to equate water in American literature with an epic, male struggle. Melville's Ishmael in *Moby-Dick* speaks for all such texts in remarking that "all rivers and oceans" offer "the image of the ungraspable phantom of life." [10] It serves a masculinist ecology to identify the most physically energetic of waters as male.

"Old Man," however, is also gendered female despite Faulkner's own design, which at best expresses an ambivalence about the legitimacy of the female in the male water world. But Faulkner worked not only from the literary tradition of male—but also of female—aquatics. Call it a parallel ecology, but from the nineteenth century, American texts affirmed the fact of water embodied, of liquid represented with the solidity of the female human body. Typically, health and dynamic energy in aqueous incarnation are shaped in female terms. In Margaret Fuller's "Leila" (1841), published in *The Dial*, the title character is a suprahuman female figure who "circulate[s] as the vital fluid" while "rivers of bliss flow forth at her touch." [11] In promotional pamphlets for the first U.S. national park, Arkansas's spa resort at Hot Springs, it is Hygiea, the goddess of health, who stretches out her beautiful arms to offer health in the form of nature's own healing waters. [12] In *The Awakening* (1899), Kate Chopin's once-scandalous novel of a woman's developing social-sexual consciousness, the personified sea envelopes a woman swimmer in its bodily embrace. These and other texts show aquatic fluidity personified both in female and feminine terms, with sex and gender allied in the embodiment of water.

When in "Old Man" Faulkner presents a woman of reproductive age—a woman ready at any moment to give birth—he necessarily doubly genders the ecology of the Mississippi. To the convict, admittedly, the woman in calico is a loathesome caricature of the Greta Garbo or Helen (of Troy?) whose daring rescue he fantasizes about (abetted by the flow of pulp fiction smuggled into the prison). The convict repeatedly describes his actual burdensome companion (and responsibility) in terms of her "deformed swell of belly," *"female meat,"* a belly "swelling and unmanageable" (126, 130).

But what is swollen and unmanageable if not the river? The vocabulary of woman and of Old Man River are remarkably similar. Faulkner's decision, moreover, to make this woman of reproductive age, pregnant and giving birth, allies "Old Man" with female aquatic ecology. More, it allies the flood with the female body. Faulkner was heir to—and in turn produced—a lexicon defining the female body precisely in terms of a flood. Indeed, Faulkner reproduced a vocabulary found from the nineteenth century and continuing through the twentieth in the gynecological-obstetrical literature of allopathic medicine. One woman physician recommended a hard bed, elevated and warmed feet, and nonstimulating diet as treatment for "flood-ing," a recurrent term in the allopathic literature, as is "gushing" and phrases on "blood that flowed in a stream," of "excessive" and "immoderate flow."[13]

Because the medical terms replicate those to be found in texts on environmental waters, there is a certain interchangeable vocabulary of riparian and female function. Rivers and lakes are presented as exhibiting the very pathological symptoms of women's reproductive health crises. There are the "swollen" streams and tributaries contributing to "great floods," including the Mississippi River headwaters area.[14] Waters are "turbid" and "discharge" themselves.[15] Streams flow "sluggishly" and need to rest but require "drainage."[16]

The tumescence in Faulkner's "Old Man," then, is both female and male. And Faulkner mirrors the woman's bodily fluids—by definition, of parturition—with the convict's own blood and bleeding. The convict is hemophe-liac, bleeding profusely from blows sustained from the skiff, thereby lying in a "watery scarlet puddle," "bloody as a hog," subject to "an apparently inex-haustible flow of blood from his nose," and identified by his "blood streaked face" (122, 127, 128).

The embedded joke in the text in which hemopheliac and hermaphrodite are confused has a point: gender slides into sexuality, and the sexualities are both, interchangeably, male and female (203). The term made famous in Stanley Kubrick's 1964 film *Dr. Strangelove* is applicable to the sexualized ecology of the Mississippi in flood: its matrix is "vital bodily fluids."

A gendered human ecology as evidenced in material culture is also pres-ent in the flood in the form of the debris in what Faulkner calls "the spittle-frothed, debris-choked water": an entire barn, planks, small buildings, bodies of drowned (yet antic) animals, entire trees leaping and diving like porpoises"; sharp gables of houses, mules; "entire towns, stores, residences, parks and farmyards"; "bridges and fences" (57, 62, 129, 132, 133, 135–36, 148, 205). The list is more than wreckage, more than an index of the power of unchanneled water to wreak havoc. The livestock, homes, demarcated boundaries (fences), social linkages (bridges) mix in an indiscriminate con-fluence of life in the human and natural worlds. The slurry of artifacts of the built environment is a sign system of the rural and urban, of agriculture and industry and artisanry, of domesticity, of every realm of human endeavor. It is ecology as a dynamic, defamiliarized exhibition of the range of human activity as it passes in a kind of panoramic, scrolling exhibition.

2

But significantly, the convict sees this aquatic slurry as a human material culture from which he, as a prisoner, is excluded. By definition of his status as convict, he has no stake nor share in the material culture surrounding him in the water. And Faulkner makes this point: "the land they [the prisoners] farmed and the substance they produced from it belonged neither to them who worked it nor those who forced them at guns' point to do so." He goes on, "As far as either convicts or guards were concerned, it could have been pebbles they put into the ground and papier-mache cotton and corn-sprouts which they thinned" (26).

This separateness from the world of husbandry and making—of manufacture—is crucially important in "Old Man." This world of human ecology is structured upon principles (or if one wishes, ideology) of property possessed and shaped in the name of agriculture, industry, domestic life, and so on. The convict protagonist's exclusion from all this leads a reader of "Old Man" to a specific aspect of human ecology which positions Faulkner with the social realist tradition from which his admirers long sought to separate him. The fundamental fact of the narrative is its protagonist's status as convict. He has no other name, as Faulkner explicitly and repeatedly makes clear, not even a one-syllable nickname.

We might glance beyond the text of "Old Man" to map the conditions of the protagonist convict and his fellow inmates, which is to say, the conditions referent to Faulkner's text. A recent study of Parchman Farm, David Oshinsky's "*Worse than Slavery*" (1996), tells us that "by 1915 white convicts comprised about 10% of the prison population," though by 1925, two years before the flood, "the Parchman superintendent reported that the white population was growing 'by leaps and bounds'" to 280 [attributable to Prohibition with its criminalization of one drug, alcohol]. Whites, says Oshinsky, were performing "the same tasks as the Negro convicts [with] much the same routine," though whites "hoped for jobs as carpenters, mechanics, truck drivers, maintenance men, or 'dog boys' who trained the hounds." "Anything beat picking cotton all day in the Mississippi sun."[17]

A self-sufficient operation by 1915, Parchman had "a sawmill, a brickyard, a slaughterhouse, a vegetable canning plant, and two cotton gins. The plantation was divided into fifteen field camps, each surrounded by barded wire and positioned at least a half-mile apart. . . . First offenders were caged with incorrigibles, and adults with juveniles, some as young as twelve or thirteen. . . . Each field camp had a 'cage'—a long wooden barracks with barred windows where the inmates ate and slept. . . . [the dormitories] had bunks stacked side by side along the walls, with two or three feet in between."[18] "Throughout its history," Oshinsky writes, "Parchman used the trusty system, in which selected inmates, called trusty-shooters, watched over the regular convicts (known as gunmen, because they toiled under the guns of the trusties)."[19] In design, Oshinsky writes, Parchman "resembled an antebellum plantation with convicts instead of slaves. Both systems used captive labor to grow the same crops in identical ways."[20]

In "Old Man," Faulkner tells these basic facts to his reader in a parenthetical message, that "there is no walled penitentiary in Mississippi; it is a cotton plantation which the convicts work under the rifles and shotguns of guards and trusties" (21). But at the outset, readers learn Faulkner's stance on the state of this criminal justice system. A failed youthful romance of train robbery as an expression of a young man's "personal best" prompts a fifteen-year sentence, while a fellow inmate (the paunchy, pale convict) has received 199 years for a crime committed by someone else, who escaped. One hundred ninety-nine years—of which Faulkner writes, "this incredible and impossible period of punishment or restraint itself carrying a vicious and fabulous quality which indicated that his reason for being here [in Parchman] was such that the very men, the paladins and pillars of justice and equity who had sent him here had during that moment become blind apostles not of mere justice but of all human decency, blind instruments not of equity but of all human outrage and vengeance, acting in a savage personal concert, judge, lawyer and jury, which certainly abrogated justice and possibly even law" (23). As for the protagonist convict, he sought justice at a "blind font" and is "defrauded of liberty and honor and pride" (21).[21]

The imagery of treatment of the prisoners sustains Faulkner's critique. Chained ankle to ankle, they are, like livestock, "herded" by armed guards (and "herded" is a term Faulkner will use repeatedly) (24; cf. 56, 58, 60). Driven to the flood zone in a truck, they are "packed like matches in a upright box or like the pencil-shaped ranks of cordite in a shell" and "shackled by the ankles to a single chain [which was] riveted by both ends to the steel body of the truck" (52). Faulkner continues: "the twenty-two convicts [are] packed like sardines into the truck bed and padlocked by the ankles to the body of the truck itself" (55). As the truck wheels sink under water, one convict's panic represents the visceral fear of all: "They're going to drown us! Unlock the chain!" (55). Faulkner uses the moment to heighten readers' awareness of the helpless prisoners' precariousness. Chained to the truck bed, they would surely drown if the truck sank or overturned. Faulkner uses the term which the historian of Parchman invoked in the 1990s when he, Faulkner, wrote that the convicts watched the approach of the flood "with that same amazed and incredulous hope of the slaves . . . who watched the mounting flames of Rome" (25).

At the levee work site, these quasi-slaves, unlocked from the truck, are then "shackled ankle to ankle in pairs . . . shackled in braces like dogs at a field trial" and left to stand (and eat) in the rain by guards "who would not think about getting them out of the rain" (56, 57). They stand "immobile, patient, almost ruminant, their backs turned to the rain as sheep and cattle do" (57).

The story or plotline of "Old Man" segues between opposing characterizations of the protagonist convict on the one hand as a patient ruminant, yet on the other a resourceful and personally and socially responsible citizen. Tasked with rowing in a borrowed skiff to a bayou to retrieve a stranded woman and man, the convict uses the resources of reflex and reason, fueled by his energy of rage. We recall that he smolders in outrage at the pulp novelists, and this rage is readily transferred to the woman who represents not erotic desire, but reproduction. Several descriptions of his relentless paddling evince the energy of this sleep-deprived, underfed man— for example, "From some ultimate absolute reserve . . . which adumbrated mere muscle and nerves, [he is] continuing to flail the paddle right up to the instant of striking, completing one last reach, thrust and recover out of pure desperate reflex" (124).

Faulkner offers his interpreters, as always, an embarrassment of riches. The narrative is readily interpreted along an axis of routinized homosocial agrarian routines at Parchman versus the crazed picaresque episodic flood sequences with the woman. Faulkner invites this reading, describing prison life as "that monastic existence of shotguns and shackles" which is "secure from women" (130).

"Old Man" lures the literary critic, moreover, to the compelling issue of narrative design, first because of its place in *The Wild Palms* and, in addition, because much of the story is recounted through flashbacks. The protagonist convict, once again installed at Parchman, recounts his adventures to the second convict, who had initially set forth on the skiff and reported his workmate drowned. Faulkner himself entices interpreters to narrative focus per se with such guideline statement as this: "and now when he told this, despite the fury of element which climaxed it, it (the telling) became quite simple . . . as though he had passed through a machine-gun's barrage into a bourne beyond any more amazement: so that the subsequent part of his narrative seemed to reach his listeners as though from beyond a sheet of slightly milky though still transparent glass, as something not heard but seen—a series of shadows, edgeless yet distinct, as smoothly flowing, logical and unfrantic and making no sound" (147). In effect, Faulkner invites readers to test out his narrative theory.

Or we can discuss the internal debate between literary and popular (pulp) writing, between high culture and the popular—especially when we learn that the convict's former girlfriend goaded him to attempt the robbery because she herself fantasized about the gangster life of Al Capone.

Readers, alternatively, can revert to the Christian symbolism of the trinity, since the convict hears the voice of the Old Man three times and is tempted in the wilderness and can be linked to the story of Noah. Or one can go the Oedipal interpretive route, as the son contends with the power of the Old Man. It may be tempting, in addition, to regard "Old Man" through Michel Foucault's theory on criminalization as social repression.

Foucault's *Discipline and Punish: The Birth of the Prison* (1979), how-ever, lets readers bypass the specifics of actual prison politics and actual prison conditions in modern America. It proves less a heuristic wedge into Faulkner's text than a circumvention of it. For "Old Man" is Faulkner's trenchant statement on human ecology centered in the criminal (in)jus-tice system. We have seen how firmly Faulkner frames "Old Man" with diction of human degradation in—and injustice of—the prison system. Its corruption extends beyond the prisoners to their supervisors, public offi-cials, indeed to the ballot box. Faulkner's exposition and imagery make utterly clear his position. The text thereafter juxtaposes the prisoner-as-ruminant against prisoner-as-rehabilitated-citizen. If Twain used the river to exhibit episodically the development of Huck's conscience, so Faulkner shows the convict's mettle tested, his fitness to live in the world. He res-cues and protects the woman and infant as long as he must in the equiva-lence of a half-century of marriage (a domestic partnership on which Faulkner expounds at length) (212–13).

The convict demonstrates resourcefulness in service to his assignment (paddle lost, he toils to fashion another from a splintered plank). He guards the property—the skiff—which must be returned to its legitimate owner. He tries to refuse the journey to New Orleans, negotiating for release from a New Orleans-bound steamboat in conversation with a manipulative physician, and this "hill-billy" proves adept in a cash econ-omy when he enters into a steady partnership with a riverman, a cajun "bayou-rat" with whom he hunts alligators and sells the hides for cash money (214). He is committed to work, not as drudgery but a source of identity: *"I forgot how good it is to work"* (221). "Herded" like cattle, shackled like a dog, packed like a sardine, viewing the flood as a Roman slave had watched the great fire, this convict nonetheless proves himself a citizenly man. Faulkner's is a rite-of-passage plot to responsible manhood. What redress in this human ecological arrangement?

The convict's "reward" is ten years added to his sentence in a cynical manoeuver by prison and state officials who thereby duck the conundrum of reincarcerating a convict presumed to be dead and pardoned. The bureaucratic task of freeing the convict without staining the officials' career records seems just too complicated. And so the convict is reconvicted on a trumped-up charge of attempted escape and sentenced to an additional decade in prison. He has no recourse. He will be released at age forty-four.

No good deed unpunished? Certainly readers can enjoy the heavy irony, irony itself a longterm staple of formalist reading. But irony is too smugly satisfying, and what's more, the ironist is complicit with the status

quo, with a corrupt system in which the prison and state politicians know-
ingly sacrifice a convict's freedom for the sake of their careers. Instead,
civic anger at injustice and indecency is the apt response—the ecologically
ethical response. Faulkner works to guide and evoke that response, for "Old
Man" shows his engagement in civic values and material conditions. It
shows Faulkner's outrage at social injustice in America. "Old Man" is caustic in its treatment of officialdom and socially reformist in its theme.

Reexamined in the twenty-first century, "Old Man" thus redirects readers to a yet newer Faulkner whose text(s) may serve as the lens through
which scholars and students may seek an understanding of urgent contemporary sociocultural issues.[22] If the Great Depression of the 1930s
awakened Faulkner's sense of social injustice, literary studies urgently
need the socially ecological Faulkner at the opening of this new century.
Just as the Faulkner of the inner world and of modernist stylistics was an
imperative for postwar generations, so Faulkner as social realist is equally
imperative at this juncture. "Old Man" shows how the primary text by the
classic American writer offers new opportunities for a redirection of literary studies at a moment of national, human ecological peril.

NOTES

1. See Lawrence Schwartz, *Creating Faulkner's Reputation: The Politics of Modern
Literary Criticism* (Knoxville: University of Tennessee Press, 1988), 108.

2. See Emily Y. Eakin, "The Latest Theory Is that Theory Doesn't Matter," *New York
Times* [National Edition], April 19, 2003: A17. This summary of a University of Chicago scholarly symposium, sponsored by *Critical Inquiry*, on April 11, 2003, exposes leading theorists'
rejection of theory itself as a heuristic useful for understanding of sociocultural crises. The
symposium participants included Henry Louis Gates, Homi Bhabba, Stanley Fish, Fredric
Jameson, W. J. T. Mitchell, and others, all reportedly in consensus that neither psychoanaly-
sis, structuralism, Marxism, deconstruction, nor postcolonialism were to be considered con-
senting to efficacious sociocultural critique.

3. See Thomas L. McHaney, ed., *"The Wild Palms": Holograph Manuscript and
Miscellaneous Rejected Holograph Pages*. William Faulkner Manuscripts 14, Volumes 1 and 2.
New York: Garland, 1986. Faulkner's original title for the separate but complementary novellas,
Old Man and *The Wild Palms*, was "If I Forget Thee, Jerusalem." As McHaney remarks, the
text has had an unusual publication history, the "Old Man" section appearing repeatedly as a
short novel in a form Faulkner did not approve (x). Though *The Wild Palms* and *Old Man*
were published independently as separate paperbacks in divers editions, McHaney quotes
Faulkner's statement to his editor that "'dismembering THE WILD PALMS will in my
opinion destroy the over-all impact which I intend'" (x). Accordingly, critics have worked to
demonstrate the complementarity of the two narratives. See, for instance, Richard Godden,
Fictions of Labor: William Faulkner and the South's Long Revolution (Cambridge: Cambridge
University Press, 1997), 199–232.

4. Schwartz recounts the decision in 1946 to include the "Old Man" in the Viking
Portable Faulkner in order to help increase "popular appreciation of Faulkner's works"
(59–60). See *The Portable Faulkner*, ed. Malcolm Cowley (1946; revised and expanded edition: New York: Viking, 1974), 479–80.

5. See John Barry, *Rising Tide: The Great Mississippi Flood and How It Changed America* (New York: Simon and Schuster, 1997).

6. Cowley, 479.

7. *The Wild Palms* (1939; New York: Vintage, 1990), 20, 205. Subsequent citations are made parenthetically.

8. Barry's *Rising Tide* corroborates these facts.

9. See Donald Worster, *Rivers of Empire: Water, Aridity, and the Growth of the American West* (New York: Pantheon, 1985).

10. Herman Melville, *Moby-Dick* (1851; New York: Penguin, 1986), 94.

11. See Margaret Fuller, "Leila," in *The Dial: A Magazine for Literature, Philosophy, and Religion,* 1, 4 (April 1841), 464, 466.

12. See Cecelia Tichi, *Embodiment of a Nation: Human Form in American Places* (Cambridge: Harvard University Press, 2001), 176–91.

13. See Mary Melandy, *Perfect Womanhood for Maidens, Wives, Mothers* (Boston: James H. Earle, 1901), 100; Fleetwood Churchill, *On the Theory and Practice of Midwifery* (Philadelphia: Blanchard and Lea, 1863), 449; Samuel Ashwell, *A Practical Treatise of the Diseases Peculiar to Women* (Philadelphia: Lea and Blanchard, 1845), 112, 105; George T. Elliot, *Obstetric Clinic* (New York: Appleton, 1868), 223, 224.

14. See Israel C. Russell, *Rivers of North America* (New York: Ginn, 1895), 22, 232, 233.

15. A. A. Humphreys, *Report on the Physics and Hydraulics of the Mississippi River* (Philadelphia: Lippincott), 94, 197.

16. Russell, 37, 259.

17. See David M. Oshinsky, *"Worse than Slavery": Parchman Farm and the Ordeal of Jim Crow Justice* (New York: Free Press, 1996), 162.

18. Ibid., 130–39.

19. Ibid., 140.

20. Ibid., 139.

21. "Font," of course, refers doubly to the source of the legal system as well as the type fonts of the pulp fiction which incited fantasies of train robbery.

22. According to the August 2002 report from the Department of Justice, by the end of 2001, one in thirty-two adults in the United States was behind bars, on parole, or on proba- tion—totaling 6.6 million people in the nation's correctional system, some two million per- sons incarcerated, the highest rate in the world, 700 per 100,000 citizens (while the Canadian and European countries average 80 to 121 per 100,000). "We've come to rely on the criminal justice system as a way of responding to social problems in a way that's unprece- dented," said Marc Mauer of The Sentencing Project, a nonprofit agency that conducts research on criminal justice policy issues. See *The Tennessean,* August 26, 2002, 7A. See also Joseph Hallinan, *Going Up the River: Travels in a Prison Nation* (New York: Random House, 2001) and Tara Herivel and Paul Wright, eds., *Prison Nation: The Warehousing of America's Poor* (New York: Routledge, 2003).

The Land's Turn

Philip Weinstein

Faulkner and Ecology: the topic may seem a bit willful, an attempt to align "our man" with some contemporary non-Faulknerian preoccupation. The more I reflected, however, the more appropriate this topic became. Not only because Faulkner's brooding imagination appears, itself, to be ecologically oriented, but also because "ecology" is hardly a recent concern. Probably derived from the Greek term *oikonomia*—home management, or "economy"—"ecology" involves the traffic between particular ("home-based") needs and the larger, always limited, resources available for meeting those needs. Like economy, ecology assumes scarcity, and therefore a reasoned deployment of limited social goods and natural resources. Concern for ecology is older than recorded history itself—is a staple of oral cultures—and the "ecological" element of Faulkner's work attaches to his most atavistic convictions. The "ecological" is the prediscursive in Faulkner's work that rebukes the endless spewing of speech.[1] It is no accident that the "ecological" lodges in that which does not speak—in the big woods that resist man's talky invasion, in the raging river that punishes any attempt to cross it, in the mule that symbolizes the very stubbornness of inertia. Put otherwise, the "ecological" in Faulkner refers to a territory of human norms premised on scarcity and shaped to a noncapitalist paradigm.[2]

Older than history: all oral societies managed to achieve their fundamental goal—survival—only by respecting ecological values. In his study of African societies, British historian Basil Davidson notes that, throughout the 1960s–1980s, liberated, postcolonial native regimes sought to imitate the prestigious economic models of their departing conquerors (British, French, Portuguese). Such models—based on a post-Enlightenment middle-class and a technological infrastructure permitting capitalistic progress—proved disastrous in Africa. As Davidson characterizes the precolonial practices that were *not* followed, a full-fledged ecological philosophy emerges into view. He writes: "Each of these ... societies, from lineage group to clan to cluster of clans, had to shape its behavior to fit its environment, its possible resources in food and shelter, its scope for political development.... The rules had to be explanatory so that people ... would understand why survival depended upon following them.... Therefore, they had to be the fruit of painstaking observation and analysis of soils and seasons and all the manifest diversities of nature, including human nature. In short, they had to be severely reasonable ... the very reverse of the blind dictates of superstition that nineteenth-century Europeans supposed to reign supreme on the 'dark continent.' "[3] The all-important goal of these noncapitalist cultures, generation after generation, was sustainability, not progress.

Older than history: oral cultures envisage history quite differently than literate ones do. With respect to Christianity this difference proved decisive, for what invading Christian colonizers could regard African natives and not see a people at least 1500 years behind the revealed truth: primitives, not yet aware of the good news that Christ brought so long ago? John Mbiti has shown that many African languages articulate temporality itself in ways tellingly different from the languages of the progressive West. Most African verb tenses, he shows, focus on the present, the immediate past, and the immediate future; the other tenses speak of the more distant (but still remembered) past and, beyond that, the sacred departed past (the realm of the spirits). *No verbs exist for an abstract future years away*: life is grasped, instead, as a concrete phenomenon moving past one, backwards, from the near future into the present, then to the recent past and finally to the distant past. The seasons, likewise, are demarcated not as abstracted months on an abstracted calendar, but as activity-filled periods—of planting or harvesting or building—that make up the concrete reality of the passing year.[4]

What has this to do with Faulkner? Ask the trees, the river, the horses, and the mules: if they could speak, they could tell you. And they would never say, as Thomas Sutpen does, "You see, I had a design in my mind. . . . To accomplish it I should require money, a house, a plantation, slaves, a family—incidentally of course, a wife. I set out to acquire these."[5] "Design . . . acquire": no nonwestern culture ever committed itself to such abstract conceptualizing, such insistent mapping of future time and space. Sutpen's "design" is as singular in its pursuit as aboriginal men's behavior was communal, shaped according to long-engrained norms.[6] And shaped at a level deeper than conscious thought or speech: the French sociologist Pierre Bourdieu describes such prediscursive shaping of individual behavior as *habitus*. Bourdieu's notion of habitus dissolves the oppositions between individual motive and social limitation, free and determined, that tend to polarize Western liberal thought. Instead, habitus involves recurring objective conditions which, over time, individuals have unthinkingly absorbed into their own reckoning, turning such reckoning into active dispositions. Bourdieu writes: "Because the dispositions ... inculcated by objective conditions ... engender aspirations and practices ... compatible with those objective requirements, the most improbable practices are excluded . . . as *unthinkable*."[7] Boiled down, as Faulkner might say, to six or eight words, viable habitus ensures successful ecological practice. Individuals seek what can be achieved within the available resources.

Bourdieu's natives act normatively (but *not* predictably: they are still free) within the flexible frame of their habitus, moved by dispositions deeper than conscious choices. Bourdieu describes these dispositions as "second natures." "The 'unconscious,'" he goes on to claim, "is never anything other than the forgetting of history which history itself produces by incorporating the objective structures it produces in the second natures of habitus: 'in each of us . . . there is part of yesterday's man; it is yesterday's man who inevitably predominates in us, since the present amounts to little compared with the long past in the course of which we were formed and from which we result. Yet we do not sense this man of the past, because he is inveterate in us; he makes up the unconscious part of ourselves.'" (79).[8] Such thinking is far from Freudian individualism: the unconscious is our forgotten social being, not our repressed personal desires. The unconscious part of ourselves, the part rooted deeper than choice, the part unthinkingly attached to yesterday's man and yesterday's world: Bourdieu's habitus, that inertial, long-gathering resistance to the new, coils at the heart of Faulkner's ecological imagination.

One's image of Faulkner does not reduce to the reactive traditionalist this model might suggest. Rather, the oldest strata in him, so to speak, is ecological: that inertial sense of things that, scandalized by the "abruption" of the new, seeks to escape, or to rebuke, such bewildering incursions. His Yoknapatawpha County thus shapes up as a precarious ecosystem itself established only by the inveigling and uprooting of a native population, and thereafter menaced, recurrently, by further crises, incursions, these driven by long-inculcated convictions and practices of opposing races, classes, and regions.[9] Put otherwise, Faulkner's work achieves its gravity because the wounds to body and spirit it records seem more stubbornly rooted, less open to therapy, than the more individualist dramas of a Fitzgerald or Hemingway. Whole ways of life are opposed and under attack. The resonance of these troubles seems to intimate the wounded land itself—the land that's "going to turn and destroy us all someday" (AA 7)—a kind of injury that goes deeper, and lasts longer, than mere individual pain. What makes this drama intractable is that the agents committing and receiving the damage are motivated by forces and orientations located beneath thought. Outrage is Faulkner's emotional signature because his protagonists act in accordance with unthinking cultural training. His great work dramatizes habitus against habitus, an agon waged between the yesterday's men predominating and inveterate in the men of today.

To find these yesterday's men he needed not Jay Gatsby but the mountain man Thomas Sutpen—not the tomorrow-ridden world of urban climbing but the yesterday-suffused world of a rural culture.

Habitus: cultural training that over the course of generations shapes individuals deeper than spoken discourse. Even Joe Christmas realizes "that a man would have to act as the land where he was born had trained him to act."[10] If it took generations of cultural training for Colonel Sartoris to find it normal to fire that gun upon unarmed Nathaniel and Calvin Burden, it took, no less, generations of cultural training for Nathaniel and Calvin Burden to find it normal to place themselves in front of Sartoris's gun. Yoknapatawpha County serves as the site, thus, of long-brooded scenarios of oppositional training confronting each other, contesting each other, and (with few mediating positions available) destroying each other. Habitus against habitus, both inalterable. Before turning to this violence in *Absalom, Absalom!*, let me sketch out the collision of opposing habituses in Faulkner's work. For if viable habitus just *means* a culture of subjects moving efficiently through familiar pathways of space and time, the Faulknerian canvas spectacularly refuses to stage precisely this. Rather than narrate normative movement, Faulkner attends to subject motion gone dysfunctional, incorrigibly awry, and heading toward either of two extremes: slow (too slow, intolerably slow) or fast (too fast, suicidally fast).

Slow, too slow: consider the ode to the mule in *Flags in the Dust*. "Steadfast to the land . . . impervious to conditions . . . [embodying] sheer and vindictive patience . . . misanthropic . . . misunderstood . . . moved neither by reason, flattery, nor promise of reward,"[11] the mule emerges as a mute signpost of long-ingrained, precapitalist Southern realities: daily and disfiguring labor upon the land, a patience wrought into him by immemorial repetitions, a gathered stubbornness of identity that nothing can deflect, that we recognize best when, desiring to get ahead, we try to hurry him up. A liminal creature, deeply inert, he straddles the line between sleep and waking, stasis and motion, as though he incarnated the inconceivable slowness of natural process itself. Immune to temptation, he is eternally what he is, even if this is other than what we want him to be, seeming to symbolize the gritty precapitalist South, and to rebuke every gadget inventable that might signal progress, getting ahead, rising.

Change mule for horse, and a more complex pattern emerges, since Faulkner's horses are both too slow and too fast. (The latter trait emerges unforgettably in the spotted horses no one is going to domesticate, a speed that intoxicates and disorients the peasants motionlessly regarding them.) Jewel's horse, however, reveals both more-than-human speed and more-than-human resistance to human control over that speed. "Then they are rigid, motionless, terrific, the horse back-thrust on stiffened, quivering legs, with lowered head."[12] A similar man-horse tension recurs in *Light in August*: Joe Christmas desperately beating McEachern's horse, trying to fly to Bobbie: "The stick still fell; as the progress of the horse slowed the speed of the stick increased in exact ratio. . . . Yet still the rider leaned forward in the arrested saddle, in the attitude of terrific speed" (LA 210). Silhouetted here is nature's inertial resistance to furious human purpose, frantic human design. If we change horse for dog, we get the haunting scene of Houston's dog blocking Mink's attempt to put Houston's corpse away, appearing and reappearing (despite Mink's ever more vicious attacks upon it) to thwart Mink's project.[13] You can't get away with this, such animal behavior silently says. Or in Sutpen language: this is a design that's not going to work, it goes against the grain of inertial nature itself. In such scenes everything hostile to the puny human figure's insistence on *imposing his will* seems to coalesce into the figures of mule, horse, and dog.[14]

Faulkner critics have long been attentive to Faulkner's brooding landscape, likewise silently resistant to human project. Most spectacularly, there is the raging river of "Old Man" and *As I Lay Dying*. It is antagonistic to human design; you can't submit yourself to that water and remain yourself. "The clotting which is you" runs the risk of dissolving "into the myriad original motion" (AILD 110). About such nonhuman implacability Doc Peabody reflects: "That's the one trouble with this country: everything, weather, all hangs on too long. Like our rivers, our land: opaque, slow, violent" (30). The inalterable self-sameness of the river appears here as more elemental than human project, more powerful than the *projectedness* of human project, as if the way that a reality (any reality) has long endured as itself counts for more than the way any character may press it to alter. Such atavistic self-insistence recalls Freud's proposal of an instinct older than the pleasure principle, beyond the pleasure principle: "*It seems, then,*" Freud writes, "*that an instinct is an urge inherent in organic life to restore an earlier state of things* . . . [thus expressing] the inertia inherent in organic life."[15] Instinct would be that in us that is prior to our identity and utterly unteachable. In this light we might reflect on the unparalleled *stubbornness* of Faulkner's characters, the assumption in his plots that whatever you are, deep down, elementally—at the level of "*central I-Am's private own*" (AA 112)—that's what you're going to be, all the way, to confrontation, annihilation, Gethsemane and crucifixion. Faulkner's mixed-race tragedies refuse the end run attempted in the plot of *passing*, as though such a progressive way of sidestepping race trouble amounted to a refusal to grant the trouble its genuine, long-gathered, all-destabilizing gravity.

This inertial stance appears recurrently in Faulkner's blacks, where it has a range of registers. "Too slow" is how Jason Compson reads such blacks, all blacks, as he scornfully muses: "like Roskus the only mistake he ever made was he got careless one day and died."[16] The text doesn't "forget" such scorn, though, and later Jason's own frantic motion makes him come a cropper. His head pounding with pain, he seeks to persuade one of the black boys in Mottstown to drive him back to Jefferson: " 'Is you do one wants to go to Jefferson?' he [the boy] said. 'Yes,' Jason said. 'What'll you charge me?' 'Fo dollars.' 'Give you two.' 'Can't go fer no less'n fo' " (313).

Quentin sees similar black imperturbability, and while it is similarly out of his reach (he is no less frantic than Jason), he at least has the wit to admire it. "Unimpatient" is his term for characterizing the unhurried black man on the mule, as the modern train rushes Quentin toward Jefferson. "Unimpatient": the term implies an ecological capacity to retain one's long-acquired stance toward the world despite the speed-insistent technologies of modern capitalism, to manage—when "patient" is no longer viable given the ubiquitous pressure—to not get caught in "impatient" but rather to find one's way past the newfangled obstacles, back into a patience that is now "unimpatience." Faulkner's poor whites sometimes manage "unimpatience" as well—witness Armstid and Winterbottom's traditional jockeying over the cultivator in *Light in August*, or the Bundrens' implacable delivery of Addie's body to the earth awaiting it (no matter the obstacles).[17] However complicated by private motives, these events unfold according to the inertial rhythms of shared habitus.

A willingness to rest within the dimensions of one's long-inculcated and confirmed identity: it is no accident this traditional virtue is mainly observed in Faulkner by its breach. Habitus enters his fictional world as rebuke, as resistance to change, as prejudice, but rarely as viable norm. Habitus does not prosper: Faulkner's protagonists typically shatter, and are shattered by, habitus. Yet his fiction is not drawn to just any iconoclastic character. In fact, Faulkner's most resonant twentieth-century habitus-destroyer— Flem Snopes—is represented almost wholly through the lenses of others. Could it be because this figure, expertly at ease with the moves required for acquisition and progress, this rural capitalist, is simply outside the field of long-brooded pieties (of habituses) Faulkner seems to require of his subjects when he chooses to go in deep? Is Flem kept representationally at arm's length because, deep down, he has no long-matured, socially inculcated "central I-Am's private own," and is thus immune to the outraging of such a center?

By contrast, when Lucas Beauchamp engages in his own Flem-like form of legerdemain, outwitting the whites who would outwit him, he is swiftly brought back into line, receiving from the earth an ecological rebuke: "the entire overhang sloughed. It drummed on the hollow kettle . . . and boiled about his feet and, as he leaped backward and tripped and fell, about his body too, hurling clods and dirt at him, striking a final blow squarely in the face with something larger than a clod . . . a sort of final admonitory pat from the spirit of darkness and solitude, the old earth, perhaps the old ancestors themselves."[18] The moving earth reveals the gold coin that will catalyze Lucas's later efforts to rise, but that "admonitory pat" seems to say, in earth talk, "beware: if there is buried treasure here, it means to stay buried." Lucas eventually realizes, after one too many trials, that "to find that money aint for me" (101). The very phrasing is redolent of a speechless inertial order rebuking the human desire for labor-free upward mobility.

Slow, too slow: elements of ecological stasis appear as the rooted resistance to violently imposed change; they serve to silhouette the abruption of fast, too fast. The shattering that occurs when events of break-neck speed burst upon traditional practices is virtually the hallmark of Faulknerian narrative. Remove the violence of the too-fast airplane and there is not only no Bayard Sartoris or *Pylon*, there is no William Faulkner coming back to a-now-understood-as-terminally-too-slow Oxford, Mississippi. You can no more imagine his work prior to the modern technology of car and airplane than you can imagine it later in the postmodern technology of virtual reality. In the former there would be only inertial slowness and the chicanery that abuses it (he might have become a minor Balzac), in the latter there would be only inhuman speed and the dizzy subject-morphing that accompanies it (he might resemble a DeLillo). Instead his moment is vintage early twentieth-century modernism. He still knows (imaginatively knows) the mind's dependence upon the ecological rhythms of a culture's habitus, but he knows these sanity-producing rhythms only as under assault.

Flight in Faulkner is incandescent because its speed is unmanageable. For Bayard, for the pilots in *Pylon*, flight means the ecstatic risking— wrecking—of identity. In early Faulkner the speed of a car can be equally destructive: "She [Temple] sat and watched rigidly and quietly as Gowan, apparently looking straight ahead, drove into the tree at twenty miles an hour. The car struck, bounded back, then drove into the tree again and turned onto its side. She felt herself flying through the air. . . . She scrambled to her feet, her head reverted, and saw [the two men] step into the road, the one in a suit of tight black and a straw hat. . . . Still running her bones turned to water and she fell flat on her face, still running."[19]

Too fast: Faulkner is not only drawn to scenes of uncontrollable speed, but his writerly identity emerges as one who can *write* speed, the speed of the mind hurtling into moments for which it has no preparation. Benjy's bellowing registers the anguish of being moment-by-moment unprepared, and in this he is echoed by Quentin's "*Wait I'll get used to it in a minute wait just a minute I'll get"* (115). Stream-of-consciousness technique appears (first in Joyce, later in Faulkner) as that use of language appropriate for the velocity of modern life: ungrammatical, fragmented, sharp edged, hurtling into the past before it is even fully thought. Stream-of-consciousness revises the prose of realism in order to bring it up to technological speed.

Such speed in Faulkner issues into wreckage, violence. Think of Joe Christmas careening into Bobbie's room: "He opened the door. He was running now; that is, as a man might run far ahead of himself and his knowing in the act of stopping stock still. The waitress sat at on the bed. . . . She sat with her face lowered, not even looking at the door when it opened. . . . And in the same instant he saw the second man. He had never seen the man before. But he did not realise this now" (214). Not just that he gets badly beaten about thirty seconds after this passage, but beaten by a man he has never seen. Other examples of violent shock in Faulkner will occur to every reader, the common element being that his characters never do get used to it.

Too fast, too slow: the shattering of expectation (appropriate subject-motion through space and time) is everywhere in Faulkner. "Wait!" Shreve cries out in *Absalom!*—echoing the distress of all first readers of that novel who cannot catch up to its speed. More, Faulkner's dilemmas don't "come right" even if you do wait. Too fast is forever too fast, no mediating reforms are on the way, and "go slow now" is slower than anyone seeking reform can accommodate.[20] The race dilemma Faulkner confronted would never come right by way of any slowness he could envisage, just as the inane racial advice offered to Charles Bon's son by Grandfather Compson avails nothing: "and your grandfather speaking the lame vain words, the specious and empty fallacies which we call comfort, thinking *Better that he were dead, better that he had never lived*" (AA 166). Such inalterable wrongness, such culturally mandated disaster, is virtually Sophoclean in its gravity. What's wrong in Faulkner is *really* wrong. I turn now to *Absalom, Absalom!* as the Faulknerian canvas that plays out this agon on the grandest scale.

There are at least six different settings in *Absalom, Absalom!*—this is the Faulkner novel that does most with its settings—but I shall focus on the ecological charge of only two of these (West Virginia and New Orleans) as they impact a third, Jefferson. As Shreve implies through his refusal to let Quentin call Sutpen's mountain home West Virginia, there was no West Virginia in the early 1800s. This territory becomes West Virginia when, on the eve of Civil War, it repudiated slavery—at least in part because it had no cotton or tobacco crops dependent on slavery—and declared its separateness. The political and economic concerns motivating this separation are inseparable from ecological factors: an entire society organizing itself differently here, with different work rhythms, different landscapes to manage and thus different crops, as well as a different structure of class and race formations that inculcate subject norms. There are no aristocrats in *Absalom's* West Virginia, no blacks, no insistently defined property rights.[21] It is a sort of rough Eden, this fantasied mountain territory in which a little boy grows up, innocent of difference. The others he sees surrounding him are of his essential kind—maybe stronger, maybe better clothed, but still versions of his potential self—a commonality of roles and behaviors that function as habitus: "Because where he lived the land belonged to anybody and everybody and so the man who would go to the trouble and work to fence off a piece of it and say 'This is mine' was crazy; and as for objects, nobody had any more of them than you did because everybody had just what he was strong or energetic enough to take and keep, and only that crazy man would go to the trouble to take or even want more than he could eat or swap for powder or whiskey" (179).

I say "fantasied" because Faulkner goes beyond sociological sobriety here, imagining a culture somehow free of money itself, in which there simply do not exist the alienations and abstractions Marx aligns with all Western societies premised on money and private property. As always with successful habitus, the culture's daily realities regulate a learned normative traffic between subjects and other subjects—norms absorbed into the body's unthinking practices. A man stepping into a ring with others in order to test his physical mettle is one of those practices, and surely Sutpen's wrestling with his slaves is as much an act of mountain nostalgia as it is a demonic assault upon Southern pieties. But of course the point is that in the South it *is* an assault—the South where the black slave body is variously dreamed of, despised, and beaten, but never publicly embraced or intimately abused like white bodies.

Sutpen leaves the mountain, but the mountain does not leave him. It is "yesterday's man" who enters that ring, an entry he seems to propose (as often with Sutpen) more in blankness than in malice. Likewise, his outrageous proposal to Rosa later simply spills out of him; it is hardly calculated, despite Shreve's insistence, to blast Rosa out of his orbit (he needs her cooperation if he is to get his legitimate son). Rather than acting like a demon here, he appears (as with Ellen after the wrestling match) surprised, bemused, blank: his gestures have spurred responses he never intended. Is it too much to speculate that we see in him not Mr. Compson's figure of agile resourcefulness ("*Given the occasion and the need, this man can and will do anything*" [35]), but rather the reverse, a blank and disoriented vertigo born of too much traveling, of conflicting habituses? He is no less bewildered in Grandfather Compson's office in 1865, wondering what mistake he made. Grandfather Compson thunders at him: "Didn't the very affinity and instinct for misfortune of a man who had spent that much time in a monastery even, let alone one who had lived that many years as you lived them, tell you better than that?" (213). Put otherwise, how could you *not* have learned not to do what you did? Have you no sense of what is appropriate, what goes with what, what follows what? These are the questions one poses to a man deprived of what we call common sense, a man without habitus, though in this case it's a man with too many habituses (as he had too many sons): one habitus that says you get in the ring with men you want to master, another habitus that says you refuse to acknowledge the very existence of your own son if he carries a speck of black blood. Nothing in Sutpen seems native any longer, can be taken for granted, nothing that might appear instinctive (no residual feeling for Bon's distress, for example). His jostling habituses lose their regional viability, yet continue to shape him at a level deeper than choice, directing his moves rather than clarifying his mind.

Demonic, Rosa calls him, but she ends her chapter with a more revealing description of his disorder: *"Because he was not articulated in this world. He was a walking shadow. He was the light-blinded bat-like image of his own torment cast by the fierce demoniac lantern up from beneath the earth's crust and hence in retrograde, reverse . . . clinging, trying to cling with vain unsubstantial hands to what he hoped would hold him, save him, arrest him"* (139). Terminally maladaptive, Sutpen has traveled too much. Absorbing the ecological norms of incompatible cultures, he remains baffled, beneath and beyond the tactics available to consciousness. His colliding allegiances cancel each other out, and the mountain boy who trusted his hands as the gauge for measuring whatever was true about life ends his own life utterly confused by the mess he has made with his "vain unsubstantial hands."

If West Virginia encountering the Tidewater is a disaster, even worse is New Orleans transposed upon Northern Mississippi: the ecological nightmare of Charles Etienne St. Valery Bon's "environed blood."[22] Born in a New Orleans in which he "could neither have heard nor yet recognised the term 'nigger', who even had no word for it in the tongue he knew who had been born and grown up in a padded silken vacuum . . . where pigmentation had no more moral value than the silk walls and the scent and the rose-colored candle shades" (AA 161), this child is seized by Clytie and transported—without explanation or even a shared language—to a Northern Mississippi where the space he inhabits has altered seismically, beyond assimilation:

(the rags of the silk and broadcloth in which he had arrived, the harsh jeans and homespun which the two women bought and made for him, he accepting them with no thanks, no comment, accepting his garret room with no thanks, no comment, asking for and making no alteration in its spartan arrangements that they knew of until that second year when he was fourteen and one of them, Clytie or Judith, found hidden beneath his mattress the shard of broken mirror: and who to know what hours of amazed and tearless grief he might have spent before it, examining himself in the delicate and outgrown tatters in which he perhaps could not even remember himself, with quiet and incredulous incomprehension).... (162)

Recognizing yourself in a mirror: Jacques Lacan has bewitched a generation of critics into seeing, in this mirror scene, the founding institution of (Western) culture within the not-yet-subject. The infant sees in the mirror a radiant image, centered and mobile, of who he-is-to-be. The image proposes an unattained imaginary wholeness that spurs the infant into the social framework he would make his own. The mother's eyes confirm the infant's desire and launch the forward-moving progress through time that, for Lacan, is simultaneously alienation and "maturity." Either way, the physics of the scene organizes space as a mirroring frame in which the infant projects his desire-fueled image of himself-to-be. The drama is projective, individualistic; its motor is orientational, its aim patriarchal. In Lacan's argument about the mirror stage, the structure of a culture's liberal norms is being encountered, identified, and pursued.

Bon's son's mirror operates in reverse. It shows him the chasm between what he was and what he is, each stance underwritten by generations of cultural training. Every present item of clothing reads as the betrayal of a former item of clothing. His New Orleans-furnished body has been intolerably displaced by his Mississippi-furnished body, none of this his own choice. As in Lacan, this is an identity-launching moment, but it inaugurates not a centering but an implosion. Charles Etienne St. Valery Bon materializes as a culturally incoherent being, torn between here and there, now and then. He has no ecological model that might resolve this ideological tearing. The habituses of Puritan Northern Mississippi and Catholic New Orleans, the jagged racist present and the harmonious race-neutral past, share him equally and without possibility of mediation. He joins these incompatible orientations in the form of crucifixion.

Identity, as always in Faulkner, operates as social coding that shapes the body; and Bon's son's body is marked by contradictory social scriptings that permit no erasures. One needs an infrared light to read the black man in this white man, but he makes it easy by guaranteeing, through premeditated acts of violence, that he be recognized as impossibly both, at once. Performing white and black codes to fiendishly intelligible effects, a cultural semiotician before the term was coined, Charles Etienne chooses for a wife exactly the kind of black woman that white and black alike will decode (for opposed reasons) as scandalous. Alert to every nuance of the cultural codes that entrap him, he naturalizes nothing, learns nothing. Time cannot heal him, nor space accommodate him, nor mores fit him; his clothes are irreparably wrong before they become bloodied as well. He does not so much communicate through language as strike through gesture. Time, space, mores, clothes, and language permit the functioning of cultural habitus only so long an organizing culture can impose its norms. By contrast, *Absalom, Absalom!* reveals, for its characters who cross cultural boundaries, an impossible living space, an ecological disaster. As with Sutpen, yesterday's child rages inside Charles Etienne, lodged speechlessly in the most intimate physical assumptions of his New Orleans childhood, these at war with the most intimate physical assumptions of his Mississippi adulthood.

"A man will talk about how he'd like to escape from living folks," Byron Bunch muses in *Light in August*. "But it's the dead folks that do him the damage. It's the dead ones that lay quiet in one place and dont try to hold him, that he cant escape from" (75). The dead, I suggest, may be as influential in Faulkner's fictional world as they are in any African oral culture. Hugh Kenner once remarked that, to produce his crucial effects, Faulkner needed a multi-generational history;[23] and I take this to mean that Faulkner has an ecological imagination, attuned to long-inculcated traditions about how individuals move in space and time. That which is impersonal, inertial, group-formed—the heavy weight of time-soaked norms (however prejudicial)—trumps the individualist projects of today and tomorrow. Yet Yoknapatawpha County offers no positive alternative to change, no viable backwater of peaceful continuities. Traversed by speed and violence, riddled by brutal tensions of race, class, gender, and region, it is a microcosm of American (indeed, hemispheric) troubles, not a sanctuary of escape from them. Surely the ideas of sanctuary and immunity loom so large in Faulkner's work precisely because he was unable to secure them.

Faulknerian ecology, I conclude, means something grimmer than the benign causes we currently group together under the notion of ecology. Rather, it points to his atavistic sense for the inertial, for impersonal forces immune to individual will and likely at any moment to torpedo the progressive reach of individual projects. "Breathing is a sight-draft dated yesterday," Will Varner notes in *The Hamlet*,[24] that which surrounds us predates and outweighs our designs. Such imminent shattering catalyzes Faulkner's imagination, highlights the pathos of his dreams of peace. He is a writer of would-be habituses, subverted might-have-beens. His most compelling psychological territory is that of unhealing wounds; his most radiant pain is that of the inability to forget. As Rider puts it eloquently,

"Hit look lack Ah just cant quit thinking. Look lack Ah just cant quit" (GDM 120).

Faulkner's work is marked by an irrepressible yet doomed desire to "quit thinking," to find a sanctuary beyond the reach of thought, to escape. Three related terms for this hopeless quest are immunity, insanity, and intoxication. His most memorable characters long for immunity, and it cannot be accidental that three of his protagonists—Benjy Compson, Ike Snopes, and Jim Bond—live out their insanity as a subjective space spared the outrages endured by the sane. Faulkner himself, we know, sought hopelessly and ritualistically to drink himself into oblivion—that form of return-to-infancy forgetting (clothes removed, bottle at his mouth) that ends with a bursting head, a cotton tongue, renewed consciousness, and more tormenting memories. We are the lucky ones finally, not he, that his projected escapes failed, and that only in the act of writing itself—"in the raging and incredulous recounting (which enables man to bear with living") (AA 130)—was he able, not to elude his demons, and even less to face them down, but rather to engage them through words, and live to tell it. In his tragic work a dark ecology prevails. The rebuke is delivered. The wounded land itself turns and destroys: it is the land's turn. In the wake of such disaster nothing gets righted, but everything, finally, gets written.

NOTES

1. Prediscursive, yes, but likewise historically fueled: the pell-mell progressive upheavals that characterize capitalism rouse what I am calling Faulkner's ecological rebuke, in the name of inertial, sanity-confirming routines.

2. Stephen Toulmin has argued at length that the Cartesian model underlying Western modernity is anti-ecological. In its rigid separation of human from natural domains—of the realm of freedom and spirit from that of law and matter—this Cartesian model conceptualizes the material world as an unrelated, objective realm passively awaiting subjective mapping and control. By contrast, ecological thinking begins by positing human subjects as irrevocably immersed within shared biological and physiological networks: such subjects sustain themselves only by sustaining these contextual networks. See "The Far Side of Modernity" in Toulmin's *Cosmopolis: The Hidden Agenda of Modernity* (New York: Free Press, 1990).

3. Davidson, *The Black Man's Burden: Africa and the Curse of the Nation-State* (New York: Random House, 1992), 80–81.

4. See John Mbiti, *African Religions and Philosophy* (London: Heinemann, 1969), especially chapters 1–2. It is no accident that ecological thought attaches so powerfully to the realities of time passing. Preliterate societies foregrounded what modern (capitalist) societies have been learning the hard way: that the survival of life systems is inseparable from an acceptance of the processes of death and renewal wrought into the very meaning of survival. As many of the papers in this volume attest, Faulkner's characters' dreams of monumentality and immortality are incompatible with the ecological trajectory of all living (and dying) things. Such biological change is not only normal but seems to be hard wired into the systems subtending organic life.

5. Faulkner, *Absalom, Absalom!* (New York: Vintage International, 1990), 212. Subsequent citation from *Absalom* refers to this edition; page numbers will be indicated, parenthetically, after the citation.

6. However foreign to the norms of Jefferson, Mississippi—as well as to the norms of the mountain culture where he grew up—Sutpen's design remains, of course, normative to the hilt. He takes it wholesale from the Tidewater practices that damaged him earlier, and he never thereafter calls its "normality" into question. For this reason, preapproved and unchallenged, it shapes his later behavior in the manner of habitus.

7. Bourdieu, *Outline of a Theory of Practice* (1972), trans. Richard Nice (Cambridge: Cambridge University Press, 1977), 77. *Habitus* resembles *ideology* enough for the reader to wonder why I use the one term rather than the other. The reason is that, within Western liberal discourse (descending from Marx and amended by Althusser), *ideology* is a negatively charged term that tends to assume a subject's illusory take upon the real. The tonic aspect of *habitus*, however, is its positivity, its rootedness in the social imaginary. Habitus denotes socially inculcated, unthinkingly appropriate modes of individual behavior, rather than the mystified stances that a power system proffers, as ideology, for complicit subjective consumption. Put otherwise, *habitus* belongs to a non-Western vocabulary of social trust, even as *ideology* belongs to a Western vocabulary of social suspicion. That said, it is all too easy for Western critics to oversimplify *habitus* and imagine non-Western societies as possessing a seamless social order that has in fact never existed.

8. Drawing on the same notion of unthinking incorporation of past attitudes (physical as well as mental), Henry Bergson writes: "The past collects in the fibers of the body as it does in the mind and determines the way we walk and dance as well as the way we think" (*Matter and Memory* [1896], cited in Stephen Kern, *The Culture of Time and Space: 1880–1914* [Cambridge: Harvard University Press, 1983], 41).

9. Edouard Glissant's *Faulkner, Mississippi* (trans. Barbara Lewis and Thomas C. Spear [New York: Farrar, Straus, and Giroux, 1999]) launched a more extensive investigation of the American South within the larger history of the hemispheric South—a history replete with colonial invasions, the rise and fall of the slave trade, and the commercial pathways linking Europe, Africa, and the Caribbean that enabled this traffic. It is increasingly clear that any polarity pitting the American South against the American North both reduces the South's complexity and furthers the illusion of U.S. history as "exceptional."

10. Faulkner, *Light in August* (New York: Vintage International, 1990), 255. Subsequent citation from *Light in August* refers to this edition; page numbers will be indicated, parenthetically, after the citation.

11. Faulkner, *Flags in the Dust* (New York: Random House, 1973), 267–68.

12. Faulkner, *As I Lay Dying*, in *Faulkner's Novels: 1930–1935.* (New York: Library of America, 1985), 9. Subsequent citation from *As I Lay Dying* refers to this edition; page numbers will be indicated, parenthetically, after the citation.

13. For recent commentary on Mink's dog as symptomatic of Faulkner's natural world, see Theresa Towner, "Unsurprised Flesh: Color, Race, and Identity in Faulkner's Fiction," in *Faulkner and the Natural World: Faulkner and Yoknapatawpha, 1996*, ed. Donald Kartiganer (Jackson: University Press of Mississippi, 1999), 49–50.

14. It should be clear that I am describing, not a metatextual reality, but rather a discursive structure operative in Faulkner's work. As such, his work participates in a (romantic) genre in which, however assaulted and abused, inhuman nature remains an implicitly moralized force, capable of erupting irresistibly in human affairs and revealing their "puniness."

15. Quoted from *Beyond the Pleasure Principle*, in *The Freud Reader*, ed. Peter Gay (New York: Norton, 1989), 612.

16. Faulkner, *The Sound and the Fury* (New York: Vintage International, 1990), 251. Subsequent citation from *The Sound and the Fury* refers to this edition; page numbers will be indicated, parenthetically, after the citation.

17. As these examples make clear, Faulknerian "inertia" is never just a phenomenon of "nature": it is shaped by differential social groups who have managed over time to sustain the viable conventions I have been calling habitus. Such long-gathered conventions regulating race and class interaction are inherently precarious, vulnerable to the "abruption" of colonial and capitalist forces that may be released (as in the cases of Sutpen and Flem Snopes) by the entry of a single all-disturbing figure.

18. Faulkner, *Go Down, Moses*, in *Faulkner's Novels: 1942–1954*. (New York: Library of America, 1994), 29–30. Subsequent citation from *Go Down, Moses* refers to this edition; page numbers will be indicated, parenthetically, after the citation.

19. Faulkner, *Sanctuary*, in *Faulkner's Novels: 1930–1935*. (New York: Library of America, 1985), 205. Subsequent citation from *Sanctuary* refers to this edition; page numbers will be indicated, parenthetically, after the citation.

20. "Go slow now" is of course Faulkner's notorious phrase of the early 1950s, admonishing blacks not to pursue their civil rights at a pace swifter than their actual deserving. For unpacking and dissent, see Charles D. Peavy, *Go Slow Now: Faulkner and the Race Question* (Eugene: University of Oregon Press, 1971).

21. As Charles Sydnor puts it in *The Development of Southern Sectionalism* (Baton Rouge: Louisiana State University Press, 1948), "Most of the opponents of slavery lived west of the Blue Ridge Mountains—a land where there were few slaves, a land whose white inhabitants believed that they had been abused and misgoverned time and again by the politically dominant east. Most of the defenders lived in the Tidewater and Piedmont, where there were more blacks than whites" (228). Thanks to John Matthews for this reference.

22. The following argument about Charles Etienne de Saint Valery Bon draws substantially on my essay "Cant Matter/Must Matter," in *Look Away: The U.S. South in New World Studies*, ed. Jon Smith and Deborah Cohn (Durham: Duke University Press, 2004), as well as, slightly altered, in my forthcoming study entitled *Unknowing: The Work of Modernist Fiction*.

23. See Hugh Kenner, *A Home-Made World* (New York: Knopf, 1975), 205–6.

24. Faulkner, *The Hamlet*, in *William Faulkner, Novels 1936–1940* (New York: Library of America, 1990), 1019.

Environed Blood: Ecology and Violence in *The Sound and the Fury* and *Sanctuary*

Eric Gary Anderson

1. "his own environed blood"

Few readers of Faulkner would contest the observation that his fiction contains moments of gruesome, horrific violence. Few would question the rightness of the Faulkner and Yoknapatawpha Conference's 1996 theme, "Faulkner and the Natural World." And few would deny that blood flows in many directions in his body of work, touching on issues of lineage, kinship, race, miscegenation, disposition, crime, and punishment.[1] But when it comes to linking these three Faulknerian givens, few have made much headway. I propose that blood, environing, and violence *do* work together, ecologically, in his fiction, and that these interrelationships in all their traumatic intensity help broaden and deepen our understanding of how his characters experience and articulate pain and loss. For my purposes, "environing" is not exactly the same thing as a sense of the natural world. It cannot easily be explained by way of a literary technique such as setting, a literary genre such as pastoral, or a mythos such as wilderness. It does not, in Faulkner, work quite as conventionally as these categories often do, in part because it involves an aggressive physicality that (often) emphasizes the strangeness of blood-soaked places. In other words, I read blood by way of ecology, the study of relationships between organisms and their environments, and I argue that such relationships often take the form of problematic convergences, often bear strange fruit, and typically raise nagging questions about, among other things, the violence of environing and the environing of violence.

Before turning to *The Sound and the Fury* and *Sanctuary*, though, I want briefly to discuss *Light in August*, the novel that provides my key phrase "environed blood." Thinking of the ghosts of congregations past and of a present congregation for whom he himself is a kind of ghost, the Reverend Gail Hightower listens to a distant strain of "Protestant music" and "seems to hear within it the apotheosis of his own history, his own land, his own environed blood."[2] Hightower, from his accustomed seated position, imagines that "the past week has rushed like a torrent" (368) and the fluctuating world seems to be heading catastrophically toward "the abyss" while at the same time resolving itself into a unanimity that doesn't include him: "now on the brink of cataract the stream has raised a single blended and sonorous and austere cry" (368). The three Christian churches of Jefferson blend into a single voice calling for an unambiguous response to the ambiguously blooded Joe Christmas. Throughout this passage, Hightower remains alone, betrays little or no interest in working on Christmas's behalf, and dissociates himself from the townspeople he persists in seeing as "them" rather than "us"—and yet the notion of "his own environed blood" intimates that he has a place here, and a deeply embedded blood relationship with this place.

But how do place and self, environing and blood, come together to form some sort of working relationship, and why is Hightower, of all people, the character thus environed? Discussions of the novel's nature-mindedness, including its pastoral elements, usually center around Lena Grove. Lawrence Buell, for example, suggests that Lena is a "Madonna/ Earth Mother" type within a larger context of "environmental realism," while Diane Roberts remarks on Lena's "inarticulate . . . fecundity" and her role as "the fertile presiding goddess of an apparently restored order."[3] An excellent though necessarily very different case can be made for Joe Christmas's nonchalant and/or hostile immersions in nature; Christmas moves in and out of pastoral trappings, especially when stalking women, and witlessly plays the role of "clodhopper" to Bobbie Allen's streetwise urban prostitute (206) without having the slightest idea of what pastoral is and how pastoral characters are supposed to behave. (Joe at one point *kills* a sheep.) His negotiations of country and city accentuate his inner rustic clown but ultimately make for mock pastoral if not anti-pastoral. Of course, the major characters in *Light in August* are neither agrarian nor indigenous to Jefferson, Mississippi; Lena, for example, ends up hitting her migratory stride rather than settling into a particular local environment. Hightower rambles—mentally—while sitting for hours on end in the window of his bungalow, engulfed in his domestic, masculine spoor: the dirty dishes and rank furnishings that mark his predictable yet unsettled mind. Having once struck his congregation as "a sort of cyclone that did not even need to touch the actual earth" (62), he still seems pretty far removed from that "actual earth" and from the intimate fusing of earth and self that the phrase "environed blood" implies.

But violence and (to some extent) regeneration through violence[4] bind him to this particular place (as they also bind Joanna Burden to her particular place). The house of Hightower (like the house of Burden) is a house of blood in at least two senses: it passes down a bloody, place-based lineage that in turn environs the blood of living descendants, and it becomes, in the narrative present, a bloody crime scene. To make the connection

between blood and place more explicit, Faulkner quite purposefully presents Hightower's family history in the chapter immediately following the
murder of Joe Christmas in Hightower's bungalow. About three generations back, his grandfather was killed in Jefferson, during the Civil War—
another fusing of blood, environing, and regeneration through violence.
And after the grandson excitedly settles in Jefferson, acts of violence
involving his wife, himself, his house, and his acquaintances continue to
bind him to this particular place, rather than to wrench him away from it.
It's not exactly that violence begets violence, but for Hightower, violence
begets something like rootedness in place and a commitment to his own
particular, peculiar strain of participatory and rather bloody regionalism.

I hasten to emphasize here that "environed blood" does not necessarily
denote race first and foremost, although race is clearly of huge importance
to each of the novels I discuss.[5] Perhaps because whiteness has been less
visible than most any other color when it comes to race, Faulkner treats
Hightower's "environed blood" not as racial but as racialized, implicated
in Southern cultural constructions of race. But, as I have been suggesting,
Hightower is also (and more explicitly) "placialized," grounded in an
uneasy convergence of physical environment, inherited memories of
familial violence, and, finally, eyewitness experience of bloody death in his
own house. All this comprises "his own environed blood: that people from
which he sprang and among whom he lives who can never take either
pleasure or catastrophe or escape from either, without brawling over it.
Pleasure, ecstasy, they cannot seem to bear: their escape from it is in violence, in drinking and fighting and praying; catastrophe, too, the violence
identical and apparently inescapable" (367–68). Violence, an "apparently
inescapable" escape, is in his blood and this blood is in his place—literally
as well as figuratively. For Hightower as well as for Faulkner, this sort of
convergence is twisted and garbled, inevitable and claustrophobic, *and*, I
argue, ecological at root.

This paper investigates the hinge, in Faulkner's major early fiction, that
connects environing to a sometimes bloody and almost always blood-
driven violence. As it turns out, the ecologies that most powerfully lay
hold of characters' minds and readers' experiences are not nurturing,
happy, organically unified, and generally functioning so much as they are
suffocating, traumatic, bloody, and generally dysfunctional. Examining
the criminal narrative *Sanctuary* alongside the family romance *The Sound
and the Fury*, I want to argue that both bring to light the compulsive if
not nightmarish elements of interrelatedness, that crucial—and often
romanticized—ecocritical concept. Moreover, the characters who most
intensely and insistently think ecologically (or position themselves in or
against "nature," or simply find themselves entangled with or otherwise

up against nature) are very troubled characters indeed. Environing is a form of turbulence, a symptom of something like a terminal disease, even a reason for suicide or murder; the ecology of the South rattles, deadens, and even kills. "Man the sum of his climatic experiences Father said. Man the sum of what have you":[6] archly ironic as he so often is, Quentin's father as filtered through Quentin's memory is nevertheless more than half right. With or without the racializations that more familiarly circulate around Southern notions of blood, these troubled convergences and mixtures very much sum up the literary and cultural ecology of William Faulkner's South.

2. Ecodysfunctions

The term "ecocriticism," in Lawrence Buell's view, is a "semineologistic label" for a "unidoctrinalist imputation"; this lurking, polysyllabic unease and dissatisfaction perhaps has to do with the very flexibility and amorphousness of the field itself.[7] As Buell points out, "ecocriticism still lacks a paradigm-inaugurating statement like Edward Said's *Orientalism* (for colonial discourse studies) or Stephen Greenblatt's *Renaissance Self-Fashioning* (for new historicism)."[8] Making things still more open-ended, Scott Slovic observes that "not a single literary work anywhere utterly defies ecocritical interpretation, is off-limits to green reading."[9] Ironically, this sense of loosely bounded inclusiveness comes in the wake of the now fairly well-known and acknowledged limitations of ecocriticism's earlier days, especially its seemingly instant canon (Thoreau, Muir, Leopold, Abbey, *et al.*) comprised almost entirely of white American male nonfiction "nature writers." Buell adds that the movement's early days also featured other "parochialisms" such as emphasis "on country landscapes, on traditional conservationist or preservationist thinking at the expense of other environmental(ist) persuasions (particularly the environmental justice movement), and on modes of criticism excessively reactive against poststructuralist or cultural studies models instead of on direct constructive engagement."[10] Agreeing with Buell and at the same time extending his remarks, Krista Comer points out that ecocriticism often focuses on a short list of preferred western places, chiefly the Rocky Mountains and the American (much more often than the Mexican) Southwest. Its "view of nature," she writes, is "holistic . . . 'innocent,' and transparent, while it simultaneously sums up a vague environmentalists' agenda: the desire for a more 'real' or environmentally sane life can be found in simpler living and a retreat from a postmodern world that decenters what ideally should be the 'whole' self." In other words, ecocritics favor "pure" wilderness and "a love of wide-open, 'wild' spaces; a penchant for the mystical, which is

also the 'natural,' American Indian; the suggestion of redemptive possibility; a disavowal of the industrial or technological; and representations of
woman as nature."[11] Obviously, ecocritics such as these betray little incli-
nation toward places such as northern Mississippi, which, after all, pretty
much defy their expectations every step of the way.

Faulkner, likewise, frustrates these designs, so much so that it can be
difficult to "place" him within conventional ecocritical confines. (Indeed,
as recently as the mid 1990s, a conference on "Faulkner and the Ecology
of the South" might very well have been seen—by ecocritics—as a bit
diversionary.) But it is also clear that Faulkner's fiction has much to do
with ecology, that he is very interested in the functionings and the "careers"
of particular socially constructed human communities as they interact
with the natural world and with other built communities. Maybe what we
need to do is define ecocriticism a little differently, to clarify its openness
to fiction and, by extension, to Faulkner. My working definition takes
the form of a list of four hypotheses, the first two of which loosen the
link between ecocriticism and the writing of nonfiction: 1. Ecocriticism
doesn't necessarily require that literary critics have an extensive working
knowledge of the biological sciences. 2. Environmentally inclined literature doesn't necessarily concern itself with "accurate" observation of
places. It allows for writerly license, in other words. It also acknowledges
that "environment" doesn't always mean "the natural world"; when we
talk, for example, about nature and nurture, heredity and environment,
we are talking about more than the flora and fauna of a person's youth.
And, closer to home for literary critics, all literary representations of environments are "built": textually constructed. Environmental realism can
only go so far. 3. Natural or constructed or both, ecologies by definition
bring different types of things together to create a living, breathing, surviving ecosystem. 4. But these ecosystems are not always stable; they fluc-
tuate dynamically and sometimes break down, age, become less viable. In
fact, this instability can be beneficial: an unstable, even "dysfunctional"
ecosystem is better able to adapt to changing environments and survive
disturbances.[12] Ecocriticism therefore can and should examine dysfunctional interrelationships; as William Howarth puts it, "Ecocriticism seeks
to examine how metaphors of nature and land are used and abused."[13]
That is, it seeks to examine textual representations of both productive and
abusive relationships between people and places. My work investigates
the implications of this working definition by, again, arguing that in
Faulkner's early major fiction, there is a powerful, underestimated relationship between the traumas or other violent experiences of particular
characters and the ways those characters articulate and reflect their traumas ecologically. How are metaphors of nature and land used and abused

in Faulkner? In roughly the same ways the metaphor-making characters themselves have been, or believe they have been, used and abused.

3. "the honeysuckle got all mixed up in it": *The Sound and the Fury*

Although mentioned only once in the volume *Faulkner and the Natural World*, *The Sound and the Fury* is, as I have already begun to suggest, a significant ecological text. As criticism of the novel amply documents, readers have gotten caught up in its various other challenges: its narrative structure, its portrayals of family and race relations, its psychoanalytic and mythic ramifications, and more particularly for my purposes, its downplaying of explicit relationships among the four sections.[14] Since 1929, the novel has compelled its readers to articulate relationships among sections and characters and, in so doing, to take a potentially ecocritical approach. But that approach still needs to be taken considerably further, and to do so I would point to traumatized characters such as Benjy and Quentin Compson, who give ecological expression to their various psychic and physical wounds as a way of voicing or otherwise bringing to consciousness their troubled relationships with other members of their family.[15] *The Sound and the Fury* is, after all, a novel about family relationships, and although these relationships are less overtly violent, graphic, and criminal than the not-so familial ones in *Sanctuary* and *Light in August*, *The Sound and the Fury* is nevertheless very interested in ecologies of loss and the loss of ecologies—in the environing of trauma and the traumatizing of environments. In this novel Faulkner gives concerted attention to interrelatedness, particularly when the relationships in question are broken, damaged, and/or obsessive.

Along these lines, it is noteworthy, even stunning, that the four principal narrators in *The Sound and the Fury* are so similarly environed and yet so verbally and mentally distinct from each other. It's as though Faulkner imagines four different world views that double as four different yet partially overlapping ecosystems.[16] The narrator of the final section is the most meteorologically inclined of the four and gives considerable attention to the confined and confining ecologies of the Compsons, to which I will briefly return. Jason bears what John Matthews has called an "unconscious grief" which perhaps plays out in his relative unconsciousness to his ecological surroundings as well as in the physical, natural world he *does* notice: a banal, mundane world of boll weevils and fice dogs and undifferentiated bushes and trees.[17] But I want to focus mainly on Quentin and Benjy. Benjy's physical wound helps to explain the prevalence of wasteland imagery in the opening section, which is of course more or less filtered through his problematically limited point of view, but I am more interested in the not-so-desolate elements of the environments he sees and remembers. What he hangs on to, with great certainty and with vividly sensual memory, is that his sister Caddy is herself an ecosystem—which means in part that Benjy processes all ecologies through both his closeness to Caddy and his loss of that closeness. Caddy, he still remembers, smells like leaves, like trees, like rain; *"Then I saw Caddy, with flowers in her hair, and a long veil like shining wind. Caddy Caddy"* (SF 24). How does a sense of place develop? from ever-accumulating experiences and memories of interrelationships with particular natural and built environments? Benjy doesn't accumulate—or organize—so much as he holds fast to powerful emotions provoked by what is immediately before him and at the same time haunted by a name, a smell, a moment out of his past.

These hauntings are complicated and probably intensified by the Compsons and Gibsons, who fence him in and place him in an unending state of both surveillance and regression: his obvious physicality notwithstanding, he is constantly described as fading or vanishing, constantly being asked to go away, constantly being told to "hush." In other words, he is haunted and he is also constructed, by his family, *as* a haunt. And when, as here, interrelatedness comes to be associated with ghostliness, it signals what Mark Seltzer, in a very different context, calls "the radical failure of distinction between subject and place."[18] Too much ecological contact, especially when coupled with Benjy's already-diminished mentality and forced removals, can intensify a sense of loss to the extent that the differences between places and selves, between pastures and people, are utterly confounded. Of course, as Noel Polk reminds us, Benjy never directly tells us that he was moaning or otherwise trying to express his pain and loss; his narrative "self" describes the stimulus, the trigger, and then jumps to someone else's response to his response—someone else's "hush."[19] In the absence of conventional memory, he responds symbolically, repetitively, even fetishistically to particular objects or places that connect in some way to the ecology of his home place: a flower, a jimson weed, a smell of rain or leaves or trees. These hauntings emphasize and reemphasize who or what he has lost as well as what he has never had—a sense of recovery from trauma. Finally, then, ecology for Benjy—"the natural" (SF 97)—is a nightmarish, frequent reminder of absence, loss, and trauma that are, for him, "apparently inescapable."

Quentin, too, is haunted by the seemingly inescapable, but in stark contrast to Benjy, Quentin dwells on and in his subjective responses to natural and built environments, describing in great, even loving detail the occasion, shape, and quality of his own particular kinds of moans. Quentin is more consciously literary—lyrical, figurative, allusive—in his turns to the natural world as well as in his accounts of the built environments of Cambridge and its outlying districts. In this sense he holds a more conventional, stylized, detached view of the natural world than does Benjy, who plunges beyond naivete in his symbolic imagination and comes closer to something like raw, primal figuration. Put another way, Quentin uses the word "symbolise" and Benjy, more of a William Carlos Williams disciple, but without the ideas, doesn't.[20] Quentin casts himself as a sort of Prufrockian isolationist positioning himself in aesthetic and anaesthetic relation to his surroundings. And yet like Benjy, he very much reads himself and the natural world in physical as well as figurative relation to each other, as a way of trying to read himself and Caddy in physical as well as figurative relation to each other. As such, he constructs and experiences the natural world as a venue for a troubled, traumatic, blood relationship.

In broaching incest, for example, Quentin devises an "unnatural" analogy: "The arrow increased without motion, then in a quick swirl the trout lipped a fly beneath the surface with that sort of gigantic delicacy of an elephant picking up a peanut" (SF 71). Setting aside the question of whether trout have lips, we see Quentin standing by a river that reminds him of a stream back home, thinking passionately about Caddy, and doing what he tells us the three boys with fishing poles do: "making of unreality a possibility, then a probability, then an incontrovertible fact, as people will when their desires become words" (SF 72). His own desires, which he understands to be checkered if not unnatural, become words that express an unnatural and somewhat fictive ecosystem in action. Bringing elephants and trout together, lips and all, his disjunctive figurative language estranges the natural here and elsewhere: the Italian girl, whom he calls "sister," is "a little dirty child with eyes like a toy bear's and two patent-leather pigtails" (SF 76), his blood sister lay with him *"in the wet grass panting the rain like cold shot on my back,"* and he also remembers *"the water building and building up the squatting back the sloughed mud stinking surfaceward pocking the pattering surface like grease on a hot stove"* (SF 84, italics in original).

In many places in his section, Quentin rehashes his obsessive, fevered fantasy of an incestuous or borderline incestuous encounter with Caddy by way of imagery that in some way skews or denatures the ecology of the South. These images point up that even when physically removed from the South, he imaginatively transports his Southern home place with him to the North and infuses that particular home ecology with a loaded, highly charged power that the North cannot match. His trauma is grounded, place-based. There is a constant interplay of interiors and exteriors, or, more precisely, there are relationships between the South he physically inhabits and the South he mentally reconstructs. For example, in what is for my purposes one of the most important passages in the section, Quentin remembers that "Sometimes I could put myself to sleep saying that ['when will it stop'] over and over until after the honeysuckle got all mixed up in it the whole thing came to symbolise night and unrest I seemed to be lying neither asleep nor awake looking down a long corridor of gray halflight where all stable things had become shadowy paradoxical all I had done shadows all I had felt suffered taking visible form antic and perverse mocking without relevance inherent themselves with the denial of the significance they should have affirmed thinking I was I was not who was not was not who" (SF 103). In the insistently liminal place that he describes and dwells in here, Quentin's very being, his most basic sense of who he is, gets "all mixed up." But what he says here is that "the honeysuckle got all mixed up in it," the honeysuckle acting as the Southern environmental signifier that stands in for the erotic, sexual mixups he feels for Caddy. In his mind, he imagines "a long corridor of gray halflight," a doubly liminal interior space made even less restful by the presence of the nagging, offending, seductive honeysuckle. Quentin's abstract expressions of shadowy confusion and paradox, his mixings of affirmation and denial, are inseparable from the concrete, sensual, *and* symbolic honeysuckle which links his troubles to a Southern ecology that "got [and gets] all mixed up in it." Ecological interrelatedness symbolizes and reiterates a fractured, painful, dysfunctional family relationship.

Quentin's presentation of the ecologies of the South and the North is full of such moments. At one point in the long description of his nocturnal encounters with his sister, Caddy's "face looked at the sky it was low so low that all smells and sounds of night seemed to have been crowded down like under a slack tent especially the honeysuckle it had got into my breathing it was on her face and throat like paint her blood pounded against my hand I was leaning on my other arm it began to jerk and jump and I had to pant to get any air at all out of that thick gray honeysuckle" (SF 92). And then, moments later, "when I lifted my hand I could still feel crisscrossed twigs and grass burning into the palm" (SF 92). The honeysuckle seems to mutate into paint; blood pounds against a hand, against blood; the honeysuckle suffocates him; his hand and the land press against each other, and this ecological Mississippi burns into his skin, marking and traumatically environing him as surely as the ditch he and Caddy arrive at marks the traumatized land: "she walked into me she gave over a little the ditch was a black scar on the gray grass she walked into me again she looked at me and gave over we reached the ditch" (SF 93). He himself is a scarred place she still walks into.

4. "cringing rearward in furious disintegration": *Sanctuary* and Criminal Narrative[21]

And speaking of the black ditch, much can be said about Faulkner's linking of environing, violence, and blood in *Sanctuary*, where once again the blackened earth bears a scar that has something to do with human as well as ecological erosion and loss: "The road was an eroded scar too deep to be a road and too straight to be a ditch, gutted by winter freshets and choked with fern and rotted leaves and branches" (S 192). *Sanctuary* begins with a problematic convergence near that scarred dirt road that is not exactly a road: a strangely pastoral and at the same time menacing and confounding accidental meeting between the lawyer Horace Benbow and the criminal Popeye. "From beyond the screen of bushes which surrounded the spring, Popeye watched the man drinking. A faint path led from the road to the spring" (S 181). This opening scene perhaps mimics a new-world encounter in the wilderness, but with a strange suppression of both identity and motive. Just as "the broken sunlight lay sourceless" (S 181), so too is there a sourcelessness to this scene, which leads to questions about where these two men hail from, why they are there, and whether this land is in fact their land.[22] Mirror imagery, with all its narcissistic ramifications, suffuses the scene, suggesting a twisted sort of closed-circuit *intra*relatedness and an ensuing "radical failure of distinction between subject and place" that problematically supplants the productive convergences that characterize a healthy ecosystem. The desire for self-reflection plays out in the context of a Southern ecology that at first seems ironically serene but that very shortly thereafter and without premeditation begins to resemble the criminal Popeye more and more, to look and act more like a blackened, traumatized, stunted, yet powerful ecosystem. His manner of inhabiting this ecosystem—and its way of interacting with him—is well captured by his pitiful cringing away from a swooping owl and also by Temple Drake's insulting joke: "What river did you fall in with that suit on? Do you have to shave it off at night?" (S 213).

The characteristic which most closely and ironically aligns this ecosystem with human figures in the novel, and particularly with Popeye, is the general absence or failure of husbandry. Temple's joke implies that Popeye can't even tend himself properly; the moonshiners' criminal habitat is not really tended much at all, and (to embrace the tautology) a place that lacks tending is, in this novel, a dangerous place, a crime scene. As I have suggested, the characters and the land at times inadvertently resemble each other in *Sanctuary*; at other times they recoil from each other, but they rarely if ever collaborate in an ecologically open way. For example, Temple Drake's urinary encounter with the land finds her running, "snatching her feet up almost before they touched the earth, the weeds slashing at her with huge, moist, malodorous blossoms" and then arriving at "a dry runlet" near "the bottom of the hill [where] a narrow scar of sand divided the two slopes of a small valley. . . . Among the new green last year's dead leaves from the branches overhead clung, not yet fallen to earth" (S 242). Suggestive as "huge, moist, malodorous blossoms" might very well be to a person with a full bladder, what they and much else in this natural environment have in common is their excess: the blossoms are too big and smelly, the leaves are too late in falling, the valley is scarred, the runlet is dry—and the girl is dislodged from her familiar habits, too exposed and too vulnerable. She is out of place in a place that is itself out of whack. In this way she can be compared to the ecosystem she races through and urinates on, or it can be said to reflect something of her present experience, but the person and the place do not appear to be acting in tandem.

Sanctuary more often describes and even practices something like "cringing rearward": a receding, a retreating, a moving away, a cancelling out, and at worst an undoing to the point of destroying selves and relationships, including possible relationships between characters and environments. Thus Popeye "looked about with a sort of vicious cringing" (S183) as the owl flashes by, and then springs and crouches against Benbow, "clawing at his pocket and hissing through his teeth like a cat" (S 184); Benbow, in the act of backpedalling from an unhappy marriage, is let go after a brief and ambiguous captivity; Temple incessantly springs away from others, moving, in Philip Weinstein's apt phrase, "like a deranged wound-up toy,"[23] and at one point "could feel all her muscles shrinking like severed vines in the noon sun" (S 220); Ruby Lamar is compelled to move away from various "homes" and eventually simply disappears, fate unknown; the blind old man at the old plantation also vanishes from sight, as if left behind or thrown away; and the old plantation house is in the process of reversion when we first see it and then abandoned again, this time by the criminals, simply left behind so far as the narrative is concerned, the better to revert back to reversion. The novel itself, as it develops, moves away from physical, natural ecosystems and toward a variety of enclosed interior spaces: rooms, jail cells, cars, and bars. And its author famously stepped back from his own production, describing it as a novel based on a "cheap idea" and cranked out to make money.[24] On many different counts, from characters to settings to authorship, husbandry is a problem; places, people, and things are not tended so much as they are temporarily tolerated and then, like the scars on the land, ditched.

What all this pulling away and falling apart and retreating amounts to is difficult to say; maybe that is the point. The tendency toward reversion, disintegration, ephemerality, emptying out, "a peaceful vacuum" lies at the heart of the book and helps accomplish what Eric Sundquist has called "the book's intense superficiality."[25] Not only is this novel fascinated by surfaces and leery of depths, though; it also works to render such binaries inoperable. For my purposes, the most interesting of these seductive yet fractured binaries is the one that pits the "natural" against the "unnatural" or machinelike. Joseph Reed sees *Sanctuary*'s natural world as itself a sort of machine, an "it" that "can perform a dazzling series of emotional impersonations" but cannot truly disguise "its impotent omnipresence," its "indifferent neutrality."[26] According to Reed, "Nature surrounds human actions but keeps its distance."[27] Or perhaps, as I have been suggesting, *Sanctuary* presents the much more terrifying possibility that its ecologies do not keep their distance but instead crowd, reflect, attack, and spurn humans for reasons that are simply not clear. In addition to the swooping owl and slashing weeds, there is the glorious spring day, described in great detail, that heralds Temple's return to Jefferson hemorrhaging, raped by a boy-man who whinnies like a horse when he violates her. And there is the tool Popeye uses to rape her, a corncob that later "appeared to have been dipped in dark brownish paint" (S 376); the corncob has "impersonated" a penis and blood "impersonates" paint.

   Given these crossings and blurrings of the lines between the natural and the artificial, how can Popeye be viewed as entirely and strictly "unnatural"? While he and Benbow take their first look at each other, the narrator gazes at both in their environmental context, and what he sees when he looks at Popeye is a piece of furniture with two legs and a tight suit of clothes. Popeye first appears in nature, near bushes and a spring, and yet he "walked, his tight suit and stiff hat all angles, like a modernist lampstand" (S 183). To some degree, he looks like he was made by hand, which to at least some extent fails to placate his narcissism and makes him, admittedly, difficult to integrate within any sort of ecosystem. And yet when the narrator remarks that Popeye's eyes are like "two knobs of soft black rubber" (S 181), the simile is ambiguous; rubber *is* found in nature, but "knobs" suggests some sort of fashioning. Things get even more complicated when Popeye walks ahead of Benbow, back to the decrepit plantation house: "Where the branch from the spring seeped across it Benbow saw the prints of automobile tires" (S183). Can we formulate an analogy between the imprint of industrialized rubber on natural seepage and the impact of "two knobs of soft black rubber" on the local environment? The rubber tires can crunch deeply into the earth, but the marks they make are evanescent; so too is Popeye both fleeting and lethal. As T. H. Adamowski argues, "If Popeye reminds us of a machine (the stamped tin syndrome), one must suspect, nevertheless, that there is a 'ghost' in it" and, I would add, around it, figuratively haunting both him and us, yet at the same time figuratively "placing" even this dangerously displaced figure.[28]

But if Popeye's eyes are windows to his soul, the shades are clearly down, and both the cause and the effect of those eyes are difficult to measure. Even so, his black eyes connect to his often-noted blackness, which is the quality that most decisively links him, in ways that he does not openly or consciously seem to grasp, to his habitat on and around the old back-country plantation. Following Eric Sundquist, I take this blackness to be no more than tangentially linked to African American identity;[29] Popeye is not racially black, but, as Sundquist has argued, both the power and the impotence of a figurative blackness cling to him as they cling to and help to demarcate the dark, menacing strains of the place itself, including what Sundquist calls "the collapsed dream of the old South."[30] The gangsters have chosen as their home and hideout a place historically implicated in racial and cultural violence: "a plantation house set in the middle of a tract of land; of cotton fields and gardens and lawns long since gone back to jungle" (S 184). Its ghosts presumably include African American slaves, and this postbellum return of an antebellum slave plantation to an African (or South American) ecosystem might be taken as a good thing—except that the reversion begins *after* the black slaves have left the plantation. As such, "jungle" operates as a Euro-American sign, a modernist gesture toward primitivism, figuratively suggesting that the house under criminal occupation is a wild, unleashed, dangerous place. It is also a strangely preliterate place; the narrator mentions early on that "the jungle already lay like a lake of ink" (S 183) and in its fusing of the untapped natural (lake) and the unused technological (ink), it presents an ecological text that emblematizes the criminal ecologies of *Sanctuary*: dark, untended, yet still contaminated by some sort of human technology that might or might not someday be used to articulate a legible identity and/or to destroy it.

As the novel moves away from the old plantation house and grounds, it continues to be punctuated by sensational moments of trauma and violence, and as I have tried to suggest, these bloody affairs bear a very complex relationship to Southern nature and culture. Temple Drake at novel's end turns the book's opening New World encounter inside out, retreating from a Southern courtroom all the way to Europe, where "she seemed to follow with her eyes . . . the sky lying prone and vanquished in the embrace of the season of rain and death" (S 398). But far more striking than this rather conventional image of postwar Europe are the corncob and all that it represents. Left behind by every character who ever had anything to do with it, it nevertheless lingers, not simply as a corncob or even as a bloodsoaked corncob, but as a bloodsoaked corncob that "appeared to have been dipped in dark brownish paint." Violence, nature, blood, and the performative—the dipping and the displaying—converge here, on and in an alien corncob that, much like Quentin Compson's all-too-familiar, paintlike honeysuckle, epitomizes William Faulkner's ecology of the South in all its traumatized and traumatizing interrelatedness.

5. Conclusion: "the earth going through my clothes"

In *Dirt and Desire*, Patricia Yaeger presents a long and convincing revisionist catalog of the characteristics of Southern women writers working between 1930 and 1990. Number fourteen on her list is the observation that literature by Southern women writers treats place as "always a site where trauma has been absorbed into the landscape"[31]—or, as Rosa Coldfield puts it in *Absalom, Absalom!*, the South is "a land primed for fatality and already cursed with it."[32] I want to suggest that something similar drives Faulkner's handling of place, at least in the novels under discussion here. In *The Sound and the Fury*, to mention just one more brief example, Quentin Compson thinks: "I lay there feeling the earth going through my clothes" (SF 95). Is the earth his lover, penetrating his clothes to reach the skin within, or is the earth a pickpocket, rifling through his clothes, or are the earth's fingers really Quentin's own? Does he autoerotically mistake or substitute the earth for himself? The ambiguity of this sentence is marvellously weird, and it bespeaks a troubled, uncomfortable, figurative intimacy with the earth itself, a strain of ecological psychosis. What Quentin remembers is that he was violated by the earth, and what he carries with him even to Massachusetts are ecological memories of his traumatic relationship with Caddy. Benjy goes further still (without of course ever leaving Jefferson); Benjy's Caddy, as I have suggested, *is* an ecosystem that smelled like leaves, like trees, like rain. So, too, do the criminal ecologies of *Sanctuary* capture the bloody, predatory, and at times hapless actions of characters at best uneasily environed. So, too, do the ecologies Hightower so uncomfortably inhabits reveal something of who he is and something of what the South is as well as something of who he is not and something of what the South is not. The turn to ecology in Faulkner's South—the terrible trials and failures of character after character caught in the act of something like interrelatedness—signifies the trauma and blood violence of the South and its people.

NOTES

1. For discussions of blood in Faulkner's fiction, see, among others, Michael Davidson, "Strange Blood: Hemophobia and the Unexplored Boundaries of Queer Nation," in Timothy

B. Powell, ed., *Beyond the Binary: Reconstructing Cultural Identity in a Multicultural Context* (New Brunswick: Rutgers University Press, 1999), 39–60 and especially 48–50; Theresa M. Towner, "Unsurprised Flesh: Color, Race, and Identity in Faulkner's Fiction," in Donald M. Kartiganer and Ann J. Abadie, eds., *Faulkner and the Natural World: Faulkner and Yoknapatawpha, 1996* (Jackson: University Press of Mississippi, 1999), 45–65; Jay Watson, "Writing Blood: The Art of the Literal in *Light in August*," in *Faulkner and the Natural World*, 66–97; and Joseph R. Urgo, "Menstrual Blood and 'Nigger' Blood: Joe Christmas and the Ideology of Sex and Race," *Mississippi Quarterly* 41:3 (Summer 1988): 391–401. Studies of Faulkner and race are of course also useful in relation to constructions of blood; see for example Patricia McKee, *Producing American Races: Henry James, William Faulkner, Toni Morrison* (Durham: Duke University Press, 1999); Barbara Ladd, *Nationalism and the Color Line in George W. Cable, Mark Twain, and William Faulkner* (Baton Rouge: Louisiana State University Press, 1996); Doreen Fowler and Ann J. Abadie, eds., *Faulkner and Race: Faulkner and Yoknapatawpha, 1986* (Jackson: University Press of Mississippi, 1987); Thadious M. Davis, *Faulkner's "Negro": Art and the Southern Context* (Baton Rouge: Louisiana State University Press, 1983); and Eric J. Sundquist, *Faulkner: The House Divided* (Baltimore: Johns Hopkins University Press, 1983).

2. William Faulkner, *Light in August* (New York: Vintage, 1985), 367. Subsequent references to this text are made parenthetically.

3. Lawrence Buell, "Faulkner and the Claims of the Natural World," in *Faulkner and the Natural World*, 4. Diane Roberts, *Faulkner and Southern Womanhood* (Athens: University of Georgia Press, 1994), 172, 173.

4. For detailed discussion of this idea, see Richard Slotkin, *Regeneration through Violence: The Mythology of the American Frontier, 1600–1860* (1973; Norman: University of Oklahoma Press, 2000).

5. Moreover, linkages between race and blood are so problematic that I don't have time to address them in this essay; see note 1 for a selected bibliography of Faulkner scholarship on this topic, and, for an interesting (though not Faulknerian) discussion of these convergences, see Chadwick Allen, *Blood Narrative: Indigenous Identity in American Indian and Maori Literary and Activist Texts* (Durham: Duke University Press, 2002). The linkages between racial mixing and ecological interrelatedness are also beyond my scope here, though fascinating and very much in need of critical investigation.

6. William Faulkner, *The Sound and the Fury*, ed. David Minter (New York: W. W. Norton, 1987). Subsequent references to this text, abbreviated SF, are made parenthetically.

7. Lawrence Buell, letter, "Forum on Literatures of the Environment," *PMLA* 114:5 (October 1999): 1091.

8. Ibid.

9. Scott Slovic, letter, "Forum on Literatures of the Environment," *PMLA* 114:5 (October 1999): 1102.

10. Buell, letter, 1091–92.

11. Krista Comer, *Landscapes of the New West: Gender and Geography in Contemporary Women's Writing* (Chapel Hill: University of North Carolina Press, 1999), 126–27.

12. For different but complementary perspectives on this point, see Richard Dawkins, "Aggression: Stability and the Selfish Machine," in *The Selfish Gene* (New York: Oxford University Press, 1976), 71–94, and Neil Evernden, *The Social Creation of Nature* (Baltimore: Johns Hopkins University Press, 1992), especially 6–16. For a critique of Dawkins, see Jon Beckwith, *Making Genes, Making Waves: A Social Activist in Science* (Cambridge: Harvard University Press, 2002). A good ecology textbook can also help guide the nonspecialist through these concepts and issues; see for example Eugene P. Odum, *Ecology and Our Endangered Life-Support Systems*, 2nd ed. (Sunderland, Mass.: Sinauer Associates, 1993), especially 38–67. I am indebted to Matthew Wynn Sivils for helping me to understand these ecological principles and for pointing me toward Dawkins and Evernden.

13. William Howarth, "Some Principles of Ecocriticism," in Cheryll Glotfelty and Harold Fromm, eds., *The Ecocriticism Reader: Landmarks in Literary Ecology* (Athens: University of Georgia Press, 1996), 81.

14. These and other matters have been abundantly discussed in the critical literature on *The Sound and the Fury*. Useful and readily available collections of critical essays on this novel include Stephen Hahn and Arthur F. Kinney, eds., *Approaches to Teaching Faulkner's "The Sound and the Fury"* (New York: MLA, 1996); Noel Polk, ed., *New Essays on "The Sound and the Fury"* (New York: Cambridge University Press, 1993); and Michael H. Cowan, ed., *Twentieth-Century Interpretations of "The Sound and the Fury"* (Englewood Cliffs, N.J.: Prentice-Hall, 1968).

15. In developing this ecocritical approach, I bear in mind that the concept of interrelatedness, particularly in relation to dysfunctional ecosystems, helps work against critical master narratives. Dawn Trouard, in an excellent essay, reads these master narratives as "the critical myths" of *The Sound and the Fury* and includes among these myths "the fiercely defended notion of the book's coherence, or at least of a coherence accomplished through an unshakable faith in Caddy's centrality and unity" (24–25). Trouard's feminist approach and my ecocritical one overlap in a number of ways: both mark the novel's as well as the criticism's fault lines, both do so in part by dismantling received binaries, and both focus attention on what she calls a "thematics of loss" (28) while noting how this thematics plays out in a variety of physical and cultural geographies. Trouard gives important attention as well to how characters and their natural and built spaces in *The Sound and the Fury* are gendered. Although I do not engage her arguments more fully and directly in my essay, I have benefited from them; they help clear a space for, among other things, ecofeminist readings of *The Sound and the Fury* and of all Faulkner. See Trouard, "Faulkner's Text Which Is Not One," in *New Essays on "The Sound and the Fury,"* 23–69.

16. Or, as Donald Kartiganer puts it, "Each of the four sections of the text situates itself in a verbal universe of its own. . . . Common to all the sections is their utter remoteness from each other and their freedom from any criteria by which the validity of their perspectives may be measured." See Kartiganer, "'Now I Can Write': Faulkner's Novel of Invention," *New Essays on "The Sound and the Fury,"* 77. My ecocritical emphasis on interrelatedness leads me to see the four sections of the novel as not quite utterly remote from each other, even though, as Kartiganer observes, no narrative point of view in the novel is reliable and even though, so far as I can tell, none of these narrative points of view has read—and none would have much interest in reading—his own section of the book, let alone any other section.

17. John T. Matthews, *The Play of Faulkner's Language* (Ithaca: Cornell University Press, 1982), 92.

18. Mark Seltzer, *Serial Killers: Death and Life in America's Wound Culture* (New York: Routledge, 1998), 34.

19. Noel Polk, "Trying Not to Say: A Primer on the Language of *The Sound and the Fury*," in *Children of the Dark House: Text and Context in Faulkner* (Jackson: University Press of Mississippi, 1996), 99–109 and especially 106–7.

20. Benjy's dictum, were he able to formulate it, might read "No ideas. Things!" Alternatively, Donald Kartiganer points to Imagism: "Benjy's severely objective, concrete, unornamented prose resembles the Imagist movement in early twentieth-century poetry" and his "scenes . . . read like a series of Imagist poems." See Kartiganer, "'Now I Can Write': Faulkner's Novel of Invention," 80.

21. William Faulkner, *Sanctuary*, in *Faulkner: Novels 1930–1935*, ed. Joseph Blotner and Noel Polk (New York: Library of America, 1985), 289. Subsequent references to this text, abbreviated S, are made parenthetically.

22. For further discussion of this peculiar sourcelessness, see Sundquist's excellent "*Sanctuary*: An American Gothic," in *Faulkner: The House Divided*, especially 57–58.

23. Philip M. Weinstein, "Precarious Sanctuaries: Protection and Exposure in Faulkner's Fiction," in J. Douglas Canfield, ed., *Twentieth-Century Interpretations of "Sanctuary"* (Englewood Cliffs, N.J.: Prentice-Hall, 1982), 131.

24. Faulkner made this claim in an introduction which he prepared for the 1932 Modern Library edition of *Sanctuary*. This introduction, which has been much scrutinized and which should be read skeptically, is reprinted in *Faulkner: Novels 1930–1935*, 1029–30.

25. Sundquist, *Faulkner: The House Divided*, 54.

26. Joseph W. Reed, Jr., "The Function of Narrative Pattern in *Sanctuary*," in Harold Bloom, ed., *William Faulkner's "Sanctuary": Modern Critical Interpretations* (New York: Chelsea House, 1988), 21–22.

27. Ibid., 19.

28. T. H. Adamowski, "Faulkner's Popeye: The 'Other' as Self," in J. Douglas Canfield, ed., *Twentieth-Century Interpretations of "Sanctuary*," 45.

29. Sundquist, *Faulkner: The House Divided*, 57–58.

30. Ibid., 52.

31. Patricia Yaeger, *Dirt and Desire: Reconstructing Southern Women's Writing, 1930–1990* (Chicago: University of Chicago Press, 2000), 13.

32. William Faulkner, *Absalom, Absalom!* (New York: Vintage, 1986), 14.

William Faulkner, Peter Matthiessen, and the Environmental Imagination

ANN FISHER-WIRTH

"But let flesh touch with flesh"

For years after first reading William Faulkner's *Absalom, Absalom!*, I remembered the novel as beginning with wistaria, and remembered the wistaria as somehow encapsulating it—just as, for me, *The Sound and the Fury* is incarnate in the odor of honeysuckle; or *The Bear*, in the enormous tick on the inside of Old Ben's leg; or *Light in August*, in the insects that cease their clamor as Joe Christmas passes by. And so let us begin with wistaria. Ordinarily, in reading, one focuses on human interactions; insofar as one envisions the natural world, it is only as a backdrop for the human drama. But to read with an environmental imagination[1]—to attend to the more-than-human world, granting it presence and meaning, conceiving of it not as a static entity but in terms both of the interactions between humans and nonhumans and of natural process—vastly transforms one's experience of a novel. This happens, for instance, with *Absalom, Absalom!* For even in *Absalom, Absalom!*, which is absolutely obsessed with human conflicts—with racism, miscegenation, incest, betrayal, and violence—an ecological countermelody is present from its very first page.

Willing her split and distance from nature, Rosa Coldfield sits in "a dim hot airless room with the blinds all closed and fastened for forty-three summers."[2] The blinds are closed, Faulkner writes, because someone told her long ago that light and air carry heat and that dark is always cooler; the house shored up, drawn in upon itself, becomes a metaphor for her attempt to create a self equally closed, in isolation. Dressed in "eternal black . . . whether for sister, father, or not husband none knew" (1), and immured in a "coffin-smelling gloom," she has summoned Quentin Compson to inflict on him her narrative of grievance. Proposed to and then insulted by Thomas Sutpen, she has lived for forty-three years as an "embattled" virgin; by now she smells of "female old flesh," though she also looks like a "crucified child" (2). Her feet, on legs too short to reach the ground, have an air "of impotent and static rage" (1); they are clearly a synecdoche for her life, which is lived in changeless fury. A cold field, an unbloomed rose, as Rosa talks to Quentin she creates for him the vision "out of quiet thunderclap" of Sutpen as God the Father, tooled by the "wild blacks . . . the captive architect . . . the shovels and picks and axes" (2), and this vision leads inexorably to all the rest that follows. She is like Proust's teacup, out of which flowers Faulkner's tragic, diabolical Combray. Yet all the while, as her voice drones on forever, "grim haggard amazed," another story is told, a story of freedom and renewal: in the sparrows' "random gusts" as they come and go outside; in the wistaria vine by one shuttered window, "blooming for the second time that summer" (1).

My focus in this paper is not primarily on the story *Absalom, Absalom!* tells of conflict between humans. Instead, it is on the wistaria—the presence that makes itself known despite Rosa's closing the house against it— and on what this wistaria represents. Nor is my focus primarily on Rosa Coldfield, for *Absalom* foregrounds a gendered narrative of patriarchy, of conflict between males, played off against a landscape which in terms of the environmental imagination reveals itself to be much more than landscape. Specifically, of course, the novel foregrounds Thomas Sutpen, who rises from Appalachian poverty and shame to become a planter in north Mississippi: as Quentin puts it, to drag "house and formal gardens violently out of the soundless Nothing . . . creating the Sutpen's Hundred, the *Be Sutpen's Hundred* like the oldentime *Be Light*" (2–3). And, as Faulkner commented on the novel: "[T]he theme is a man who outraged the land, and the land then turned and destroyed the man's family."[3] Nor, as the title of my paper suggests, is my focus only on *Absalom*, but also on three recent novels by the contemporary American writer Peter Matthiessen—*Killing Mister Watson* (1991), *Lost Man's River* (1997), and *Bone by Bone* (1999)—for the protagonist and themes of the Watson trilogy closely parallel those of Faulkner's novel.

An internationally famous environmental activist and writer, Matthiessen based the trilogy on nearly twenty years' research into the life of E. A. or E. J. Watson, a historical settler in South Florida whose death by posse in 1910 has, over the years, made him a legend in that part of the world. Unlike Faulkner's *Absalom*, Matthiessen's novels foreground environmental issues. They span the mid-nineteenth to mid-twentieth centuries and describe in detail the process of development and environmental degradation: how the Everglades and Thousand Islands have been transformed from wilderness into sugarcane plantations; how the Native Americans have been driven out; how the native species, such as plume birds, fish, and alligators, have dwindled in number or vanished; and how dredge and fill, ditches, roads, railways, and bridges have created what one character describes as the fulfillment of "the American Dream": "Condoms a-risin on the Sun Coast Skyline in just a thrillin silver line. . . . Sunset on the Golden Gulf, just a-glintin off them condoms."[4] A passage in *Lost Man's River* about Watson's son Lucius articulates the trilogy's environmental vision most powerfully. Lucius sits in a graveyard, musing on the dead, feeling "humbled by the great age of the granite." Flesh touches with flesh, human with more-than-human, as his "blood-filled finger" makes contact with the "dry crust on the stone . . . derived from black lichens millions of years old—blind algae and fungi working minutely with wind and rain and sun to obliterate man's scratchings on this upright rock hewn from granites heaved up into the sun and air by planetary fire" (143–44). Suddenly, Lucius realizes how bitterly he longs for a way of life he has not known:

> The loss of simplicity, was that it? Loss of the simple harmonies and truths, the earth's natural order and abundance? Perhaps that ruin, mourned by the earth itself, was the most profound of all life's losses, underlying all the rest. Not fear of death . . . but deep generic dread of the death of earth as witnessed in the despoliation of the New World, the great forests and rivers of America, the wilderness and the wild creatures, still abundant in his childhood, now fragmented and broken or bound tight by concrete, poisoned everywhere by unnameable pollutions. (144)

Absalom, Absalom! contains a passage very much like the first lines I've quoted here; at one point Judith speaks to Quentin's grandmother of how "little impression" (130) one makes in life, until

> all of a sudden it's over and all you have left is a block of stone with scratches on it provided there was someone to remember to have the marble scratched and set up or had time to, and it rains on it and the sun shines on it and after a while they don't even remember the name and what the scratches were trying to tell, and it doesn't matter. (131)

But whereas Lucius's awareness of obliteration leads him to conclude that "in the end there was no sanctuary except free self-relinquishment into the eternal light of transience" (L 144), Judith's similar awareness leads her instead to a Modernist desire, to preserve and pass on the artifact, the beautiful final letter she receives from Bon. Published in 1936, predating the contemporary environmental movement, *Absalom, Absalom!* is not per se an environmental novel. Nevertheless, thinking of Faulkner together with Matthiessen allows us more clearly to see the environmental imagination at work in Faulkner, and to realize its persistence, even in a world that absolutely wills its destruction, as a poetic countertext to the wastefulness, the heartbreaking stupidity, of the human tragedy. After reading

Peter Matthiessen, and given my own ecocritical orientation, *Absalom, Absalom!* means something very different to me than it may to the Faulkner establishment. Throughout *Absalom*, an environmental subtext occurs in Faulkner's lovely phrase, "trees [are] drawn in ink on a wet blotter" (195). At the narrative level, there is at work an environmental imagination, which at the level of the novel's human action is everywhere ignored.

But first, what *are* the similarities between Faulkner's and Matthiessen's novels?

In a recent letter, Peter Matthiessen informed me that he read all of Faulkner's novels by the time he finished college, *Absalom, Absalom!* included, "but that was almost a half century ago and I've never gone back." Therefore, he claimed, Faulkner's influence "is little to be seen in my own fiction."[5] However, whether or not he was consciously working under Faulkner's influence, the similarities are stunning; as Matthiessen himself writes, "these wild figures (Thos. Sutpen and E. J. Watson) may be parallel incarnations of the many inspired ruthless entrepreneurs whose huge failings brought them to grief on . . . our wilderness frontiers" (letter). Like Faulkner, Matthiessen creates a protagonist of enormous charisma who passes his childhood in white poverty. Thomas Sutpen begins his life in West Virginia, in a log cabin "boiling with children," where "the land belonged to anybody and everybody and so the man who would go to the trouble and work to fence off a piece of it and say 'This is mine' was crazy" (230). Faulkner describes this life as egalitarian, and Sutpen as innocent; having no basis for comparison, he does not think of himself yet as poor white trash. E. J. Watson, in contrast, is born into a family of "Clouds Creek aristocracy"[6] in Edgefield, South Carolina, but upon returning from the Civil War his shiftless, alcoholic father soon loses the ancestral lands and he becomes as poor as Sutpen. Sutpen's fall into shame and self-loathing occurs abruptly, after the family has moved to Tidewater Virginia, on the day he carries a message to the plantation door and is told by the house slave to go around back. Watson's shame and self-loathing are more gradual. Abused by a sadistic father and an equally sadistic mother, he finally runs away to sharecrop for the cousin who has taken over his father's lands, but soon realizes the scorn in which his female relatives hold him for his smell, his clothes, his lack of education (B 43). The effect, however, is the same. Abjected in the flesh, humiliated by the shibboleth of caste, each adolescent is forever changed by this experience. Watson vows to make himself almighty. Though Sutpen first intends to revolutionize the system, as Jay Watson and others have argued,[7] making it possible for a boy like himself to be welcome at the front door, by the time he returns from Haiti, he too vows to make himself almighty. Each clears the wilderness in Mississippi or Florida with slave or derelict labor, and makes a fortune off cotton or sugarcane. Having dragged "house and gardens out of virgin swamp, and plowed and planted his land with seed cotton which General Compson loaned him" (37), Sutpen becomes "the biggest single landowner and cotton-planter in the woodpile" (71). Watson builds Chatham Bend, which one character describes as "a fine plantation, I can see it yet, the boathouse, sheds, that dock, that strong white house!" adding that "All the point of [Watson's] whole life was in that cane patch he had made with his bare hands in the meanest kind of snake-crawling scrub jungle."[8]

Ironically, however, because of his iron will to triumph and control, each man loses everything in the end, loses especially the sons who would provide a reason and a future for his dynasty. Sutpen, of course, founders on race. Shamed not by the house slave, who is merely an empty signifier, a "child's toy balloon with a face painted on it" (240), but by the planter behind the house slave, whose communicated disdain makes him feel that he and his family are "cattle, creatures heavy and without grace" (245), he determines that if he cannot shoot the planter he will *be* him—only to find that his attempt to "class off" (as Zora Neale Hurston puts it in *Their Eyes Were Watching God*,[9]) to rise to a position of command and invulnerability, creates Bon, the repudiated son, the "nigger in the woodpile" (71). As Richard Godden writes, for all Sutpen's attempts to deny it, he "knows that what he breathes is the breath of slaves, and that he will breathe it no matter where he sits in the hierarchy."[10] Issues of race pervade Matthiessen's novels, too. One central thread involves Henry Short, the only black man in the posse, and whether, being black, he dared to fire his gun; and another involves the black convict labor Watson supposedly kills when he cannot pay them—his own "nigger in the woodpile," in Faulkner's phrase, or, in Matthiessen's, "The-nigger-blood-that-would-not-wash-away" (B 342). But the Watson novels do not share the obsession in *Absalom* with miscegenation. Watson himself has a couple of "backdoor" families, and sexual relations with women of both races; unlike Sutpen he doesn't repudiate his women, or even particularly hide them. Instead, what brings Watson down is violence. A mostly loving patriarch, a mostly good provider, he trails a string of suspicious deaths behind him, connected partly with what he thinks of as his "Jack Watson" side—the ruthless, despairing product of his culture and his father—and partly with his need to maximize profits.

These legendary self-made men, archetypal Americans, create empire upon what Faulkner calls "the tranquil and astonished earth," despoiling it for an idea, pulled, Faulkner says, from the "soundless Nothing" (3). Faulkner's phrasing bespeaks an environmental awareness, one's awareness of which is perhaps intensified by concurrently reading Matthiessen, who understands fully and in anguished detail the extent of the damage that Watson is involved with: Watson, not only a brilliant farmer who can, for instance, grow tomatoes where no one else can and whose cane syrup is the best to be had, but also a capitalist developer who lays down his life, committing the murders that finally get him killed, for "Progress!" The four hundred pages of *Absalom*, the 1,200 pages of the Watson trilogy, contain much environmental history, all of it dismal. And yet ambivalence characterizes the portrayal of both protagonists, both full of derring-do, individualists, heroes—and so, to give voice to this ambivalence, Faulkner creates Quentin, and Matthiessen creates Lucius, each a peaceable but tormented, intellectual "son" whose life work becomes an attempt to find out the "father"'s truth and if possible honor his name.

This leads to one of the strongest similarities between Faulkner's and Matthiessen's novels: the restless, seemingly endless renarrativizing, the desire to arrive at what Faulkner calls the "fourteenth image of [the] blackbird."[11] Like *Absalom*, *Killing Mister Watson* divides its narrative up among several interested parties: in *Absalom*, of course, these are Rosa, Mr. Compson, Quentin, and Shreve; in *Killing Mister Watson*, they are primarily those in some way connected with the posse that kills Watson, though Matthiessen includes other voices and also historical sources. *Lost Man's River* carries the story forward into the adulthood of Watson's second son, Lucius, whose own happiness has wrecked on the sins of his father. A history professor, Watson's pseudonymous biographer, Lucius has made it his aim to prepare a list of his father's killers—and the action of the novel largely consists of his driving around Florida seeking additional information about Watson's life and death. An overly long novel, *Lost Man's River* does, however, issue at last in Lucius's breakthrough discovery from his long-lost brother Rob that Watson, in fact, was a murderer. This bleak accession of truth is set against the backdrop of various attempts either to preserve or to destroy the abandoned Watson homestead, now part of federal lands—against the backdrop, that is, of the further destruction of Florida. Like *Absalom*, the novel ends with a fire that destroys the house and with a doomed black survivor.

If *Lost Man's River* is Matthiessen's "Quentin" story—"*I dont. I dont! I dont hate it! I dont hate it!*" (A 395), *Bone by Bone* resembles the narrative of Sutpen's biography in chapter 7 of *Absalom*. It presents a fuller, deeper, psychologically complex, and therefore more likable Watson—a child traumatized by an abusive father; a young boy haunted by the terrible fate of his relative Selden Tilghman, who is tarred and feathered and finally killed for his opposition to slavery; a passionate, loving husband driven mad and cruel with grief when his adolescent wife dies giving birth to his first son, Rob. In this novel, Matthiessen reverts to the consolations

of an omniscient narrator, attempting to find—or create—a deep truth to
Watson. Yet even here, the more he wants to, the less he can explain him.
"You want the truth," a character remarks in *Lost Man's River*. "Where
you aim to find it? . . . He'll tell you his truth, he'll tell his, I'll give you
another. Which one you aim to settle for and make your peace with?"
(472). Moving toward his death in *Bone by Bone*, Watson does attain a
tragic self-acceptance, realizing, finally, "For taking a life, one paid with
one's own soul," and, with regard to his own split personality, "E. J. Watson
was Jack Watson or had become Jack Watson long ago" (400–1). But for all
the attempts to account for him, what drives the man is a mystery, and as
he dies, Matthiessen's narrative dies as well, into poetry. Here are the last
two pages of *Bone by Bone*; the change in typeface marks the transition
from the first to the second page:

finish it? that what he said?
    well he sure is finished   shot to pieces godamighty
    never got to three

                    who shot first, then?

            moon masks   mouths
        eyes come   eyes go

                            a star

        in starlight shadow

                how the world hurts

                        a star

    this world is painted on a wild fine metal (409–10)

   The final page, beginning with "moon masks," is particularly important,
for it offers a vision of the self which is quite different from anything else
in the Watson trilogy. A student of Zen Buddhism for nearly forty years,
Matthiessen arrives here at a place where the thick self drops away. The
self, which has seemed throughout the novels to be so imperious, so insistent, dissipates into an emptiness beyond narrative, containing images and
one feeling—"*hurts*"— surrounded by white space on the page. This
beautiful passage, which moves toward a vision of the *incorporeal*, is quite
different from a passage, equally beautiful, near the end of *Lost Man's
River*, which expresses instead a vision of attunement to the world, of
what Maurice Merleau-Ponty will call the "*intercorporeal*,"[12] (emphasis

mine), that characterizes deep ecology. "The only 'truths' of E. J. Watson," Lucius comes to realize,

> were the intuitions rising at each moment—for example, that during his long years on the Bend, his driven father, whether or not he had ever paused to listen, had heard the song of an ancestral white-eyed vireo, all but identical to the dry wheezy trill which even at this moment came and went over the thump and pop of the rain-banked fire. The Calusa Indians had heard it, and the Harden clan and the old Frenchman, and a pretty little girl named Lucy Dyer, and even the lean and hungry [murderer] Cox, alone on this storm-battered river, awaiting the return of Mr. Watson. In the stark wake of hurricanes and fire, the delicate bird went on and on about its seasons. (521)

As the French photographer Henri Cartier-Bresson has recently remarked, summarizing his final sense of experience, "There is only the present . . . the present—and eternity."[13] Therefore, the Watson trilogy finally becomes, not a journey toward truth, but a journey toward compassion. As in Matthiessen's nonfiction masterpiece *The Snow Leopard*, there is terrific grieving—though here, it is focused outward, not on the self, but on the brilliant, driven Watson, who was once "a wary boy," who "occupied earthly time and space" in the "sun of the old century in Carolina," but who knew too much of "privation, rage, and suffering," and was destroyed (L 53). Like the story of Thomas Sutpen, the story of E. J. Watson is told and retold, refracted, twisted, lied about, confessed. Like Quentin, Lucius desperately longs to be able to "settle for" (L 472), make his peace with, one or another version of events. But the deeper the investigations go, the more the truth reveals itself to be—to invoke Melville's word—"inscrutable." And so, both Faulkner's and Matthiessen's novels finally relinquish the dream of the final, complete narration, the dream of certain knowledge, and "overpass to love" (A 331).

* * *

Now I want to return to Rosa, midway through the novel, to one of her gorgeous, baroque meditations on the body. She is telling Quentin about Bon's death, about how Wash Jones rode to town, to her gate, and shouted out that Henry had shot Bon, "Kilt him dead as a beef" (137). She is telling Quentin how she hurried to the house, only to be stopped by Clytie's hand on her arm as she ran up the stairs, and how, despite her social conditioning, she was not anything as simple as amazed or outraged at the touch of a black woman's hand on her "white woman's flesh." This is because, she says,

> there is something in the touch of flesh with flesh which abrogates, cuts sharp and straight across the devious intricate channels of decorous ordering, which

enemies as well as lovers know because it makes them both:—touch and touch of that which is the citadel of the central I-Am's private own: not spirit, soul; the liquorish and ungirdled mind is anyone's to take in any darkened hallway of this earthly tenement. But let flesh touch with flesh, and watch the fall of all the eggshell shibboleth of caste and color too. (144)

"But let flesh touch with flesh"—the phrase may serve as leitmotif for this essay. Rosa refers to human contact—to Clytie's hand on her arm, barring her access to the room where Bon lies dead. But the phrase may also be seen as extending beyond the human, as bringing us once again into the presence of the environmental imagination.

One cannot simply separate nature from culture or culture from nature, cannot talk about a natural world utterly independent of human agency and consciousness, or about human agency and consciousness utterly independent from the natural world; this realization is central to ecocriticism. Rosa thinks to herself, "But let flesh touch with flesh." Throughout *Absalom, Absalom!*, in phrases and passages that may at first seem merely ornamental, merely descriptive, Faulkner reminds us that beneath or beyond the "eggshell shibboleth" of class and race—the human abstractions that admit some, ban others, and wreak such havoc—there is the living, physical universe of stars and cedar trees, hound dogs and horses, wistaria and mud, and of ourselves as biological organisms, as "mammalian meat" (151), in Rosa's powerful phrasing. *Absalom, Absalom!* is anything but a novel in which characters exist or could exist in a state of oneness with nature; instead, Faulkner uses natural imagery to evoke a world that the characters block, deny, abuse. However, Faulkner's awareness is not simply that the natural world lies underneath the human drama, but that something *else* lies underneath, of which the natural world is an embodying. In the words of the French phenomenologist Maurice Merleau-Ponty, this something else is "flesh."

In *The Visible and the Invisible*, his last, unfinished work, Merleau-Ponty articulates a philosophy for which Rosa's musings are remarkably apt. Merleau-Ponty writes that there is no such thing as an isolated action or an isolated self—that, for instance, my hand can feel only because it can also be felt: my left hand touches my right hand because my right hand touches my left hand; or, Clytie touches Rosa because Rosa touches Clytie. The toucher "takes its place among the things it touches, is in a sense one of them" (133). Just so, Merleau-Ponty reminds us, I can see because I can be seen, and my seeing is another kind of touching, a "palpation with the look." Then—dismantling the primacy of the gaze which, much feminist and other theory has argued, is central to illusions of dominion—he points out that "since the same body sees and touches, visible and tangible belong to the same world" (134), a world we make contact with only because we are bodies.

In an earlier work, *The Phenomenology of Perception*, Merleau-Ponty writes that he seeks to discover "the world which precedes knowledge, of which knowledge always *speaks*."[14] Here, he calls this world "flesh"; the living universe is "the flesh of the visible" (118). It is not matter, he says, nor mind, nor substance. It is that *of* which we are, that *in* which we are, both touching and touched, both seeing and seen. We are fundamentally and irrevocably embodied subjects. The body, "the thickness of [our] flesh," is our means of going "unto the heart of the things" (135), of communicating with others and experiencing ourselves as part of flesh itself, which radiates "everywhere and forever . . . an individual . . . also a dimension and a universal" (142). Like Lucius in the passage about the vireo in *Lost Man's River*, but perhaps unlike Matthiessen at the end of *Bone by Bone*, Merleau-Ponty does not speak of the incorporeal, but rather of the "intercorporeal"; we are embedded in an environment that extends always beyond what we touch and see, "a presumptive domain of the visible and the tangible" (143).

Not surprisingly, Merleau-Ponty's philosophy has been central to much recent environmental thought. As David Abram writes in *The Spell of the Sensuous*, he undoes the hierarchical binaries of Cartesian philosophy such as those that privilege mind over body, reason over feeling, or human over nonhuman, and seeks instead a "phenomenology that takes seriously our immediate sensory experience" in a "wild-flowering proliferation of entities and elements, in which humans are thoroughly immersed."[15] For, Abram asks, "Does the human intellect, or 'reason,' really spring us free from our inherence in the depths of this wild proliferation of forms? *Or on the contrary, is the human intellect rooted in, and secretly borne by, our forgotten contact with the multiple nonhuman shapes that surround us?*" (49). In relation to this world, Merleau-Ponty writes, "every scientific schematization is an abstract and derivative sign-language, as is geography in relation to the countryside in which we have learnt beforehand what a forest, a prairie, or a river is" (P ix). The environmental imagination situates us here, among the wildly proliferating, interconnected and interpenetrating systems that make up the living universe. As Louise Westling remarks in a recent essay on Merleau-Ponty, "We are bodies for whom meaning is dynamic, participatory attunement to the world in the particular situations where we find ourselves at any given moment. . . . [T]here is no clear distinction between subject and object or mind and body or each of us and the things around us."[16] If this indeed is true, if flesh touch with flesh, how could "caste" and "color" be other than eggshell shibboleths?

Faulkner's ecological vision in *Absalom, Absalom!* has much in common, I think, with the phenomenology of Merleau-Ponty. There are passages in the book that powerfully express this vision, which is bitterly resisted by its human characters. Because these are passages, however, that may be nearly invisible unless one reads with an environmental imagination, I would like now to focus on several, hoping to open up a relatively unexplored dimension of the novel.

At a crucial juncture, in Quentin's account to Shreve, Sutpen says to the girl who has just given birth to his baby, *"Well, Milly, too bad you're not a mare like Penelope. Then I could give you a decent stall in the stable"* (193). This, of course, is the ultimate insult—the blow to her grandfather's pride that gets Sutpen killed—because it places the human order lower than the animals. Sutpen speaks this way not only because he despises Milly but also because the baby is a girl; a son and heir would promptly gain a place in the realm of the Father. Desiring to perpetuate patriarchy's illusion of dominion, Sutpen denies here both the literal flesh of his child and the "flesh" in Merleau-Ponty's sense: not matter, but what emerges at the moment of contact between beings, in relationality. But Faulkner's inversion is cunning: the human male—and, the *white* human male—mates brutishly, callously, whereas, as Quentin says earlier, the *"black* stallion" has "a son born on his wife Penelope" (192, emphasis mine), a mare that remains a mare but is nonetheless linked with the human realm of signification, since her very name epitomizes nobility and marital fidelity.

Some descriptive passages in the paragraphs that follow further enrich the ecological vision of the novel. First comes the comic levelling of Sutpen on his way to the grave, riding *"in his homemade coffin, in his regimentals and sabre and embroidered gauntlets, until the young mules bolted and turned the wagon over and tumbled him, sabre plumes and all, into a ditch"*(194). Decked out in the accoutrements of what Zora Neale Hurston calls "positions and possessions" (79), Sutpen is simply dead here and can be tossed across the boundary he has struggled to maintain, back into the ditch, back into abjection. Furthermore, the proper punishment for those who deny relationality and do violence to the productive body is to be reduced forcibly to what they cannot affirm for themselves: their condition as meat. Killed by Wash Jones's scythe, Sutpen has lain *"quiet and bloody and with his teeth still showing in his parted beard"* (193)—an image highlighted by the similar but gorier image of E. J. Watson, shot down on the beach, "Crusted with blood-black sand and blind, with bullet-smashed teeth, nose and lower lip half shot away . . . and sand fleas hopping all over the whole mess" (K 359).

Equally revealing, far more lovely, are some passages from *Absalom* that follow the account of Sutpen's botched funeral. Shortly thereafter,

Shreve reminds Quentin of a story Quentin has told: of a gray day in the past "after it had rained all night" (195), when Luster and Quentin and Mr. Compson first stumble upon the Sutpen family graves. In an unspecified voice, these paragraphs follow:

> [Quentin] looked up the slope before them where the wet yellow sedge died upward into the rain like melting gold and saw the grove, the clump of cedars on the crest of the hill dissolving into the rain as if the trees had been drawn in ink on a wet blotter—the cedars beyond which, beyond the ruined fields beyond which, would be the oak grove and the gray huge rotting deserted house half a mile away.
>
> . . . It was dark among the cedars, the light more dark than gray even, the quiet rain, the faint pearly globules, materialising on the gun barrels and the five headstones like drops of not-quite-congealed meltings from cold candles on the marble: the two flat heavy vaulted slabs, the other three headstones leaning a little awry, with here and there a carved letter or even an entire word momentary and legible in the faint light which the raindrops brought particle by particle into the gloom and released; now the two dogs came in, drifted in like smoke, their hair close-plastered with damp, and curled down in one indistinguishable and apparently inextricable ball for warmth. Both the flat slabs were cracked across the middle by their own weight (and vanishing into the hole where the brick coping of one vault had fallen in was a smooth faint path worn by some small animal—possum probably—by generations of some small animal since there could have been nothing to eat in the grave for a long time). (195–96)

This passage is one of the most extraordinary in the novel. It neither advances the plot nor comments on the characters' psyches, but it offers the fullest expression of the novel's environmental imagination. Countering Rosa's determination to freeze into bitterness, or Sutpen's to freeze into dynasty, there is all the natural imagery of process: the light and dark, the rain, the generations of beasts, and the passage of seasons. Countering the torment of human touch repressed, betrayed, denied, there are the dogs curled together into a ball for warmth, enacting the only peaceful contact in the novel. Countering Sutpen's dreams of grandeur, there are the letters on the gravestones, flickering in and out in the rain and gloomy light, as if all the namings of human history appeared then vanished, appeared then vanished. And countering the horror of abjection, the maniacal obsession with the "eggshell shibboleth" of class and race, there is Faulkner's laconic comment on ourselves as food for possums.

Faulkner's remark about the land that I quoted at the beginning of this paper, that it "turns and destroys" Sutpen's family, is easy to accept without question. It is, however, an example of anthropomorphism, and not in fact true. The land does not "turn" nor take revenge. Any land that is abused will soon fail to support its human population. And Mississippi, we all know, was abused. Sutpen begins to clear his land in the 1830s. In this, he is part of a general onslaught. Mikko Saikku reports in *The Evolution of a Place* that during the 1850s alone acreage in cultivation in the Yazoo-Mississippi Delta "doubled or even tripled";[17] forests were cleared, cotton was planted, the soil was quickly depleted, more forests were cleared, more cotton planted, more soil depleted, and so on. Rosa eating ditch-weed, Sutpen going mad over the ruin of his fields are simply the logical outcomes of an extractive economy. Just so Sutpen's house, which he wants to stand for his dynasty, is simply a physical object; there is no ulterior meaning in its gradual collapse. This natural process carries all human bodies with it as well; what the patriarch aspires to—the nonrelationality, the incorporeality, of complete dominance and dominion—is swept up in, negated by, the organic processes of *flesh*. Reminding us of this, when Quentin and Rosa go to the house at the beginning of chapter 9, Faulkner writes of it "as if the wood of which it was built were flesh"—like Rosa's bitter body itself, breathing and reeking "with a smell of desolation and decay" (383).

And yet also Faulkner writes of the house, as it looms "jagged," "square and enormous," "for an instant as they moved, hurried, toward it Quentin saw completely through it a ragged segment of sky with three hot stars in it as if the house were of one dimension, painted on a canvas curtain in which there was a tear" (382–83). He uses metaphors of theater such as Matthiessen also comes to at the end of *Bone by Bone*, when "the world is painted on a wild fine metal" (410). One remembers Lear's complaint in the storm, his kingship lost: "When we are born, we cry that we are come/To this great stage of fools."[18] Or Prospero's words near the end of *The Tempest*, his realm given up, his magic powers fading: "Our revels now are ended."[19] Human culture, the stars, all of existence itself, seem illusory, a stage set.

Yet though these metaphors sit oddly with the metaphors of flesh, both kinds call into question the traditional dichotomies between human and more-than-human. We are destroying the world. Novels of struggle and loss, *Absalom, Absalom!* and the Watson trilogy show us part of how, and why. For whether or not it be, finally, illusory, the world is ecological. The human animal, "mammalian meat," is utterly a part of the flesh of the visible.

NOTES

1. The phrase is Lawrence Buell's. See his *The Environmental Imagination: Thoreau, Nature Writing, and the Formation of American Culture* (Cambridge: Harvard University Press, 1995).

2. William Faulkner, *Absalom, Absalom!* (New York: Modern Library, 1993), 1. All subsequent references are to this edition and, when necessary, will be indicated by A.

3. Joseph Blotner, ed., *Selected Letters of William Faulkner* (New York: Vintage Books, 1978), 78–79.

4. Peter Matthiessen, *Lost Man's River* (New York: Vintage Books, 1997), 500. All subsequent references are to this edition and, when necessary, will be indicated by L.

5. Letter to the author from Peter Matthiessen, 25 July 2003.

6. Peter Matthiessen, *Bone by Bone* (New York: Vintage Books, 1999), 11. All subsequent references are to this edition and, when necessary, will be indicated by B.

7. Jay Watson, "And Now What's to Do: Faulkner, Reading, Praxis," *Faulkner Journal* 14, 1 (Fall 1998): 70. See also Dirk Kuyk, *Sutpen's Design: Interpreting Faulkner's "Absalom, Absalom!"* (Charlottesville: University Press of Virginia), 17–19.

8. Peter Matthiessen, *Killing Mister Watson* (New York: Vintage Books, 1991), 336. All subsequent references are to this edition and, when necessary, will be indicated by K.

9. Zora Neale Hurston, *Their Eyes Were Watching God* (Urbana: University of Illinois Press, 1978), 210.

10. Richard Godden, *Fictions of Labor: William Faulkner and the South's Long Revolution* (Cambridge: Cambridge University Press, 1997), 61.

11. Frederick L. Gwynn and Joseph L. Blotner, eds., *Faulkner in the University: Class Conferences at the University of Virginia, 1957–1958* (Charlottesville: University Press of Virginia, 1959), 273–74.

12. Maurice Merleau-Ponty, *The Visible and the Invisible*, ed. Claude Lefort, trans. Alphonso Lingis (Evanston: Northwestern University Press, 1968), 143. All subsequent references are to this edition.

13. John Banville, "Secret Geometry," *New York Review of Books* (3 July 2003): 19.

14. Maurice Merleau-Ponty, *The Phenomenology of Perception*, trans. Colin Smith (London: Routledge and Kegan Paul, 1962), ix. All subsequent references are to this edition and, when necessary, will be indicated by P.

15. David Abram, *The Spell of the Sensuous* (New York: Vintage Books, 1997), 48–49.

16. Louise Westling, "Erotic Embrace with the Flesh of the World" (unpublished essay), n.p.

17. Mikko Saikku, *The Evolution of a Place: Patterns of Environmental Change in the Yazoo-Mississippi Delta from the Ice Age to the New Deal* (Helsinki, Finland: Renvall Institute, University of Helsinki, 2001), 149.

18. William Shakespeare, *King Lear* (Baltimore, Maryland: Penguin Books, 1973), IV, iv.

19. William Shakespeare, *The Tempest* (London: Penguin Books, 1999), IV, i.

My thanks to Jessica Fisher, Joseph Urgo, and Jay Watson for their help with this essay.

The Enemy Within:
Faulkner's Snopes Trilogy[1]

Michael Wainwright

Inheritance is never a given, it is always a task.[2]

There is no inheritance without a call to responsibility. An inheritance is always the reaffirmation of a debt, but a critical, selective, and filtering reaffirmation.[3]

Ecology is the study of plants, or of animals, or of peoples and institutions, in relation to environment. For example, I live in the village of Shepperton, England; the counties of Surrey, Middlesex, and Berkshire form my accustomed environment of which the River Thames is an important constituent. Many organisms thrive in and about the river but one species in particular has stimulated scientific interest in recent years, the Chinese mitten crab.[4] This nonindigenous crustacean has proved to be surprisingly resilient in its new surroundings. In Darwinian terms, the crab is ecologically fitted to the temperate environment offered by the Thames.

Closer to the southern states of America, one discovers the rampant spread of kudzu, a vine native to Japan, but one that is well-suited to the Mississippi basin.[5] Or, to come to Faulkner, one recalls his commentary on cotton farming in the South. Cotton had been introduced from Mexico, but within the transplanted seed lay the larvae of a parasitic scourge, the boll weevil. By the early twentieth century this parasite had, in Faulkner's words, "taken over the southern earth."[6] Or, to take an example from Faulkner's literature, consider an invader from the Old World, one brought to America on European ships, one that has colonized the Jefferson of *Requiem for a Nun*. "[M]igrants too," these English sparrows, birds that "came all the way from the Atlantic coast as soon as the town became a town."[7] An English legacy of an *other* sort, these intruders roost in the courthouse cupola; foreign once again, but this species too is fitted to Yoknapatawpha.

The dome of Jefferson's hall of justice may be dominated by sparrows, but the building itself symbolizes the dominance of another species,

Homo sapiens; and in the struggle for existence, as Darwin makes clear, although contestation takes place between organisms that are biologically differentiated from one another, evolutionary pressure is greatest between members of one's own species.[8]

Faulkner, writing after the epistemological break effected by Darwin's *On the Origin of Species by Means of Natural Selection*, recognizes the crucial aspects of mankind's struggle for existence. "Man's environment," Faulkner argues, "is the only thing that changes. He must change with it. He will cope with it. The problems he faces today are the same ones he faced when he came out of the mud and first stood on two legs."[9] The importance of ecological pressures is primary in Faulkner's artistic mind, as extracts from his colloquies at the University of Virginia confirm: "I'm interested primarily in people," he professes, "in man's conflict with himself, with his fellow man, or with his time and place, his environment [where] by environment I mean his tradition, the air he breaths, his heredity, everything which surrounds him."[10] The South formed Faulkner's familiar topology, "the only really authentic region in the United States," a territory in which he identified the persistence of a deep, indestructible bond between man and his environment.[11] For Faulkner, Mississippi remained a Darwinian country, "still in the seethe and turmoil of being opened and developed and, in a sense, civilised,"[12] and he links this impulse to establish communal stability to the aesthetic sense, a proclivity that keeps humankind "trying to paint the pictures, to make the music, to write the books."[13] This Darwinian circumambience therefore includes the written word and the recipients of that text: "the writer," Faulkner insists, "has got to write in terms of his environment, and his environment consists not only in the immediate scene, but his readers are part of that environment too."[14] The Faulknerian paradigm, a particularly astute representation of Darwin's philosophy, is a model from which evolves the Snopes trilogy that comprises *The Hamlet* (1940), *The Town* (1957), and *The Mansion* (1959).

These novels consider the ecology of Mississippi, as represented by Faulkner's fictitious Yoknapatawpha, documenting the evolution of human habitation in the southern wilderness from the settlement of Frenchman's Bend to the town of Jefferson. *The Hamlet* opens the trilogy with this account of the local terrain and man's relation to that topology:

> Frenchman's Bend was a section of rich river-bottom country lying twenty miles southeast of Jefferson. *Hillcradled and remote, definite yet without boundaries, straddling into two counties and owning allegiance* to neither, it had been the original grant and site of a tremendous pre-Civil War plantation, the ruins of which—the gutted shell of an enormous house with its fallen stables and slave

quarters and overgrown gardens and brick terraces and promenades—were still known as the Old Frenchman place, although the original boundaries now existed only on old faded records in the Chancery Clerk's office in the county court house in Jefferson, and even some of the once-fertile fields had long since reverted to the cane-and-cypress jungle from which their first master had hewed them.[15]

This description makes clear nature's disregard for human ordinance, but the definite topology of Frenchman's Bend—"*hillcradled*" as it is— ensures that this land remains an enclosed space. In *On the Origin of Species* Darwin describes the evolutionary consequences for such enclosures. Of Farnham in Surrey he writes:

> Here there are extensive heaths, with a few clumps of old Scotch firs on the distant hill-tops: within the last ten years large spaces have been enclosed, and self-sown firs are now springing up in multitudes, so close together that all cannot live. When I ascertained that these young trees had not been sown or planted, I was so much surprised at their numbers that I went to several points of view, whence I could examine hundreds of acres of the unenclosed heath, and literally I could not see a single Scotch fir, except the old planted clumps. But on looking closely between the stems of the heath, I found a multitude of seedlings and little trees, which had been perpetually browsed down by the cattle. In one square yard . . . I counted thirty-two little trees; and one of them, judging from the rings of growth, had during twenty-six years tried to raise its head above the stems of the heath, and had failed. No wonder that, as soon as the land was enclosed, it became thickly clothed with vigorously growing young firs.[16]

Protected from the outside by its terrain, Frenchman's Bend is a form of Darwinian enclosure, one that has attained an evolutionarily stable state: a condition in which the mixture of ecological strategies employed by its inhabitants is in equilibrium.[17] The local populace are settled. Even so, with evolutionary forces ever present, such a balance remains liable to invasion from without. At a human level, the burgeoning global population of the twentieth century makes this vulnerability to outsiders especially pronounced and, as migratory pressure builds, foreignness becomes a source of anxiety to indigenous populations. In *The Hamlet*, the spread of tensions related to immigration is evident in the irony of obfuscation that pervades the region's history: the wilderness's first master, the eponymous Frenchman of the Bend, is now almost forgotten.[18] A foreigner had established the hamlet, but this descent provides the inveterate community with little comfort in the face of outlandishness. But what, or who, constitutes this danger?

From the perspective of a Darwinian hermeneutic, three broad divisions can be applied to an analysis of immigration and evolutionarily stable states: the *foreigner*, the *outlander*, and the *extrinsic stranger*. The category of *foreigner* is divided in racial terms: the African, the Caucasian, the Semite, and the Asian. Immigrants of three subcategories are tolerated within a stable state of the fourth as long as (un)written laws of racial segregation are observed. The *outlander* category describes those of one's own race who hail from beyond state boundaries whilst the term *extrinsic stranger* denotes individuals of one's own race and state who originate from outside one's parochial ambit.

In Jeffersonian terms, the Chinese laundryman and the two Jews singled out by Charles Mallison in *The Town* exemplify the benign *foreigner*.[19] Racial difference enables locals to readily identify these men, a foreign presence that poses no threat to communal stability: segregated and alone, these outsiders are not "just kinless but even kindless."[20] In the southern states, the Caucasian subcategory consists of two main types: the Mediterranean and the Northern European. Both of these categories are acceptable in Yoknapatawpha because they constitute the Old World antecedents of the majority of Caucasian residents.[21]

In terms of Faulkner studies, the second category, the *outlander*, describes those Caucasian Americans who hail from beyond Mississippi. Homer Barron in "A Rose for Emily" is one such immigrant; his origin arouses local concerns about his intentions toward Miss Grierson—the dramatic irony of this anxiety only appearing after her demise.[22]

The third category, the *extrinsic stranger*, comprises those Americans of the Caucasian race who live within Mississippi but outside the district in question. Of these characters, most of those who live close to this boundary have personal histories and family genealogies known throughout the inner region and are often kin-related to indigenes. Yet even extremely local *extrinsic strangers* can cause consternation as Hoake McCarron's courtship of Eula Varner affirms. McCarron is a Mississippian, he is even from Yoknapatawpha, but he is categorized according to the parochialism of Frenchman's Bend as "some foreigner from four or five or six miles away." Eula's chosen beau therefore violates "them outside boundary limits" which demarcate the locals' home ground.[23] These young men, determined to prevent an outsider sullying one of their women, act "as knights before them have probably done."[24] Driven on by a "desperate instinctive hereditary expedient" these insiders ambush the couple in the hope of deterring further intimacy between Eula and her paramour.[25] However, McCarron, fighting like "a wild stag surrounded by a gang of goats" and aided by Eula, beats off their attack.[26] Faulkner presents this confrontation as a case of Darwinian sexual selection in which "of the males, the strongest and, with some species, the best armed, drive away the weaker males."[27] The *extrinsic stranger* triumphs, the lovers consummate their relationship (despite the injuries sustained by McCarron during the fight) and Eula's daughter is conceived.

Durable and potent, the *extrinsic stranger* is certainly disconcerting, but this category provides an even more worrying variant: the *extrinsic alien*, the nonparochial local whose personal history and genealogy remain apocryphal. Paradoxical, the *extrinsic alien* is that most dangerous of intruders, the mutinous mutation, the enemy within. Such an alien appears to be at one with his community yet remains unallied to communal interests. These mutineers need not necessarily be further evolved nor more mutable than the norm; they may simply benefit from their new surroundings, an ingenuous environment that presents fewer checks on their expansion. "Many cases are on record," writes Darwin, "showing how complex and unexpected are the checks and relations between organic beings, which have to struggle together in the same country."[28] When an *other* species breaches an enclosure these internal constraints may prove to be ineffective.[29] This is especially true of efficacious *extrinsic aliens* whose likeness to indigenes initially masks any difference.[30] Their presence only materializes when their extensive infiltration appears as a contraindication to the robustness of that community.

For instance, the Chinese mitten crab was first detected in the Thames in 1935, but the ecological damage effected by this species has been identified only recently. As a sand extractor, the destruction of many river islets is assured by the crab's progress upstream.[31] Little can be done to halt their advance. Or, take kudzu as an illustration, a plant that has been present in Mississippi since 1937, but one that goes unmentioned in Faulkner's work; it is not, as one might expect, the bitterweed recalled by Malcolm Franklin. Kudzu's invasion remained unremarkable until, that is, incursion became infestation. Today, this vine has overrun more than seven million acres of southeast America. Neither of these species strictly conform to the immigrant categories detailed above, but they do provide examples of the sustained infiltration of an enclosed ecosystem. Moreover, tangible references such as these exemplify the prescience of William Faulkner's creation of that incipient species, those descendents from *Homo sapiens*, the Snopeses.

This figuration of a human subspecies became perceptible in 1925, a seminal year in which the young Mississippian visited Europe. This sojourn not only confirmed Sherwood Anderson's advice concerning the parochial essence of a writer's subject matter, but also introduced Faulkner to the work of Hippolyte Taine.[32] Taine, a professed Darwinian, believed that cultural constructions result from the interaction of three causal

elements, the *race*, the *surroundings*, and the *epoch*, an approach especially apposite for Faulkner who would later state his own "belief that
environment shaped culture rather than culture created environment."[33]
Faulkner's interest in the dynamics of ecology emerges in this period, a
time that furthermore witnessed the Scopes Monkey Trial in Dayton,
Tennessee.

These proceedings, broadcast by radio and transmitted telegraphically,
disseminated the Darwinian controversy across America and around the
world. Darwin's philosophy was in the air and, despite Faulkner's absence
from the United States during the trial, the concept of evolution certainly
permeated his mind. As a result, the parallel between "Scopes" and "Snopes"
retains critical importance especially when one recalls that the pressures
of evolution were visited on the Faulkner family in January, 1931 with the
death of their daughter, Alabama, within two weeks of her birth.[34]
Faulkner's first completed work after this trauma, a cautionary tale of mismatched genetics entitled "The Spotted Horses," attests to the unpleasant
inevitability of natural selection.

This short story would become a crucial episode in the author's consideration of the Snopes clan as they intrude upon the evolutionarily stable
state of Frenchman's Bend. Unfortunately for this region's residents, they
prosecute a single approach to human interaction, one that can be termed
an *exclusivity of doves*, ethical behavior succinctly recalled in *Requiem for
a Nun*. These are pioneering people for whom "personal liberty and freedom were almost a physical condition like fire or flood," a community that
would not interfere with the dubious mores of others as long as amoralists
"practised somewhere else."[35] Eventually, of course, a criminal gang bring
their amorality into the environs of the Bend. When captured these out-
laws are imprisoned in the community's makeshift jail, and a padlock, normally used to secure the federal mail pouch, has to be commandeered
to secure their internment. Previously the cell door had never required
fastening because local miscreants could be relied upon to remain in cus-
tody. The captive gang are not so obliging, they escape, taking the padlock
with them!

In terms of evolutionary biology, *dovelike* conduct is an unconscious
behavior program fostered by genes in which a community consists of
altruistic individuals who rarely, if ever, practice deception.[36] Unfortunately, this form of stability is vulnerable to breaches of trust, and the abusive self-interest inherent in the Snopeses, their *hawkishness*, is ideally
fitted to such an environment. So why, one may ask, are this family allowed
to remain in Frenchman's Bend? Are the indigenes completely ingenuous?

Faulkner's brilliance in presenting this invasion rests on the Snopeses'
character as *extrinsic strangers* of the *alien* variety. The Snopes family *are*

intrinsic to Mississippi, yet *extrinsic* to Frenchman's Bend.[37] At first this family appear to be another set of *dovelike* individuals who will practice altruism; any intimations of their *hawkish* nature go unrecognized by a community that is essentially naïve.[38] This naïvety even recommends the Snopeses as another set of peasants of whom the district's major landowners, the Varners, can take advantage. Jody Varner, son of the patriarch Will, complacently rents dirt farms for this very purpose. But in doing so with Ab Snopes, Jody unwittingly brings about his own displacement from society's upper echelons. Indeed, most of the Bend's residents are ignorant of Ab's reputation until the sewing-machine agent, V. K. Ratliff, reminisces about the barn-burning Ab of his childhood. Unfortunately for the Varners, this disclosure comes too late—they have already allowed Ab on to their land. In consequence, Jody employs Ab's son in the family store, hoping to forestall the destruction of Varner property. Yet this dubious insurance policy merely enables a far more efficient enemy to capitalize on the environment offered by Frenchman's Bend, an individual extremely fitted to that ecology: Flem Snopes.

Faulkner makes plain that Flem and his kin are germane to the socioeconomic times because of their biological inheritance. In *The Hamlet*, heredity is conceived in a mixture of blood blending and chromosomal terms but, as an interview in Japan indicates, by the mid-1950s Faulkner was more certain about the stamp of genetics, human behavior being driven by a "composition of hormones and genes."[39] To reiterate, *extrinsic aliens* need not be more evolved than the resident species in order to thrive in their new surroundings; their success may depend entirely upon ecological compatibility. Within the Snopes trilogy however, Faulkner figures genetic mutation in addition to environmental suitability, a combination that brings success to this emergent clan as they pervade and therefore undermine the evolutionary stability of the Bend. Genes *are* the Faulknerian basis for the Snopes family. As Joseph Urgo argues, all Snopeses are male and their characteristics, their *Snopesishness*, is carried biologically from male to male.[40] In the language of genetics, Faulkner figures each Snopes in terms of dominant gene(s) where the determining sex is male: *Snopesishness* is carried on the Y-chromosome. Females can bear the Snopes name but are unlikely to carry the Snopes gene(s).

The phenotypic characteristics of being a Snopes are exhibited in the males' supreme adaptation to the ecology of the twentieth century. Created by and molded to the socioeconomic environment, individual Snopeses fit into ecological niches from which they practice self-interest to an unprecedented extent. These men, rapacious by nature, are a parasitic affliction. Expanding the earlier Faulknerian quote emphasizes this conclusion. "[W]ith the boll-weevil already in it since, like the Snopes, he too has taken over the southern earth," cotton farming is analogous to communal benignancy with the South suffering a parasitic blight.[41]

Snopeses are a mutant form of *extrinsic aliens* with whom *Homo sapiens* will have to struggle in order to survive. Employing deception, lies, and manipulation, these mutants are often described as if they were members of an *other* species. Flem has the quality "of a spider of that bulbous blond omnivorous though non-poisonous species," Lump is a "chipmunk," whilst Mink is "a different kind of Snopes like a cotton-mouth is a different kind of snake."[42] To Ratliff this difference has a hybrid essence: trying to remember Mink's first name, he ponders, "*Fox? Cat? Oh yes, mink.*"[43] Similar thoughts emanate from the Snopeses themselves. Mink imagines himself as "a child of *another race and species*" and Montgomery Ward sums up the Snopes genealogy as "a family, a clan, a race, maybe even a species of pure sons of bitches."[44]

Flem Snopes epitomises the Snopes mutation with his personification of the *selfish gene* as the basis for capitalism.[45] Flem has a singular appetite for capital, he is rarely seen to eat or drink, and yet he constantly masticates the circumambience. Tasting the local air, Flem is concerned with figuring out the habitual disposition of Frenchman's Bend. He literally chews it over, concocting strategies for drawing the "suption" out of money and extracting all that is valuable from his environment.[46]

As these calculations become more and more finely tuned, Flem starts to figure out more and more local businessmen. As previously noted, the only presence in the hamlet to have foreseen this pervasion is Ratliff. In his eyes Flem is a Snopes vengeance weapon unleashed by Ab at the time to which it is most adapted. Faulkner's development of the Snopes history (in *The Town*) makes such a conclusion explicit. Old Ab was hanged by Colonel Sartoris for dubious horse trading during the Civil War but the Snopeses, even after numerous generations, retain a grudge. In effect, they have immolated Old Ab.[47] Their revenge, believes county-attorney Gavin Stevens, was to put a "monkey on the back of Ab's commander's descendant as soon as the lineage produced a back profitable to the monkey."[48] The Sartorises may re-establish their communal status during Reconstruction, a primacy symbolic of the evolutionarily stable state to which Jefferson has returned, but this postbellum equilibrium is precarious, a vulnerability which the Snopeses exploit in what *The Hamlet* promises as a Marxist revolution: anarchy that will level the local hierarchy.

The Sartoris and Snopes genealogies testify to this assurance. Faulkner had sketched out these family trees "one immediately after the other" while writing *Flags in the Dust*.[49] They are antithetical. The Sartoris genealogy is aristocratic, hierarchic, and has ancestral depth whereas the ancestry of the Snopeses is shallow, extensively spread, and modern.

Christian names tell of this difference. Sartoris forenames are derived from their esteemed antecedents while the Snopeses garner theirs from contemporary life with mail order catalogues, patent medicines, politicians, and even the economic catastrophe of 1929 providing suitable names. The Snopes genealogy may lack depth, but one inherent trait, their struggle for existence through cost-benefit analysis, ensures their dynasty's expansion. In comparison, the risk-taking predisposition of the Sartorises ensures their genealogy's reductiveness. A consequence of this genetic difference appears to be the extinction of the old order by the modernity of the new.

The Snopeses' most powerful response to Southern degeneration, Flem's insurgency, surfaces at Varner's store. Before this appointment Flem had labored alongside his itinerant father on a succession of rented farms. But, ensconced as store clerk, Flem promptly introduces his relatives, I. O. and Eck, into the local economy. These two cousins take over the blacksmith's business; the previous incumbent is evicted, leaves Frenchman's Bend, and never returns.[50] The next development comes at harvest time when the locals are surprised to find Flem, not Jody Varner, supervising the weighing of crops. By this time Flem has moved into the Varner house, going to work on Jody's mare. Soon touring the Varner estate in a horse-drawn buggy, Flem is subsequently seen at the Old Frenchman Place sitting in the barrel seat so readily associated with Will Varner. He appears to be usurping the landowner's position and Flem's influence spreads even further when he becomes a money lender. Earning interest from Caucasians and African Americans alike, Flem exploits both ends of the market simultaneously, and then consolidates his social standing by marrying into the modern landowning class. Although his marriage to Eula, pregnant and abandoned by McCarron, appears to be an error, one that solves Will Varner's social dilemma and one that is settled with the deeds to a valueless property, Flem's strategy actually guarantees his prosperous presence in Yoknapatawpha. With the Old Frenchman Place as his wedding gift, Will believes he has swindled his son-in-law. Flem will prove otherwise.

The newlyweds' return from honeymoon is signaled by "The Spotted Horses" episode. These wild mustangs, ostensibly the property of a Texan rancher, symbolize the spot or taint from abroad that is now to be found within the enclosure of Frenchman's Bend. These "jackrabbit[s]" are of another species and constitute a "contagion."[51] The genetic hybridity of the horses is detected in "their mismatched eyes."[52] Sold to gullible locals, these crossbreeds, another example of *extrinsic aliens*, break out of their enclosure spreading mayhem throughout the county and beyond. Faulkner confirms the correlation adumbrated between mustangs and Snopeses by positing the Texan horse trader as Flem's agent.

Ratliff is one inveterate wise enough not to get cheated in this incident and yet he, one of the most immune of locals, does get infected by Flem: he falls for the Salted Gold Mine scam. Will Varner had thought the Old Frenchman Place worthless, but Flem now sells the property to Ratliff, Bookwright, and Armstid. They are tricked into believing that the grounds to this property remain salted with Civil War gold. In this, the novel's closing episode, with the three men digging up nothing but dirt, Flem finally extracts his revenge on Ratliff for the costly reappearance of Mink's promissory notes while working at Varner's store.

And so, over the course of *The Hamlet*, Flem Snopes defeats all comers as he rises from blue-collar farm worker to white-collar usurer. The spread of Flem's ambit beyond Frenchman's Bend is compounded by the continued arrival of new Snopeses to Yoknapatawpha County.

These developments are narrated in *The Town*, a novel in which Flem evolves into a capitalist *per se*, a businessman characterised by two words, the "No," or nope, of Snopes and the "foreclose" of the money lender.[53] In terms of an evolutionary hermeneutic, Flem approaches the status of a *memeoid*, an individual taken over by a cultural construct, or *meme*, to such an extent that his own survival becomes inconsequential.[54] Flem's blind faith concerns money, money as an end in itself, money as autotelism, and *The Town* corroborates the opinion of the few discerning peasants in Frenchman's Bend that Flem would cheat his own kin as readily as he would swindle anyone else.[55]

Such observations confirm that Flem's parasitism overrides the biological inheritance of kin-selected altruism. As the epitome of the *selfish gene* Flem both eradicates his non-Snopes kin and expels unsuitable relations from his suzerainty: the death of that non-Snopes Snopes, Eck, is realized; Mink is left to rot in the state penitentiary; and Montgomery Ward is ousted from his "photographic" shop when Flem plants a substantial quantity of moonshine on the premises.

That thirty dollars were spent on this scheme bemuses Montgomery Ward. He concludes that his cousin's objective was "a little harder than Flem had expected or figgered."[56] Montgomery Ward's attempt to understand his relative's difficulty even leads to "the horrid aspersion that Flem had let lawyer Stevens and [the sheriff] Hub Hampton outfigger him," or that Flem "was subject to bad luck too, just like a human being."[57] Of course, Flem has neither been out-thought nor the subject of anthropoidal misfortune. For a moment however, Montgomery Ward believes that Flem is not "immune either to the strong and simple call of blood kinship," pleading with his cousin, "ain't blood thicker than water?"[58] This is a question that Flem does not answer. Montgomery Ward may figure in terms of pangenesis, but Flem never does: his autotelic capitalism evinces the phenotypic effects of "hard," rather than "soft," inheritance. When Montgomery Ward attempts to tilt the odds in his favor a second time by threatening to reopen his pornographic business on his release from prison, Flem responds, " '[y]ep. That's what I figgered.' "[59] Anticipating this move Flem has already collected enough evidence against his cousin to have him imprisoned for a much longer period if necessary.

Banishment of the pornographer from Jefferson is intended to protect Flem's ascendancy whilst effecting a scheme calculated to lengthen Mink's custodial sentence. If Montgomery Ward plays his part well, his early release will be secured by Flem. The mechanics of this parole have already been "figgered" along with an open railroad ticket.[60] Flem has both cousins completely figured out and even employs a third relative, Senator Clarence Snopes, to ensure that Montgomery Ward sticks to the deal. "He could have trusted me," insists Montgomery Ward, but being *hawkish* by nature Flem didn't dare discover at his age "that all you need to handle nine people out of ten is just to trust them."[61] Aspersions of Flem being out-figured, the subject of misfortune, being soft with respect to his own relatives, or trusting in others are completely dispelled as Faulkner unerringly constructs this episode in the terminology of economics. Flem, of all the Snopeses, is *the* figure of figuration, the master of capitalism, a man with a "pure and simple nose for money." Capitalism is the "pure and simple principle" by which he lives.[62] No wonder that Montgomery Ward, finally recognizing this obsession, chooses to spend his days on bail in Jefferson's jail. Only behind bars does he feel "safe from the free world, safe and secure for a little while yet from the free Snopes world."[63]

Flem is selfish, undoubtedly, but he also understands the notion of altruism, a concept that he has been abusing ever since his entry into Frenchman's Bend. His cuckoldry by Major de Spain is a prime example. Flem endures his wife's infidelity for eighteen years in order to disclose this betrayal at the most profitable of times. This disclosure ousts the Major from his position of financial superintendency, his colonial mansion, and the arms of Eula, whose suicide has been induced. Capitalizing on the town's indignity to the revelation of the de Spain affair, and as prophesied by Gavin Stevens, Flem at last gains control of that contemporary symbol of aristocratic primacy and communal stability, the Sartoris Bank.

Cynically foresighted with regard to altruism, Flem is also mightily aware of that small percentage of the population who are not *doves*: Byron Snopes's children for instance. These atavistic hybrids threaten Flem's ascendancy. Unsurprisingly, he soon returns them from whence they came, although, as an aside, evolutionary theory does suggest a contradictory interpretation of his actions. Flem's behavior could be a deviant form of kin-selected altruism. By evicting his relatives from Jefferson, he sends the Snopes genes abroad and away from the ambit of Yoknapatawpha County, an environment slowly evolving a mix of evolutionary strategies immune to *hawkish* exploitation.[64]

Free of Major de Spain, his wife, and troublesome relatives, Flem relishes his reign as bank president. He has reached the capitalist peak to which he aspired when young. However, this self-interest, Flem's capitalist agenda in which he gives supreme weight to his own desire whatever the cost to others, reveals the initial sense of nascent Marxism in the Snopes trilogy to be fallacious. This disdain for alterity equally applies to Flem's future selves so that ultimately his self-actualization, Flem's personification of self-interest theory, necessitates his own destruction. Having out-figured all others, he must figure out Flem Snopes. Ratliff's use of metaphor in the penultimate chapter of *The Town* manifests this inference. The sewing-machine agent sums up the antagonism between lawyer Stevens and bank president Snopes in this way.

> It was like a contest, like Lawyer had stuck a stick of dynamite in his hind pocket and lit a long fuse to it and was interested now would or wouldn't somebody step in in time and tromple the fire out. Or a race, like would he finally get Linda out of Jefferson and at least get his-self shut forever of the whole tribe of Snopes first, or would he jest blow up his-self beforehand first and take ever body and ever thing in the neighborhood along with him.
>
> No, not a contest. Not a contest with Flem Snopes anyway because it takes two to make a contest and Flem Snopes wasn't the other one. He was a umpire, if he was anything in it. No, he wasn't even a umpire. It was like he was running a little mild game against his-self, for his own amusement like solitaire. He had ever thing now that he had come to Jefferson to get.[65]

Ratliff believes that Flem's "game of solitaire was against Jefferson." More accurately adduced, Jefferson is the game or agency by which Flem can test *himself*.

Flem Snopes's greatest opponent may be Flem Snopes, but the community continue to suffer. In consequence, and as suggested previously, a number of behavior programs evolve to counter the banker's consuming self-interest. Some individuals, not many but a few, do offer alternatives to the *hawkishness* practised by the Snopeses and the *dovelike* ingenuousness of the proletariat.[66] These new combatants emerge from the population in a Darwinian manner since the "impulse to eradicate Snopes is," in Faulkner's opinion, "so strong that it *selects* its champions when the crisis comes."[67]

The "Centaur in Brass," Flem's attempt to defraud the county of valuable brass fittings while he is power-plant superintendent, the incident with which *The Town* opens, intimates the essence of a successful counterattack.

Flem's failure comes in the face of reciprocal altruism prosecuted by his subordinates, Tom Tom and Turl. Together, these two African Americans protect each other from their boss's rapaciousness by dumping his stolen brass into the communal water tank. Flem is forced to reimburse the county out of his own funds. The tank may remain on the town's horizon as a symbol of the Flem's spreading taint, but in addition it is a monument to a retaliatory strategy in which fraternity outwits the sharpest of *hawks*.[68]

That the response prosecuted by Tom Tom and Turl requires the passage of many years before the emergence of other effective responses to Flem's ascendance testifies to the persistence of intolerant racial politics in Yoknapatawpha. Nevertheless, *grudgers*, people who have long memories and a willingness to deny altruism to others by whom they have been previously deceived, do eventually emerge. Mrs. Hait is one example. She learns to withhold her goodwill from the Snopeses after her husband's death while assisting I. O. Snopes with an insurance swindle.[69] However, she has to remain tremendously patient to acquire the retribution she seeks, justice coming after ten years of struggle.

Of Faulkner's major figures, only Ratliff begrudges the indulgence of Ab and Flem from the outset. In the example of Snopes and non-Snopes Yoknapatawphians it is assumed that each Snopes is a *hawk* while all others are *doves*. This form of evolutionarily stable state, one in which two or more behavior strategies are prosecuted, is said to exhibit *polymorphism*. Rudimentary operational analysis assumes that each individual employs one, and only one, of the modalities found in such an environment. But Faulkner realizes that nature is rarely as straightforward as this convenient model suggests, and with the character of V. K. Ratliff he introduces a more complex approach in which his subject employs a combination of available strategies. When beyond the confines of Mississippi, when outside his home ground, when he is an outlander in someone else's accustomed environment, Ratliff displays *hawkish* tendencies akin to Flem's. Travelling to Columbia, Tennessee, the sewing machine agent views this outside territory as a "virgin African vale teeming with ivory, his for the mere shooting and fetching out."[70] Ratliff has no difficulty in selling his machines. To use terminology appropriate to his vocation, he has the region sewn up. As a salesman and restaurant owner Ratliff echoes Flem Snopes's capitalist instincts; he is the capitalist Everyman. Of a species similar to Snopes, Gavin Stevens must constantly remind himself of his friend's perspicacity. By Gavin's reckoning, Ratliff, comrade or not, is "too damned shrewd."[71] Even within the parochial ambit of Frenchman's Bend, Ratliff's shrewdness is evident from the conditional strategy he employs with respect to the Snopeses. He probes their *hawkishness*. If this exploration meets no retaliation, then he escalates the contest—the extraction of promissory notes from Mink with which Ratliff later confronts Flem in *The Hamlet* is a case in point.[72] But escalation of a conflict can be dangerous, as Ratliff's supposed victory over Flem confirms. Flem bears a grudge for longer than his adversary, whose wariness has been undermined by his initial success. With the salted mine scam, Flem redresses the balance of his account with Ratliff, and his ascendancy over the onetime restaurant owner is established.

In turn, Ratliff learns from his salted mine mistake; his skepticism with regard to *hawks* increases accordingly. So ecologically censorious does Ratliff become that he forestalls Senator Clarence Snopes's election to Congress. As Faulkner says of Ratliff, "he had accepted a change in culture, a change in environment, and he has suffered no anguish, no grief from it."[73] In other words, Ratliff develops a necessary intolerance toward pure capitalism.

Gavin Stevens is another *grudger* but one that adopts a different strategy to Ratliff's, one that stems from his group selectionist sensibilities. Stevens is morally convinced that the human collective must come before the individual. "Jefferson's got to come first," he avers, a concern he feels acutely when *in absentia*.[74] Thus, leaving for Heidleberg, Stevens passes on the responsibility for monitoring Yoknapatawpha's *extrinsic aliens* to Ratliff.[75] On his return from Europe, his attitude toward the Snopeses hardened by Montgomery Ward's behavior during the conflict, Stevens trains Flem's daughter, Linda, as an ecological agent. She matures into his *grudger* within the enemy camp that is the Snopes family.

Stevens is Flem's principal protagonist but another adversary comes from within his own clan: cousin Mink. Like Ratliff, Mink is also too forgiving in his initial response to the practice of self-interest as his involvement with his neighbor Jack Houston demonstrates. Mink believes in the spirit of the law, but many, such as Houston, do not. It is this landowner's insistence on an extra night's grazing fee, a fine stipulated by the law, that signals his murder by Mink. Flem does not attend the subsequent trial, but Mink is willing to forgive this absence until, that is, the abortive escape plot involving Montgomery Ward and the resultant extension to his prison sentence. That Flem had been without "the decency and courage to say No to his blood cry for help from kin to kin" can no longer be ignored.[76] Gavin Stevens's agent, Linda Snopes, now comes to Mink's aid. She successfully appeals for his early release, exploiting the lawyer's disbelief in the inherent selfishness of human nature to obtain the parole. Gavin has schooled Linda well, how well is yet to be revealed. Linda, wishing to avenge her mother's death, becomes, almost unbeknown to Mink, his confederate. As if their mutual strategy of grudging forges a genetic link, Faulkner figures a musteline family resemblance between this pair, a generic bond lacking between Linda and Flem.[77] Capitalizing on Mink's resentment, counting on the fact that the parolee will return to Jefferson, she is justified by his arrival at the mansion. Turning a deaf ear to this murderous presence, Linda tacitly sanctions her father's execution.

The capitalist system, personified by Flem Snopes, is the realization of the phenotypic effects of hard inheritance, and Flem's death, murder as passive suicide, is Faulkner's method of confirming the immanent autotelism, the collectively self-defeating essence, of this paradigm.[78] The Snopeses, initially identified as the mutant enemy within a benign community, are now understood to be Faulkner's figuration of genetic replicators at their most ruthless. Worryingly, it is a lesson that the peasants of Jefferson do not grasp. Marxism fails in Yoknapatawpha because of a local ethos "in which the Jefferson proletariat declined not only to know it was the proletariat but even to be content as the middle class."[79] These indigenes believe that their present condition is temporary, that they are destined to be bankers, and that eventually the Snopes Bank will be theirs. Most Yoknapatawphians retain this delusion and as a result Northern Mississippi remains an "alien capitalist waste" to those not similarly beguiled.[80] Linda retains her Marxist sympathies but, by the autumn of 1945, even her communist comrades have become "market investors." These two men, of Finnish extraction and once deemed *foreign* to the local ecology, became rich during the war and by investing this money in the stock market have achieved thorough assimilation.[81]

Linda stands alone.

Or does she?

If capitalism in the form of Flem Snopes is immoral, then Linda's figuration is no less concerning. Gavin Stevens testifies to this fear. For, despite the machinations of the Snopeses, Jefferson's county-attorney had maintained a belief in mankind's predisposition toward the good of his own species. Stevens had interpreted Linda's demand for Mink's early release as altruism, but cognizance of his protégé's motives (elucidation manifest in the shape of a British sports car) disabuses him of his group selectionist notions. Linda, compelled to engineer Flem's execution, drives from the murder scene and out of Gavin's sight, resplendent in a symbol of the economic system that tarnishes her too. Only now, with Linda's departure, does the sobering implication come home to Stevens that " '[t]here aren't any morals.' " [82] With this, his last appearance in Faulkner's canon, Gavin Stevens, the Harvard and Heidleberg trained lawyer, finally learns the painful answer to his beloved Eula's lament. " 'We've all bought Snopeses here,' " she once complained, " '*whether we wanted to or not*; . . . I don't know why we bought them. I mean, why we had to: what *coin* and when and where *we so recklessly and improvidently spent* that we had to have Snopeses.' "[83] With Gavin's enlightenment, Faulkner emphasizes that biological inheritance does not select traits at a group level; the *memes* of human morality remain forever susceptible to the genetic nature of *Homo sapiens*.

Flem's funeral compounds this suggestion with the appearance of three unknown Snopeses, men "not alien at all: simply identical," not *alien* yet distinguishable, not *alien* but *other*.[84] These normal differences suggest the ever-presence of the *extrinsic alien*, the enemy within: the genetic basis that constantly threatens the tranquillity of stable communities. The Snopeses are not mutants, they are representative of mankind.[85]

Recognition of this inherence with regard to our own species is profoundly disturbing. No wonder then that the Snopeses, a symptom of Faulkner's aesthetic of conflict between biological heredity and cultural inheritance, provided him with so much material. In Faulknerian terms, genes predispose organisms toward selfish behavior while the philosophy of ethics must be promoted by *memes*. Faulkner's aesthetic recognized this conflict more than twenty-five years before the evolutionary biologist Richard Dawkins would propound a similar argument from the perspective of genetics: this tension between intrinsic selfishness and morality playing out in Faulkner's attitude toward the apotheosis of *alienation* that is Flem Snopes. At times, especially before composing *The Mansion*, Faulkner had rather admired Flem, a man who "came from nothing with no equipment," a character whom the author had once envisaged becoming president of the United States.[86] But in 1959, in a novel that "is the final chapter and the summation of a work conceived and begun in 1925," Faulkner was forced to rub out this figure, disfiguring Flem with a gunshot to the face, his assailant using a "mud crusted" gun likened to a "fossilised terrapin," a weapon resurrected from the depths of evolutionary time.[87]

Evolution accounts for Flem. He is vanquished by an ecological condition alien to beneficent life, one that continues to be promoted in the twenty-first century, that of capitalism. Within such an environment *Snopesishness* remains a disturbing revelation with regard to the deficient nature of *Homo sapiens*. True, capitalism has evolved, but evolution fails to guarantee an ethically solvent socioeconomic system of the order permissible via the solidarity of a group conspiracy.[88] Nature's ethically flawed immanence perturbed Faulkner, sustaining his pessimistic determinism for more than thirty years and yet, taking solace from moments of optimism, he believed that future generations could take responsibility for their inheritance. Man, human but humane, solitary but partaking of solidarity, will prevail, Faulkner asserts, because "there's always someone that will never stop trying to cope with Snopes."[89]

NOTES

1. Considering the Snopes and considering the climate in Mississippi, the original title for this paper, a title inspired by S. J. Perelman, was "It's Not the Heat, It's the Cupidity."

2. Jacques Derrida, *Specters of Marx: The State of the Debt, the Work of Mourning, and the New International* (London: Routledge, 1994), 54.

3. Ibid., 91.

4. The Chinese mitten crab (*Eriocheir sinensis*) is a burrowing crab whose native distribution is the coastal rivers and estuaries of the Yellow Sea in Korea and China.

5. *Pueraria lobata*, or kudzu, is a climbing, semi-woody, perennial vine in the pea family that was introduced to the United States from Japan at the Centennial Exposition in Philadelphia, Pennsylvania, in 1876. During the Depression of the 1930s, kudzu, with its extensive root structure, was deemed an ideal solution to the South's problem of soil erosion.

6. William Faulkner, *Essays, Speeches, and Public Letters by William Faulkner*, ed. James B. Meriwether (London: Chatto & Windus, 1967), 14.

7. William Faulkner, *Requiem for a Nun* (London: Vintage, 1996), 45–46, 46.

8. Darwin writes: "the struggle will almost invariably be most severe between the individuals of the same species, for they frequent the same districts, require the same food, and are exposed to the same dangers. In the case of varieties of the same species, the struggle will generally be almost equally severe, and we sometimes see the contest soon decided: for instance, if several varieties of wheat be sown together, and the mixed seed be resown, some of the varieties which best suit the soil or climate, or are naturally the most fertile, will beat the others and so yield more seed, and will consequently in a few years supplant the other varieties." Charles Darwin, *On the Origin of Species by Means of Natural Selection; or, the Preservation of Favoured Races in the Struggle for Life*, 6th ed. (Oxford: Oxford University Press, 1996), 29.

9. William Faulkner, *Lion in the Garden: Interviews with William Faulkner, 1926–1962*, ed. James B. Meriwether and Michael Millgate (New York: Random House, 1968), 221.

10. William Faulkner, *Faulkner in the University*, ed. Frederick Gwynn and Joseph L. Blotner (Charlottesville: University of Virginia Press, 1959), 19. Faulkner, *Lion in the Garden*, 203.

11. Faulkner, *Lion in the Garden*, 72.

12. Ibid., 187.

13. Faulkner, *Faulkner in the University*, 34.

14. Ibid., 41.

15. William Faulkner, *The Hamlet* (New York: Vintage Books, 1991), 3 [emphasis added].

16. Darwin, *On the Origin of Species*, 21.

17. Richard Dawkins credits fellow evolutionary biologist John Maynard Smith with the concept of evolutionarily stable strategies: genetically predetermined behavior patterns which, if practiced by most members of a population, cannot be bettered by an alternative strategy. See Richard Dawkins, *The Selfish Gene* (Oxford: Oxford University Press, 1989), 69.

18. Faulkner, *The Hamlet*, 4.

19. William Faulkner, *The Town* (New York: Vintage Books, 1961), 306.

20. Charles continues: the Chinaman is "sundered from his like and therefore as threatless as a mule." Faulkner, *The Town*, 306.

21. But crossing the boundary between the major racial categories is unacceptable. *Light in August* documents the communal reflex to such a transgression when Joe Christmas, initially accepted as a Mediterranean, is later imputed to be a miscegene. Being an African Caucasian Joe has broken the demarcations of race, and his fate as a scapegoat is assured.

22. The carpetbaggers whom John Sartoris shoots for inciting African Americans to vote, as recalled in *Flags in the Dust*, also fit this category. William Faulkner, *Flags in the Dust* (New York: Vintage Books, 1973), 263. *Knight's Gambit* provides a number of other examples of the outlander. In "Smoke," originally published in 1934, Anselm Holland, a man who came to Jefferson "[w]here from, no one knew," and married into a landowner's family, remains to "those of us whose fathers and grandfathers had been bred here . . . an underbred

outlander." William Faulkner, *Knight's Gambit* (New York: Random House, 1949), 3. The carnival worker, Joel Flint from the 1946 short story "An Error in Chemistry," a man who remains in Yoknapatawpha when the funfair moves on and then marries a local woman, nevertheless is always "the foreigner, the outlander, the Yankee" to the inveterate community. Faulkner, *Knight's Gambit*, 109. A third example appears in the character of Buck Thorpe from "Tomorrow" (1940). Known to local young men as Bucksnort, he is seen as contemptuously virile, Thorpe also "had appeared overnight from nowhere." Faulkner, *Knight's Gambit*, 86. This collection of outlanders, Anselm Holland, Joel Flint, and Buck Thorpe, all suffer unenviable ends. The first two are murdered, the last is sentenced to death for the murder of his wife and father-in-law.

23. William Faulkner, *The Mansion* (New York: Vintage Books, 1965), 118. McCarron is Eula's choice. She chooses the most suitable mate as befits Darwinian principles. Hoake is the only suitor "wild and strong enough to deserve and match her" while "[i]t would a taken that whole generation of young concentrated [local] men to seeded them . . . magnificent loins." Faulkner, *The Mansion*, 118, 114.

24. Faulkner, *The Hamlet*, 126, 151.

25. Faulkner, *The Mansion*, 121.

26. Ibid., 122.

27. Charles Darwin, *The Descent of Man and Selection in Relation to Sex* (London: John Murray, 1996), 163.

28. Darwin, *On the Origin of Species*, 21.

29. Darwin describes such an invasion with reference to a country estate in Staffordshire where several hundred acres of barren heathland had been enclosed twenty-five years previously and planted with Scotch fir. "The change in the native vegetation," Darwin continues, "was most remarkable, more than is generally seen in passing from one quite different soil to another: not only the proportional numbers of the heath-plants were wholly changed, but twelve species of plants (not counting grasses and carices) flourished in the plantations, which could not be found on the heath." Darwin concludes, therefore, that the ecology of an enclosure can become severely altered once penetrated by a potent trespasser. Darwin, *On the Origin of Species*, 21.

30. A for the good of the species view of evolution prompts one to think of deceivers, liars, and manipulators as a different species: predators and parasites. But Dawkins follows Darwin, "we must expect lies and deceit and selfish exploitation of communication to arise whenever the interests of the genes of different individuals diverge. This will include individuals of the same species." As note 7 suggests, Darwin believes that members of one's own species are an individual's greatest threat.

31. There are further ecological implications from the explosion of the Thames mitten crab population. As an omnivorous predator the crab devours many organisms including the rare, native, freshwater crayfish.

In the United States, the mitten crab was first recorded in the Detroit River at Windsor, Ontario in October 1965. There were no further sightings until 1973, when two males and one female were caught in Lake Erie by commercial fishermen. The next instance of this crustacean in North America was not recorded until 1987, when a single specimen was captured in the Mississippi Delta, near Louisiana. In 1992, commercial shrimp trawlers in the southern San Francisco Bay reported the occasional catch of Chinese mitten crabs. Many of these were egg-bearing, and by the summer of 1994 they had spread to the northern San Francisco Bay. As important locations for the fishing industry, the sudden increase in the crab populations was considered a major threat. During the late 1980s, all mitten crab imports into the USA were banned and the law was enforced with tough penalties. Despite these measures the population in the San Francisco Bay region continues to increase.

32. Anderson told Faulkner, "[y]ou're a country boy; all you know is that little patch up there in Mississippi you started from." Faulkner, *Essays, Speeches, and Public Letters*, 8.

Although Taine's *History of English Literature* is not in William Faulkner's library, Faulkner did have a copy of *A Modern Book of Criticism* which he read in France during the autumn of 1925. Faulkner's hand-written annotations on this volume are numerous, and their tone indicates the ferocity of Faulkner's engagement with the work. Ludwig Lewisohn, ed., *A Modern Book of Criticism* (Boni & Liveright: New York, 1919). Autographed by William Faulkner in Normandy, September 1925. Phil Stone cites another Faulknerian source of Taine's hermeneutic, Willard Huntington Wright's *The Creative Will: Studies in the Philosophy and the Syntax of Aesthetics* (1916). Stone recalls that "the aesthetic theories set forth in that book, strained through my own mind, constitutes one of the most important influences in Bill's whole literary career. . . . If people who read him would simply read Wright's book they would see what he is driving at from a literary standpoint." Phil Stone cited by Joseph Blotner, *Faulkner: A Biography* (London: Chatto & Windus, 1974), 1:320.

33. Faulkner, *Lion in the Garden*, 105.

34. In an interview with Louis Daniel Brodsky from the 1980s, Estelle Faulkner's eldest grandchild, Mrs. Victoria Fielden Johnson, insists that "there was a strain of weakness in Grandmama genetically." Louis Daniel Brodsky, *Life Glimpses* (Austin: University of Texas Press, 1990), 155.

35. William Faulkner, *Requiem for a Nun* (London: Vintage Books, 1996), 9, 12.

36. Contradictory as it may appear, *dovelike* behavior evolves from the same basis as *hawkishness*: selfish genes. See Dawkins, "Nice guys finish first," *The Selfish Gene*, 202–33.

37. Ab's father is determined to gain revenge on the swindling Pat Stamper, not for monetary reasons, but because Stamper is an outsider, "a stranger," who "breaks into your house" like a burglar. Faulkner, *The Hamlet*, 38, 41. This native sensibility offsets the extraneousness of the family with regard to Yoknapatawpha as evinced when Jody Varner meets the younger Ab for the first time. He "was a complete stranger"; Jody "had never heard the name before." Faulkner, *The Hamlet*, 9.

38. Thus, Ratliff may have foreseen the trouble intimated by the arrival of the Snopes family, but "nobody else in Jefferson seemed to recognise the danger." Faulkner, *The Town*, 106.

39. Faulkner, *Lion in the Garden*, 104 [August 5, 1955].

40. Joseph R. Urgo, *Faulkner's Apocrypha: "A Fable," Snopes, and the Spirit of Human Rebellion* (Jackson: University of Mississippi Press, 1989), 172.

41. Faulkner, *Essays, Speeches, and Public Letters*, 14.

42. Faulkner, *The Hamlet*, 65, 177, 101.

43. Ibid., 99.

44. Ibid., 263 [emphasis added]. Mink's speculation is confirmed by his wife when she describes his semen as "rank poison." Faulkner, *The Mansion*, 87.

45. The *selfish gene* is Dawkins's concept: a unit of biological heredity predisposed to differential survival through replication.

46. Faulkner, *The Hamlet*, 26.

47. Faulkner, *The Town*, 33.

48. Ibid., 42.

49. Gail Mortimer, "Evolutionary Theory in Faulkner's Snopes Trilogy," *Rocky Mountain Review of Language and Literature* (Salt Lake City: Rocky Mountain Modern Language Association, 1986), 193.

50. Faulkner, *The Hamlet*, 73.

51. Ibid., 319, 303.

52. Ibid., 300. Faulkner conflates this figuration through the terminology of blood blending according to which the colts "clotted and blended and shifted among themselves." Faulkner, *The Hamlet*, 325.

53. Faulkner, *The Mansion*, 215–16. Neither can Charles Mallison imagine Flem's "hand writing anything except adding a percent symbol or an expiration date." Faulkner, *The Mansion*, 221.

54. Dawkins continues: one sees "lots of these people on the evening news from such places as Belfast or Beirut." Dawkins, *The Selfish Gene*, 330.

55. Faulkner, *The Hamlet*, 309.

56. Faulkner, *The Mansion*, 61.

57. Ibid., 59.

58. Ibid., 61, 68.

59. Ibid., 68.

60. Ibid., 70, 69.

61. Ibid., 71–72.

62. Ibid., 54, 56.

63. Ibid., 83.

64. Wallstreet Panic, who tries "to remove himself from the aura and orbit of Snopes," is a different matter. He may remain in Jefferson, but this is despite Flem and thanks to Ratliff, who guarantees him financial assistance. Faulkner explains, "I think that Wall Street Panic wasn't really a Snopes, that probably, actually, he was not a Snopes, that his father's mama may have done a little extra-curricular night work." Faulkner, *Faulkner in the University*, 33, 246.

65. Faulkner, *The Town*, 347.

66. Just as boll-weevil infestation eventually compelled Southern farmers into crop diversification.

67. Faulkner, *Faulkner in the University*, 34.

68. The water from this tank, no longer fit for human consumption, is used to wash down the streets. During this period it could be said that Jefferson is awash with phlegm!

69. Mrs. Hait's benevolence is evident from her treatment of the tramp, Old Het.

70. Faulkner, *The Hamlet*, 61.

71. Faulkner, *The Town*, 44.

72. Flem too is happy to co-operate with an antagonist to counter a more immediate threat. When his social ambition is endangered by Montgomery Ward's pornography business, Flem permanently expels his relative from Yoknapatawpha by helping Gavin Stevens and Hub Hampton effect a prosecution.

73. Faulkner, *Faulkner in the University*, 253.

74. Faulkner, *The Town*, 174.

75. Ratliff co-opts Gavin's relative, Gowan Stevens, to help him fulfil this civic duty. And, like his cousin, Gowan "got interested in it like *a game, a contest* or even a battle, a war, that Snopeses had to be watched constantly like an invasion of snakes." Faulkner, *The Town*, 106.

76. Faulkner, *The Mansion*, 396.

77. Faulkner symbolizes this bond with Linda's appearance. Once black, now streaked with a single, central white line, her hair resembles a skunk's coat. Linda appears to be of the same genus as Mink.

78. Capitalism as a destructive end in itself is not as contradictory as it appears. "When a self-interested man pays the price imposed on him by the self-interested acts of others," writes the philosopher Derek Parfit, "he regrets the fact that these people are self-interested. He regrets their bias in their own favor. But this does not lead him to regret this bias in himself." Derek Parfit, *Reasons and Persons* (Oxford: Oxford University Press, 1987), 187.

79. Faulkner, *The Mansion*, 213.

80. These are Charles Mallison's words. William Faulkner, *The Mansion*, 214.

81. Ibid., 350.

82. Ibid., 429. Note that Gavin Stevens had already compromised his high ideals by co-operating with Flem in the framing of Montgomery Ward.

83. Faulkner, *The Town*, 95 [emphasis added].

84. Faulkner, *The Mansion*, 421. Could Faulkner intend these others, one wonders, to be descendants of Flem's unnamed brother from "Barn Burning" (1939), the anonymous Snopes whom the adult Flem never mentions?

85. All of us embody the enemy within, although as Faulkner's sexual politics indicates— the genes of *Snopesishness* are determined by male meiosis are they not?—men are more blameworthy than women.

86. Faulkner, *Faulkner in the University*, 119. Faulkner, *Lion in the Garden*, 223.

87. Faulkner, frontispiece, *The Mansion*. Faulkner, *The Mansion*, 429, 398.

88. Dawkins, *The Selfish Gene*, 75.

89. Faulkner, *Faulkner in the University*, 34.

Is Faulkner Green?
The Wilderness as Aporia

François Pitavy

The discourse on ecology has taken such space in various ways of contemporary life, it has developed such new critical tools and even put on such different colors that, to try to reflect soundly on Faulkner and ecology, more precisely on the question of whether Faulkner can be drafted into something like ecological thinking, it is safe to go back to basics, that is, etymology: *oikos-logos*, the discourse on *oikos*, household, or, in a wider meaning, habitat, environment. The definition of Ernst Haeckael, the German scientist and disciple of Darwin who coined the word in 1866, merely elaborates on etymology and, pointedly, on its fundamental meaning and function, that is, relating, connecting: "the science of the relations of living organisms to the external world."[1]

The wide scope of this definition opens the way for a two-sided questioning: examining man's relation to his natural environment, an expected approach in any discussion of ecology in Faulkner's cosmos, and also his relation to his habitat, that man-made environment which Faulkner, all too often ironically, even derisively, names civilization, or Progress. So Faulkner's cosmos could be viewed as a manner of ecosystem in which man is to be perceived in relation at once to his "civilized" and to his natural environment. The two aspects are interrelated: man's relation to "civilization" can be viewed, especially in the last two decades of the Faulkner canon, as the obverse side of his relation to nature. Urban civilization versus nature, progress versus wilderness, motion versus stasis, the flow of time versus eternity: one recognizes here the major tension underlying Faulkner's work, most notably *Go Down, Moses* and the prologues of *Requiem for a Nun*, selected here for this reason. An unresolved tension (reflected in the unusual number of oxymorons in his language), full of ambiguities, as Faulkner, while loudly rejecting the more strident signs of ostensible Progress, never ceases to ask himself whether a man-nature relation is at all workable, even possible, whether man is to be held accountable for his attitude toward nature and the changes he brings to his environment.[2] Such are the first and fairly obvious concerns and questionings subsumed in the admittedly simplifying and slightly provocative question: is Faulkner green?

At first sight, Faulkner may appear as a legitimate candidate for enroll-ment: the awareness of an "economy of nature"—the phrase antedating the word ecology[3]—and the sense of man's communion with nature seem to permeate "The Old People" and "The Bear," in Go Down, Moses, to take what comes to mind first. Yet, revisiting the Arcadian nostalgia and at greater lengths the concept of wilderness, so prominent in some of Faulkner's later fiction, will tend to show that, appearances notwithstand-ing, there is in the last analysis no real man-nature interrelationship in his fiction: it is an ontological impossibility—an aporia,[4] as the second part of the title for this paper indicates.

The "Green" Faulkner in Historical Context

Before looking closely into the two novels, and the better to define Faulkner's stance regarding the poles of the tension I have identified, let me begin with a double contextualization: historical and canonical, that is, the literary and ideological, or rather national, traditions against which Faulkner can be put in perspective, and the Faulkner canon itself, as there is clearly evolution and maturation in his view of nature. This lengthy prel-ude will be no digression into literary history, but a gradual, concentric approach to Faulkner's mature thinking on ecology and already, in several instances, a comment on the two novels discussed here. Thus, circling around Faulkner will help focus the answers to the question asked in the title.

Let us first consider Faulkner in the light of the late eighteenth- and the nineteenth-century Anglo-Saxon thinking on "Nature's economy." Roughly speaking, one can trace two major and opposed traditions, the Arcadian and the humanist. The first advocates an ideal(ized) rural simplicity and contentment such as exhibited by shepherds in conventional pastoral poetry, that is, a simple life and humble submission to natural laws, the reestablishment of a sense of harmony between nature and man; it is an equalizing, democratic ideal. Conversely, the other tradition aims at estab-lishing man's dominion over nature and its inhabitants, including man himself, through the exercise of reason and hard work, in accordance with the biblical order, and in the tradition of the Enlightenment compounded by the Protestant ethic. This humanist stance, a belief in progress and civ-ilization, places man at the apex of creation, as in Genesis: it is, in fine, aristocratic and imperial (in an etymological, or ecological, not a political or social sense[5]). Briefly exploring the first tradition, the one in which Faulkner might be inscribed, will help understand his stance on progress, and his reflection on wilderness, even though it appears in the last analy-sis that he escapes easy classifications and the resolution of tensions and contradictions.

The early and best known representative of that first tradition is Gilbert White, the eighteenth-century curate of Selborne, a tranquil village in the Hampshire countryside, who published in 1789 a single book, *The Natural History of Selborne*, a book properly belonging to the next century, as White's fame came after his death and his book then became the hallmark of an Arcadian stance. He had tried to understand how all creatures were united and interrelated in a given environment, his own Hampshire countryside, but mostly to revive "man's loyalties to the earth and its vital energies" (Worster 9), to reestablish an Arcadian harmony with a nature no doubt idealized through his classical readings (Virgil's *Eclogues* and *Georgics*, themselves probably revisited by Cowper, Gray, or Thompson).

That White soon became the paradigm of an Arcadian nostalgia must be understood in the context of the agricultural and industrial revolutions then taking place in England. The agricultural revolution, with the enclosure acts of the 1750s, destroyed the remnants of a communal mode of subsistence farming and the democratic open-field system that had survived from the Middle Ages, radically transforming the English landscape. The industrial revolution brought a new mode of industrial production, in factories, thanks to the accumulation of capital and several manufacturing inventions (spinning jenny, power loom, steam engine, etc.). With that double revolution, the natural world was submitted to man's dominion (the reverse of young Ike McCaslin's attitude), and White made to emerge, in the nineteenth century, "as a focal point on the map of dream and reverie, the living memory of a world that had been lost" (Worster 14).

This double revolution, however, had already made White's ideal world obsolescent when he advocated it, as, a century later, Frederick Jackson Turner proposed an idealized and vital view of the American contact with the wilderness, to him *the* shaping force in the making of the *Homo Americanus*, precisely at the time when the end of the frontier was officially acknowledged.[6] Viewing both writers in their historical contexts, one retrospectively sees a similar tension between man's nostalgic longing for a mythified Arcadia, a desire for rebirth and rejuvenation, and conversely, especially in Turner, the sense of an ending. No contradiction here: the Arcadian strain, in White, as in Thoreau and Turner, is the stronger for being questioned by the course of history. Here again, the radical and unsolvable tension in Faulkner can be traced back to an Anglo-Saxon tradition, notably to American historiography.

If we consider the history of the American's relation to the land, it is indeed clearly not Arcadian: the colonists' errand into the wilderness was no nostalgic search for a pagan golden age, rather the reverse—a will to establish man's dominion over nature, bountiful so as to be made subservient to man's needs, and amenable to God's manifest plan that the new land be claimed in the name of political, economic, social, and spiritual progress. From the start, Christianity in America had to sever man from wild, untamed nature emotionally and spiritually, to eradicate the pagan animism of the native populations, their sense of communion with the vital spirit of a natural but unchristianized world, envisioned by the new-comers to be synonymous with evil (as is obvious at the beginning of *The Scarlet Letter*, opening on the prison door). In that respect, Faulkner's view of nature is fundamentally unchristian: Ike's initiation into the wilderness by Sam Fathers is a pagan ritual. Thus the history of the American colonization of the new world belongs to the humanist, imperial tradition. The benevolence of a bountiful nature was in itself proof that it was meant to provide for man's dominion. Here again, Faulkner goes counter to the American grain.

So did Henry David Thoreau, the first great subversive mind of modern times in America, with whom Faulkner appears to possess more affinities than has generally been acknowledged. Some filiation—an Arcadian strain—can clearly be ascertained.

Like Gilbert White looking for traces of Selborne's past in the Hampshire countryside,[7] Thoreau tried to discover in Massachusetts and New Hampshire some pockets of the primeval wilderness, indeed hardly extant in a New England natural landscape then almost extinct twenty miles west of Boston. Aware of the dwindling of natural resources, of the encroachment of civilization and of the new railroads, he longed to reconstruct the actual condition of the land prior to man's arrival and destruction: "I long for wildness . . . a New Hampshire everlasting and unfallen."[8] Everlasting and unfallen: precisely the impossible Faulkner dream, in *Go Down, Moses* and the first prologue of *Requiem for a Nun*. Thoreau had a keen sense of the discontinuity brought to nature through agriculture and technology, and he longed for the restoration of continuity. Similarly, in these two novels, Faulkner appears to long for continuity, an accessible substitute for changelessness, rather than progress. However, Thoreau knew that one cannot change the course of history, so that *in fine* the Arcadian longing in him must be ethical rather than strictly ecological or scientific: "Either nature may be changed, or man."[9] Contemporary ecological thinking says nothing else. Thoreau believed in man's spiritual progress. Conversely, though he kept asserting his belief in man in his public discourse, spiritual progress in Faulkner appears to be a delusion; hence he must believe in man's capacity to endure rather than to change the world, or even himself. He said nothing else in Stockholm.

Which is confirmed by the novel closest in tone to that speech, *Requiem for a Nun*.[10] The first prologue is a manner of mock heroic or tall-tale telling of the dream of Jefferson's founding fathers, when Ratcliffe suggests to register the arbitrary value of the lost lock, fifteen dollars, in the Book, necessarily written with a capital B (and unanimously accepted as such); thus it becomes a mock biblical foundation narrative, the outrageous Genesis-like account of the foundation of Faulkner's cosmos. This inscription in the Book "not only solved the problem but abolished it . . . from now on into perpetuity, opening to their vision like the rending of a veil, like a glorious prophecy, the Last splendid[11] limitless panorama of America: that land of boundless opportunity, that bourne, created not by nor of the people, but for the people, as was the heavenly manna of old . . .—illimitable, vast, without beginning or end . . . inalienable and immutable."[12] Such splendid vision, such limitless and immutable panorama of America, is paradoxically static and out of time (the panorama seems to preexist behind the veil to be rent, "without beginning or end")—not the glorious vision of a splendid future, but the backward-looking image of God's original chosen people, amid prophets and the manna of old (an all too revealing qualifier, somehow referring back to the "old people" in Go Down, Moses, an extinct species): this is not a representation of a new-born Republic or Commonwealth, but a nostalgic image of the lost Garden or of an imagined lost state of innocence and benevolence. It is an ahistorical vision, in contradiction to Faulkner's evocation of his own cosmos, inscribed in time, from genesis to the last ding dong of doom, a time that cannot be arrested (except by art, or artifice), so there can be "no such thing as was—only is" (LG 255). So Faulkner denies the possibility, even the legitimacy, of an Arcadian vision—which thus dwells in the same category of impossibilities as the wilderness.

Moreover, the foundation of the city rests on impure premises: the inscription of a debt in the Book is paradoxically no acceptance of accountability, but on the contrary a denial of responsibility toward future generations (the denial of an ecological stance), which abrogates the significance of the founding gesture. To compound the founders' unwitting aporia, the courthouse is first built as an adjunct to the jail, it is second in precedence and importance to a building designating the concomitance of foundation and evil. Moreover, though erected to stand as the bulwark of liberty and equality, its symbolical value is undermined by the construction itself: it is designed by a captive architect and built by slave labor. The original building in the foundation of Jefferson, the jail then becomes the only reliable witness of its future development and so-called progress, as it is told in the third prologue. So the shadow of evil antedates even the naming of the city[13] and looms over its history, an apt comment on the dramatic part of the novel, preparing for Temple's last words: "Doomed. Damned" (286). The foundation narrative here abrogates the foundation myth, making the founders' (mock) beau geste a derisive gesture.

Faulkner's cosmos, whose sole owner and proprietor he claims to be, cannot be of this world.

The Canonical Context

Descriptions of the natural world and even more the concept of an economy of nature do not appear prominently, if at all, in the works of the 1920s, and even of most of the 1930s. Moreover, and the better to define the status of nature in Faulkner, one should foreground here a trait of his descriptive technique, which significantly often does away with denotation (expected in nature writing), in favor of connotation: consequently, the less mimetic, or descriptive, his fiction is, the better susceptible of *re-presentation* (instead of mere presentation) and imaginative power, the more metonymical or metaphorical. This does not apply just to Faulkner's early work, but to the whole canon, and interestingly to the relatively late novels studied here, as for instance in the description of the Gum Tree "alive with frantic squirrels" in the final scene of "The Bear," defying any attempt at mimesis: it is "one green maelstrom of mad leaves," a "frenzied vortex" (GDM 245–46).[14] One should add here that Faulkner often resorts to smells and sounds in his representations of nature, that is, to the perceptions the less susceptible of mimesis. The creation of Benjy's extraordinary sensorial landscape rests on the same representational technique ("Caddy smelled like trees"). So that, say up to the "Old Man" sections of *If I Forget Thee, Jerusalem*, Faulkner may not really be called a nature writer. It is even doubtful that the definition applies to him at all.

Faulkner's greenery in the 1920s is self-conscious and derivative, his trees and leaves of grass are purely literary. In *The Marionettes*, the leaves and garlands, garden trellises, moon-tipped trees, romantically curved poplars mimicking in superimposed projections the lovers' bodies bending toward formal and unrealized kisses (the ever present Keatsian theme of arrested desire) are the graphic pen-and-ink inscriptions of a well-established literary tradition, derived from Verlaine, Mallarmé, and Laforgue, and which has little to do with nature *per se*.[15] They are the objective correlatives of a vague, stylized, fin de siècle sensuality, as also expressed in Faulkner's early poems and stories, and even novels.

The Wishing Tree (written in 1927) is a title emblematic of the early Faulkner's view of nature. A somewhat unconvincing fairy tale hesitating between child language and Southern vernacular, it sets as the object of a quest a tree that is significantly underrealized. The leaves of the mellomax tree are originally white, that is, blank forms which take up the colors of man's desires. As Maurice, the guiding consciousness in the story, tells an old man who is past desire: the leaves are "the color of everybody's wishes."[16] Not a literary tree this one, but a revealing mirror, or more precisely the outward projection of man's consciousness and dreams.

In *Absalom, Absalom!*, the wistaria smell may be perceived as a metaphor for feminine desire, the very aura of Rosa Coldfield (though the first paragraph of the novel does not mention the smell of wistaria). Also, permeating as it does the twilight dedicated to "rememory" (to take up Toni Morrison's language in *Beloved*), at once on Mr. Compson's gallery and in Quentin's sitting room at Harvard, it seems to be the atmospheric projection of the tense, guilt-laden quest for a white young man's identity in the South,[17] similar to the way the overpowering honeysuckle smell in *The Sound and the Fury* represents Quentin's repressed sexuality and guilt.

In the late 1930s onward, say in the "Old Man" sections of *If I Forget Thee, Jerusalem*, and then in *Go Down, Moses*, there appears in Faulkner a more mature, or preferably a more elaborate, thinking on nature, divested certainly not of its mythical connotations, but of its literary derivations and self-conscious poses—something which can legitimately be called an ecological consciousness. Hence the selection of the two novels examined here.

Faulkner's Ecological Concerns

Within this deliberately limited canon, and in the light of the American ideological context, notably the Arcadian, Thoreauvian thinking to which Faulkner is clearly heir, whether he finally accepts or rejects the heritage, can he be considered green, in line with ecological concerns? The answer remains two-sided: apparently yes, profoundly no.

The word ecology has often been extended, or degraded, into a nostalgic dirge for the dwindling of resources, a loss of the wilderness and of the Edenic promise originally inherent in the land. This is recurrent in American thinking and literature, as for instance in Crevecoeur and James Fenimore Cooper, in the revisiting of the frontier made into a powerful national myth by Frederick Jackson Turner, in the counterculture movement of the 1960s and its brief, illusory upholding of (ab)original values.

Some passages in Faulkner's later novels and in some of his essays lead one into categorizing him with those who lament contemporary urban civilization. Everyone has in mind those lashing outs at "the resonant boom and ululance of radio" (RN 637), at the jukeboxes and the bellowing amplifiers on the crowded Square, so outrageous that nobody could "be threatened with one second of silence" (ID 463), at "the automobile . . . become our national sex symbol" (ID 463–64), at the new developments replacing the old aristocratic columned mansions, where the identically built houses set on their tiny lawns are so close to one another that you can hear the next door neighbor's toilet being flushed. The new people, not even intruders in the dust of the past, are no part of a continuity or a constancy, but are the ephemeral expressions of progress:

> only the old citizens knew the jail any more, not old people but old citizens: men and women old not in years but in the *constancy* of the town, or against that *constancy*, concordant (not coeval of course, the town's date was a century and a quarter ago now, but in accord against that *continuation*) with that thin durable *continuity* born a hundred and twenty-five years ago . . .—that steadfast and durable and unhurryable *continuity* against or across which the vain and glittering ephemerae of progress and alteration washed in substanceless repetitive evanescent *scarless* waves, like the wash and glare of the neon sign on what was still known as the Holston House diagonally opposite, which would fade with each dawn from the old brick walls of the jail and leave *no trace*. (RN 641; my emphasis)

The outraged recoil from the more strident signs of progress is not the important point here, but the opposition between progress and continuity or, better, constancy, that is, between change, alteration, and conversely the signs of motionlessness, near stasis, or immutability, the word used in the first prologue of *Requiem for a Nun*. This is also the meaning of endurance in Faulkner's fiction. The two words—"They endured"—defining Dilsey in the "Appendix: Compson" evidently refer not just to the blacks surviving slavery and postslavery times, but to their reassuring permanence as fixed "landmarks" (the word applied to Dilsey in the opening of the fourth section of *The Sound and the Fury*) in a changing economic and social landscape. The vision of the motionless black man sitting on his mule, seen at a train stop by Quentin going back South, represents the same desire for permanence in the young man, a failed heir, socially and ideologically insecure.[18]

The paradox in this evocation of the jail is that progress leaves no trace, no mark, not even a scratch on a windowpane: it has no relevance, it is of no moment. The whole movement of the third prologue is one of ever-accelerating Progress taking the American earth, and not just the South, to its doom, presided over by the jail immutable through its avatars, "while the time, the land, the nation, the American earth, whirled faster and faster toward the plunging precipice of its destiny" (RN 625). Against that apocalyptic background, Cecilia Farmer represents a permanence different from that of the black man in *The Sound and the Fury*, which is that of the land itself: her "stasis" is of another order, that of the spirit, "that invincible captaincy of soul which didn't even need to wait but simply to be" (647); her permanence is not of this world, it is that of the word, the indelible scratch of her signature offered to the eyes of the passing stranger and of the future generations of readers. Her signature is another expression of that arrested motion which Faulkner recognized on the flank of Keats's urn, as he explained to Jean Stein in a formulation known almost by heart by every Faulknerian: "The aim of every artist is to arrest motion, which is life, by artificial means and hold it fixed so that 100 years later when a stranger looks at it, it moves again since it is life" (LG 253)—the exact description of Cecilia Farmer's signature. What endures at the end of the third prologue is "a fragile and workless scratching almost depthless in a sheet of old barely transparent glass" (648). The undistanced instantaneous voice of Cecilia Farmer, arising from her signature, denies the whole course of time, that is, civilization, progress, in the only way man can avail himself of: by the poet's voice, atemporal, Godlike.

Faulkner's Wilderness

The tension between constancy and progress, motionlessness and change, eternity and the flow of time, which can be traced back to the Arcadian tradition and the Thoreauvian heritage, culminates with Faulkner and even abrogates itself in the concept of wilderness. The word designates the wild space as opposed to the cleared, tamed land, but since John Wycliffe (1320–84) it is also the translation for the biblical terms representing the desert as a place of wandering, trials (hence the words barren, desolate, waste, often connected with wilderness in the eighteenth century), and also of spiritual quest (as it is shown by Christ himself in the desert, or by St Anthony), or it represents a sanctuary, or at least a refuge, for the displaced Hebrews. With the Puritans, the wilderness comes to represent the dark, unknowable, pagan space beyond the garden wall (the garden versus the wilderness is an American mythical axis that has no real equivalent in the European imagination); it becomes the locus of Satan, where his unspeakable evil rites are enacted—not God's temple, but Satan's home[19] (a remarkable border in the Puritan imagination, sending not so distant echoes in today's political philosophy). It is the expression of the Other, irreducibly nonhuman, outside man's reach and God's realm. So it is not to be humanized at all, not to be made usable: it is a place or interdict necessary to a given subject's self-definition, it must remain completely alien. Deprived of the pathetic fallacy inherent in the point of view, this is finally Ike McCaslin's position in the face of wilderness, though, being the central consciousness in "The Bear," he cannot, will not, acknowledge it.

Yet as soon as it was conquered and tamed (and its inhabitants, the Indians, christianized, or eradicated), that is, when it had been divested of its original mystery, the wilderness nostalgically became paradise lost itself, a place of original purity and mystery, forever haunting the American imagination and fiction, as in Cooper, Thoreau, and William Faulkner.[20] It stands for freedom, goodness, and is the reverse of constraint, artifice, wickedness, of what Huck Finn calls "sivilization"; it is a place of redemption and renewal, of rejuvenation, the foundation of Americanness, in Crevecoeur and Turner. But it also entails a backward-looking glance, a flight from history and modernity into primitivism (a tendency also perceptible in Turner's myth-making historiography). The wilderness no longer is to be reclaimed, as with the Puritans, but it must be resurrected, in the name of the American dream.

Possibly for such reasons, the American wilderness this side of the Mississippi River, and then the wild West, becomes a *sublime* space, that is, of an order different from that of the garden, beyond the *threshold* (the meaning of the Latin *limen*: note here that Faulkner constantly uses the wall image in the presence of the wilderness) of man's apprehension and appreciation, where he can almost see the face of God, as Moses saw the burning bush in the desert, and as Ike McCaslin saw the buck and the bear. This sublimity is also evident in the paintings of Thomas Cole, of Thomas Moran discovering the Yellowstone River, of Albert Bierstadt in Yosemite. These changes in the meaning of the concept of wilderness tend to show that, in the last analysis, it does not represent a space *per se*, an identifiable object, but the object of a quest, the reflection of man's longings and frustrations: paradoxically, it is profoundly *unnatural*.[21]

This overview of the concept of wilderness will now help redefine Faulkner's personal version of it. In *Go Down, Moses*, it becomes an unchristian metaphor of divinity, a myth divested of religious meaning but not of the sense of the sacred—a secularized version of the Old Testament God, as can be seen first in retracing the steps of the young Ike McCaslin in his ritual of initiation with Sam Fathers.

Like the Old Testament God, the wilderness is approached with awe. When Ike is about to kill his first buck, he feels the presence of the wilderness, "tremendous, attentive, impartial and omniscient" (GDM 135). The four qualifiers fit the biblical evocations of God: the word *tremendous* (i.e., inducing tremor, trembling, awe-inspiring) recurs constantly in "The Old People" and also in "Delta Autumn," in connection with the wilderness. *Omniscience* is the very attribute of God, it is also that of the wilderness, and that of its death-defying representative, Old Ben, whose knowledge or perception of Ike antedates the boy's awareness of the bear, as he realizes, saying to Sam: "You mean he already knows me, that I aint never been to the Big Bottom before. . . . It was me he was watching" (148); " 'I didn't see him,' he said. 'I didn't, Sam.'/'I know it,' Sam said. 'He done the looking' " (149). *Attention* suggests some close and personal watch over the unwitting hunters or travelers: "The wagon wound and jolted between the slow and shifting yet constant walls from beyond and above which the wilderness watched them pass" (132). And *impartial* is a qualifier Faulkner recurrently applies to images of the divinity or of destiny, often connected here with the metaphor of the Umpire. The buck itself, close by and invisible, is "perhaps conscious also of the eye of the ancient immortal Umpire" (135). The wall image, recurrent in "The Old People," reinforces this attribute of the wilderness, the indifference and impenetrability required in impartiality. So the feeling of being watched is no more than pathetic fallacy; the wilderness does not watch Ike any more than the travelers in the wagon or any one of the hunters: it ignores them. This image of an all-knowing and indifferent God brings to mind the representation of God the Pantocrator in Byzantine churches, in which the brightly colored tiles of the mosaic cover the complete rounded surface of the chancel—a God whose tremendous all-seeing eyes the awe-struck believer can never escape.

The "aboriginal" Sam Fathers, the last of those "Old People," seems not only to antedate time but to abrogate it in his narratives of old times and "vanished men": "gradually to the boy those old times would cease to be old times and would become a part of the boy's present, not only as if they had happened yesterday but as if they were still happening" (127). Sam partakes of the timelessness of the wilderness, conjuring up with his words the everpresentness of the past, a manner of eternity. The two animals whose appearance he mediates for the young Ike are the stag, out of reach and of view of the hunters except in rare moments of epiphany, saluted by Sam as "Chief, Grandfather" (137), and Old Ben, perceived as the immortal spirit of the wilderness itself. That is why Sam will not survive him: he dies, an ageless old man, soon after the spiritual death of the wilderness with that of Old Ben. Whether he dies naturally because he serves no further purpose, or commits suicide, or is killed by Boon, does not change the fact that he has become irrelevant.

The wilderness opens itself to Ike in brief moments of epiphany in which the divinity is present and all-seeing even before the viewer can see anything: he suddenly becomes aware of some presence. When the buck actually comes into sight, the mode of apparition and the light images clearly suggest a radiant epiphany: Ike "began to shake, not with any cold. Then the buck was there. He did not come into sight; he was just there, looking not like a ghost but as if all of light were condensed in him and he were the source of it, not only moving in it but disseminating it, already running, seen first as you always see the deer, in that split second after he has already seen you" (121). The appearance of the bear, present before the boy's awareness of it, reiterates the experience: "It did not emerge, appear: it was just there, immobile, fixed in the green and windless noon's hot dappling . . . dimensionless against the dappled obscurity, looking at him" (153). The killing of the buck is another moment of epiphany, a brief illumination which Faulkner calls "the moment of the buck": in the boy's mind, "the buck still and forever leaped . . . forever immortal" (132). This is an illusory poetic vision, the impossible inscription of motion and speed in the immortality of vision. For the price is the death of the animal. Only art can resolve the paradox, as Charlotte Rittenmeyer knew well when she was trying to paint not the deer by the lakeside, but Motion itself. We are once more back to Keats.

Coming out of the wilderness is a fall from stasis and timelessness, or a fall back into time—entering a world of division and fences, of "skeleton cotton- and corn-fields" (131), an experience of discontinuity and separateness, of encroaching progress. But this is precisely the world in which Ike must live, yet which he must repudiate, not only because he will not live by what his initiation into the wilderness has taught him, not only because he cannot retain the rare moments of epiphany, a metaphor for the artist's dream, but more profoundly because of a radical impossibility: the wilderness had just seemed to accept him in those fleeting moments during which the sense of belonging, of acceptance into its eternity, was an illusion. He was seen by an all-knowing but indifferent power, he was a *guest* (127), so he believed at least, never an inmate: he was ignored. He could become part of that time- lessness only in death, as Sam Fathers going back home, or as the buck or Old Ben. Choosing to survive the brief encounter with eternity is an impos- sibility he thinks he can overcome by repudiating a heritage synonymous with wrong and shame, which he discovers in the plantation ledgers.[22]

Ike is not just facing a Southern heritage of incest and miscegenation. He cannot face his own relationship with a father whose own sexuality is probably unacceptable (there are clear hints of homosexuality in him), and possibly, too, his own sexual insecurity (he will live like a hermit, sans women, in a homosocial environment), if only because in his Southerner's mind sexuality will always signify the reiteration of the original sin of the South and of that of his ancestors: miscegenation and incest. His predica- ment is more complex (and probably more painful) than that of Quentin Compson in *The Sound and the Fury*. The idealist Quentin commits actual suicide. The possibly less courageous or less intransigent Ike will do with spiritual suicide. But the Quentin of *Absalom, Absalom!* (not to be confused with Quentin of *The Sound and the Fury*) had not committed suicide because he had learned in his long journey into night that repudi- ating his heritage—the South—would be repudiating his own self.

Unlike Quentin Compson, Ike never comes to say that he does not hate the South, or unlike the narrator of "Mississippi," he cannot bring himself to love not because, but despite the wrong and the shame, "not for the virtues, but despite the fault."[23] In "Delta Autumn," Ike flees in revulsion from the young woman who carries an infant whose mixed blood literally is the black part of himself, which he refuses to acknowledge: "Get out of here! I can do nothing for you! Cant nobody do nothing for you!" (267). He does not understand that you do not buy off your wrong with a sheaf of banknotes, nor that the horn left him by General Compson, "covered with the unbroken skin from a buck's shank and bound with silver" (268), has become a meaningless memento: the buck is dead, so is the wilderness he had refused to inherit, and which is now destroyed by the encroachments of progress.

More profoundly, the wilderness *cannot* be inherited, because it is, in essence, no part of the human time. It cannot belong to anyone to bequeath, because the original appropriation had abrogated its very meaning: "on the instant when Ikkemotube discovered, realized, that he could sell it for money, on that instant it ceased ever to have been his forever, father to father to father, and the man who bought it bought nothing" (189). The earth should have remained "mutual and intact in the communal anonymity of brotherhood" (190). Lacking that, man's relationship with nature is impossible, as mutual brotherhood—the definition of an ideal impossible ecology—has been abrogated from the start, in principle. The original wrong had been not only racial, a sin against man, but natural, a sin against the land, of which the old people themselves had been guilty. The appropriation, or rather enslaving, of man, had been compounded by that of the land: the wrong cannot be undone, the double burden of the South cannot be overthrown.

As for Sam Fathers, he cannot bridge the symbolic gap between the Old People and Ike, he represents no real alternative. It is true that he appears to belong to a different species, because he has "chief's blood." But despite his innate pride, despite the respect he inspires, his blood has been fatally tainted, as his name tells: Had-Two-Fathers (123). His kingly father, *Du Homme*, who had come to power by murder, then becomes *Doom*, which makes his son his own battleground: he "was betrayed through the black blood which his mother gave him. Not betrayed by the black blood and not willfully betrayed by his mother, but betrayed by her all the same, who had bequeathed him not only the blood of slaves but even a little of the very blood which had enslaved it; himself his own battleground, the scene of his own vanquishment and the mausoleum of his defeat" (124–5). That is why, significantly, he will remain barren, just like Ike, his pupil, another failed, doomed, heir.

Such is Ike's aporetic predicament. Late in life, he can retrospectively say to the buck: "*I slew you; my bearing must not shame your quitting life.*

My conduct forever onward must become your death" (259). But his commitment to the immortal ideal of the wilderness makes no sense because
he is the killer, and will go on being a killer: of his never-to-be-born son
and, spiritually, of the mixed blood infant who is, not just metaphorically,
but genetically, a part of himself. In self-delusion, he believed "he could
repudiate the wrong and the shame, at least in principle." His rigid and
self-blinding morality of principles keeps him incapable of acting like a man
or a father and makes him unworthy not only of the wilderness, but of leaving to a dreamed-of son a heritage originally illegitimate anyway. He
thought "he would at least save and free his son"; but in "saving and freeing
his son, [he] lost him" (259). Just as he had lost the radiant immortal buck.

So his ritual initiation into the wilderness, even in brief glimpses of
epiphany, has brought Ike no revelation and left him with no heritage to
bequeath, because he did not have the courage to confront his heritage
and his own self in the mirror of the wilderness, and then to endure the
inescapable wrong and shame of his predicament. Yet he had tried to go
beyond the threshold, to enter the sacred realm, abandoning all the attrib-
utes of civilization. He then goes further than Huck Finn, who just toys
with the idea of lighting out for the Territory. But he finally lacks courage,
refuses to live up to the ideal of his initiation and dedication, which had
been the ecological ideal of relating, in the communal anonymity of brotherhood. Even such ideal had been ambiguous: who was he relating to in
the solitude of the Big Woods? As the young woman abandoned with her
child by his cousin Roth Edmonds tells him at the end of "Delta Autumn:"
"Old man . . . have you lived so long and forgotten so much that you dont
remember anything you ever knew or felt or even heard about love?"
(268). He will indeed remain barren, like his surrogate father.

In the last analysis, the wilderness must remain unknowable, tremendous and indifferent, like God, unapproachable, like a dream, and man
must remain alone, cut off from his dream, as in *The Great Gatsby* the
Dutch sailors cannot realize the vision of beauty they have from the ship
and can retain only if they remain this side of the impassable waters, this
side of realization. This is their splendid failure. The Arcadian dream of a
blessed interrelatedness between man and nature must remain just the
impossible dream of man's desire to inhabit an eternity which his tempo-
ral condition, his heritage, precludes. Such is the aporia of man's condition, as exemplified by Ike McCaslin.

A Splendid Territory of Impossibilities

The tension between the two traditions in the man-nature relationship,
defined as humanist and Arcadian, remains unresolved in Faulkner, even

though the Arcadian/Thoreauvian strain appears to be the stronger, in *Go Down, Moses* and in the prologues of *Requiem for a Nun*. Faulkner laments the encroachments of civilization as being not manifestations of progress, but of regression and loss. More profoundly, man's original sin against his brother and against the land of brotherhood, that is, the wilderness, keeps him forever cut off from that territory: from the origin, he has excluded himself from the garden of eternal youth, hardly glimpsed by the boy Ike before his own falling from grace.

So Faulkner's reflection on progress, nature, and wilderness in *Go Down, Moses* and *Requiem for a Nun* leaves him in a territory of impossibilities: this is his *locus solus*, the cosmos of his own, where he must fail splendidly. The impossible, aporetic man-nature relationship forces him to inhabit the only domain where he will not fear to tread, that of art, where he will forever try to "do the impossible" and match the work to the dream, just this side of the "pinnacle of cut perfection," beyond which there is nothing but death (LG 238). Only in art can he ever hope to conjoin the motion of life and the stasis of eternity, as on the flanks of Keats's urn. Only in the writing of *The Sound and the Fury* did Faulkner ever experience "that emotion definite and physical and yet nebulous to describe," of which Ike had only a glimpse in the wilderness. "That eager and joyous faith and anticipation of surprise" can be encountered not in the wilderness, but only "on the yet unmarred sheet beneath [his] hand, held inviolate and unfailing."[24] Inviolate and unfailing: such should have remained the wilderness. But then it precludes man's presence.

Even though Faulkner can be placed within a recognizable Arcadian tradition, he will remain aside. He is not the subversive spirit Thoreau was. He is probably more attuned to the reflection of Fitzgerald on the American dream seen as an ontological impossibility. Neither can he be called an ecologist in his vision of the wilderness. Does the acknowledged aporia make him a pessimist? Again, no. In the face of tensions and contradictions and impossibilities, he will continue to believe in man, not in the possibility of his moral progress, as did Thoreau, but in his capacity to endure.[25] Such is man's pride and his humility. The path Ike McCaslin would not follow to the end. Could not follow. Ike could not fail splendidly. This is the poet's privilege.

NOTES

1. Quoted in Donald Worster, *Nature's Economy. A History of Ecological Ideas*, 2nd ed. (1977; Cambridge: Cambridge University Press, 1998), 192. I am indebted to this classic history of ecology. Further page references to it will be given in parentheses.

2. Faulkner's view is not morally neutral, although he never poses as a moralist in his fiction, never takes a Christian stance, not even in the dramatic parts of *Requiem for a Nun*, all the Christian, post Nobel-speech readings notwithstanding.

3. One of the most admired works of Linnaeus was his essay "The Oeconomy of Nature," written in 1749 as an academic thesis, then translated into Latin.

4. From the Greek *a-poros*, no passage, no path; thus an aporia is a philosophical dead end, it designates a philosophical problem arising from an awareness of incompatible views on a given theoretical matter.

5. One must add Darwin into the ideological picture of the second half of the nineteenth century: the theory of evolution and of the survival of the fittest and, later in the century, the social interpretation of Darwinism are anything but democratic.

6. Turner's seminal essay on the reinterpretation of American history was an address delivered on the occasion of the Columbian Exhibition in Chicago, in 1893.

7. Thoreau had a copy of Gilbert White's book, and he referred to him repeatedly in his journal.

8. Journal XIV, in *The Works of Henry David Thoreau*, Walden edition (Boston, 1906), 268 (quoted in Worster 74).

9. Journal, VIII, 330.

10. The sonorous ending of the first prologue is obviously reminiscent of that of the Nobel speech.

11. The occurrence of the adjective "splendid" to qualify the founders' dream sounds like an anticipated ironic echo of Faulkner's description of the artist's impossible inscription of his dream of perfection as a "splendid failure," in the interview he gave to Jean Stein in 1956 (*Lion in the Garden: Interviews with William Faulkner, 1926–1962* [New York, Random House, 1968], 238). Further references to this interview will be given in parentheses after the quotations, with the abbreviation LG).

12. *Novels 1942–1954*, ed. Joseph Blotner and Noel Polk (New York: Library of America, 1994), 486–87. All further references to *Requiem for a Nun*, as well as to *Go Down, Moses* and *Intruder in the Dust*, will be to this volume (with the abbreviations RN, GDM, ID).

13. The original title of what became the first prologue, now its subtitle, is "A Name for the City."

14. See also this "description" of cotton blooms, "petty globules of Motion weightless and myriad even in the hand of a child" (RN 625).

15. Noel Polk has elaborately explained the context and significance of the 1920 handwritten play in his introduction to *The Marionettes* (Charlottesville: University Press of Virginia, 1977).

16. *The Wishing Tree*, illustrated by Don Bolognese (New York: Random House, 1964), 29. The single original copy was typed and bound by Faulkner in 1927.

17. See the opening of chapter 2.

18. The hymn to the mule in *The Hamlet* and in *Requiem for a Nun* (637–38) partakes of the same longing for permanence.

19. See Hawthorne's *The Scarlet Letter* and "Young Goodman Brown."

20. For a further exploration of the concept of wilderness, see the excellent essay of William Cronon, "The Trouble with Wilderness; or, Getting Back to the Wrong Nature," in *Uncommon Ground. Rethinking the Human Place in Nature*, William Cronon, ed. (New York: W. W. Norton & Company, 1996), 69–90.

21. The wilderness image haunts the American imagination more so than that of an older Europe centered around the heritage of Athens and Rome, where generally no untamed wild land was left to be claimed in the name of civilization, or of God (this remark does not consider Northern Europe, or in a broader way what lay beyond the *limes* of the Roman empire). In his essays on Italy, D. H. Lawrence elaborates on the specificity of the Italian landscape, saying that in Tuscany nature is humanized through and through and yet remains unviolated: "the intensive culture of vine and olive and wheat . . . the ceaseless industry of naked human hands [do] not devastate a country, [do] not drive away either Pan or his children./. . . the peculiar Italian beauty . . . is so exquisitely natural, because man, feeling his way sensitively to the fruitfulness of the earth, has moulded the earth to his necessity without violating it" ("Flowery Tuscany," in *Selected Essays* [New York: Penguin Books, 1950], 139). It is significant that the word wilderness, so prominent in American literature, has no proper equivalent in, say, the French language.

22. See the provocative essay by Richard Godden and Noel Polk, "Reading the Ledgers," *Mississippi Quarterly*, 55 (Summer 2002): 301–59.

23. *Essays, Speeches, and Public Letters by William Faulkner*, ed. James B. Meriwether (New York: Random House, 1966), 43.

24. "An Introduction for *The Sound and the Fury*," ed. James B. Meriwether, *Southern Review* (October 1972): 705–10.

25. "I believe that man will not merely endure: he will prevail," Faulkner proclaimed in Stockholm (ESPL 120). But it is never clear what difference he finally makes between enduring and prevailing. In the culmination of the long dialogue between the Corporal and the Old General in *A Fable*, the dialogue stops short precisely at this point: " 'Because man and his folly—'/'Will endure,' the Corporal said./'They will do more,' the Old General said proudly. 'They will prevail—Shall we return?' "

The Ecology of Uncle Ike:
Teaching *Go Down, Moses* with Janisse Ray's *Ecology of a Cracker Childhood*

THOMAS L. MCHANEY

It is easy to judge Isaac McCaslin in *Go Down, Moses* harshly for his insensitivity to ongoing human affairs. As with so many of Faulkner's characters, Ike's development of empathy snags on the barbs of the past. He rejects not just a material inheritance but the ability to share with other humans the common joys and sorrows of day-to-day existence. Faulkner critics who had studied all of Faulkner's fiction and also dealt with Faulkner's entire novel, not just "The Bear," essentially settled this point long ago. In 1959, Olga Vickery observed that rituals of initiation or transformation are pervasive in *Go Down, Moses*, but that rituals "have no value in themselves"; and thus when "outside the wilderness, Isaac is virtuous but ineffective."[1] Between the ages of twenty-one and seventy, she points out, "nothing happens to him" (133). Then near the end of his life, he condones by repetition the arrogant inhumanity of his grandfather. For Cleanth Brooks, in his 1963 book on the Yoknapatawpha novels, "the fact that [Ike's] power and influence are limited is perhaps directly related to the renunciation that he had made many years before. In divesting himself of his legacy—for the best of motives, let us say—he has thereby reduced his power to act."[2] "One can, if he likes, make a sharper indictment," writes Brooks, and he too cites the scene where James Beauchamp's granddaughter asks Ike if he knows anything about love. Here "Isaac is a failure" (273–74). In *The Achievement of William Faulkner* (1966), Michael Millgate observes "there is a sense in which it is true of Ike that what he *says* is right, but what he *does* is wrong," and Ike achieves only "the quasi-freedom of withdrawal and escape."[3]

The politeness of these condemnations, however, is subtly conciliatory regarding the Ike of the woods; and the assurances that in the woods Ike is still a hero, that he achieves wise innocence or redemption or is reborn, continued to appear in critical essays on "The Bear," and even on *Go Down, Moses*, for decades. There may, in fact, never have been an absolute movement away from the hagiography of Isaac McCaslin engaged in by such as R. W. B. Lewis, who in *The American Adam* (1955) regards Ike (using

"The Bear" only, and referring to it as a novella) as undertaking "a lifelong errand of private atonement for everything that had betrayed" the "lost hope" of the New World; or Lewis Simpson, who in 1966 still saw "The Bear" as depicting the hope of the wilderness life dashed by technology, not Ike's moral failure, a second "Fall."[4] But if Vickery, Brooks, and Millgate felt compelled to write that Ike is "virtuous but ineffective," limited in power and influence only "perhaps" because he fails to claim his inheritance ("for the best of motives, let us say"), saying the right thing but not acting in the spirit of his words, less uncommon readers were ready to express a still stronger sympathy for Ike the woodsman that he may not deserve. Despite Ike's passivity as a conservationist and his failure to mentor a successor who might preserve the unspoiled big woods, for many student readers of *Go Down, Moses* Ike remains a tragically noble woodsman and hunter.

In the context of the current ecological crisis, Ike may look even better. As a hunter who has refused to kill the ancient bear Old Ben and who vocally laments the destruction of the woods, Ike also now appears ecologically minded, and his repudiation of his inheritance, the McCaslin plantation, seems to students to make as much sense as Thoreau's anti-materialist anecdote in *Walden* pitying the unfortunate young men "whose misfortune it is to have inherited farms, houses, barns, cattle, and farming tools. . . . It is a fool's life."[5] Given Ike's apparent motives for separation, his rejection of a tainted material legacy often provokes in students no negative second thoughts about the way Ike responds to his spiritual training as a hunter or his potential as a savior, rather than a passive worshipper, of the wilderness.

Attempting to enlarge and deepen classroom debate about the consequences of Ike McCaslin's wilderness behavior among students to whom I assign *Go Down, Moses*, I have experimented with other texts to be read against the book. Toni Morrison's *Beloved*, Zora Neale Hurston's *Their Eyes Were Watching God*, and Ellen Douglas's *Can't Quit You, Baby* have proved useful. These texts speak back to *Go Down, Moses* on women's lives, on the ideological heritage of the South's racial codes, and on the ambiguities of love and hate that can flourish in places where horrors have occurred but where even victims' lives are rooted. Such texts work especially well against the inscription of female anonymity and displacement in *Go Down, Moses* that nonetheless fails to erase persistent female interventions in male folly and disaster and examples of female rebellion against patriarchal arrogance. But finding a text that throws Ike's wilderness experience into similar relief was something I did not think of until the appearance of Janisse Ray's *The Ecology of a Cracker Childhood* (1999). Ray's memoir, as it happens, dramatizes an initiation into the "wilderness"

that offers a relevant standard about the conduct of everyday life, an ecologically oriented drama that helps show readers of *Go Down, Moses*
exactly how, in T. S. Eliot's words, Ike McCaslin has "had the experience
but missed the meaning."[6]

Though contemporary and a memoir from a woman's point of view,
Janisse Ray's *The Ecology of a Cracker Childhood* closely parallels in
many ways Ike's process of reinterpreting a family and a native landscape
as one matures within the interrelated stories that help characterize both.
Ray's choices, however, are different from Ike's, and they illustrate dimensions of ecological understanding that Ike fails to achieve, not merely
because Ray's text encapsulates a polemical meditation upon a once vast,
but now vanished, Southern woodlands ecosystem. It is her candid
account of family history that illuminates Ike's choices and his decisions,
her action that confirms Ike's failure to act.

Like *Go Down, Moses, The Ecology of a Cracker Childhood* speaks of
generations rooted in a landscape that has shaped them. "I was born from
people who were born from people who were born from people who were
born here," Ray writes, and her people, like the settlers of Ike's Mississippi,
were exploiters who "settled the vast, fire-loving uplands of the costal
plains of southeast Georgia, surrounded by a singing forest of tall and
widely spaced pines whose history they did not know, whose stories were
untold. The memory of what they entered is scrawled on my bones, so
that I carry the landscape inside like an ache. The story of who I am cannot be severed from the story of the flatwoods."[7]

Like Ike's, Ray's family story is marked by difficult marriages, assertive
men going their own ways, and women who love faithfully and learn to
cope with or without the presence of their sometimes volatile mates, and
there is rapacity and shame. In Ray's case the shameful flaw in the trans-
mission of family traits is not only willfulness but also mental illness, and
the form that rapacity takes is not the play of sexuality across social barri-
ers assigned by racial codes but being a party, however small, to the almost
complete destruction of a complex aboriginal natural environment.

Ike McCaslin himself cannot say exactly that he was "born from people
who were born from people who were born from people who were born
here," since he represents only the third generation of a male line of a
family that pioneered in north Mississippi. The first generation, represented by his grandfather Lucius Quintus Carothers McCaslin, came with
slaves to accomplish a plantation. But his white cousins, the Edmonds,
who are descended from the female side begun by his grandfather's
daughter, have attained seven generations within Ike's lifetime on this
same land, and his black cousins the Beauchamps, who began their time
in Mississippi as slaves and whose family name is assigned, have attained

seven generations as well, at least three of them touched by interracial sexual exploitation and arrogant denial and reassignment of paternity.

Like the heritage that comes down to Ray through a landscape "inscribed on her bones," but also derived from family stories, Ike McCaslin's existence cannot be severed from how his inherited native landscape intertwines with stories of the McCaslin, Edmonds, and Beauchamp families that he has heard and that are so tied up with the land that they have become, often in distorted form, communal property. *Go Down, Moses* takes place primarily on a small isolated farm bordering the river jungles where Ike's people go annually to hunt. It is a place where, in the time of Faulkner's writing, as the WPA *Mississippi Guide* of 1938 recorded, "earth-rooted people . . . collectively face[d] an industrial revolution with hoes grasped tightly in their clay-stained hands."[8] Ray's book begins in South Georgia where "everything is flat and wide. Not empty. My people live among the mobile homes, junked cars, pine plantations, clearcuts, and fields. They live among the lost forests" (3).

Ike is rooted in land that in just one generation the McCaslin family transformed from wilderness to plantation, but like Ray his existence is also rooted spiritually in the diminishing primal forest his forebears entered and began to deplete, an old woods now increasingly under assault by mechanized deforestation. But Ike spends most of his year on the McCaslin farm, where, in the absence of deceased parents or even a senior white female, his cousin mentors him. Only sixteen years his senior, McCaslin "Cass" Edmonds is the preserver and transmitter of all the dimensions of Ike's heritage, telling him family stories, arranging for Ike's initiation into the mysteries of the big woods, serving as regent for the farm which Ike is being prepared to inherit.

Though there is also a farm in Janisse Ray's family, she grows up literally in a junkyard, a sump of leaking automobiles, refrigerators, farm tractors, and outmoded agricultural equipment within whose borders she and her family have their home. Ray takes much longer than Ike to receive an initiation into the woodland ecology whose ruin she comes to lament and oppose. Her father's strictness and the oddness of their habitat keep other children away, and Janisse is, in many ways, as barred from normal human contacts as a princess sequestered in a dark tower.

Faulkner's work is, of course, a fiction about made-up characters, and Ike's tragic failures ultimately result from his role as a character in a novel. Ray's work is the memoir of a writer's growing up, coming of age, and becoming ecologically minded. But like Faulkner's novel, Ray's memoir is thoroughly constructed and achieves its effects by selection of incident, order of revelation, characterization, dramatic design, and the application of something akin to the "mythical method" of Eliot and Joyce.

Ray's project began as a plan to gather a series of meditations upon the great swath of longleaf pine forests that, before timbering began, covered millions of acres of the lower South, from the Carolinas into Texas, a stand now reduced from as much as 150 million acres to roughly 10,000 acres of virgin woodlands representing the original ecosystem. Ray's object is to inspire a recuperation of that lost ecology and to point out to the unaware that managed tree farms of quick-growth pine, which now fill much of the land from which the old forest was stripped, are neither a forest nor a vital and complex ecology. But as she wrote about the longleaf pine she suspected, she explains at readings of her book, that few people were likely to buy essays about a lost forest. She would need a human interest, and so she conceived the idea of counterpointing what she had to say about the lost woodlands with a candid family story. Writing as openly and unflinchingly about her family as she writes passionately about the fate of the longleaf pine, she, like Faulkner, fashioned a story that reads like a myth, though the two books turn out very differently, and enlarges the reader's perception of what is an ecology.

Go Down, Moses, of course, announces the mythic with its title—the expectation of a hero-figure who will lead a people out of bondage. The words of the old spiritual, coded by slaves to speak of a longed-for deliverance from bondage in the American South, remind us at the same time of biblical stories of stern patriarchs on both sides of the ledger, pharaoh and slave. As does the Bible, *Go Down, Moses* contains several births of the sort that the psychoanalyst Otto Rank describes in "The Myth of the Birth of the Hero," births marked by a noble heritage, often concealed; continence or prolonged barrenness or secret sexual intercourse, along with cautionary dreams, prophecies, or cosmological portents, as a prelude to conception; abandonment of the child, often to water, and rescue by humble people, such as shepherds; revenge against the real father and then acknowledgement by him; and, finally, the achievement of honor and high position (65). The doubly mixed-race slave Tomey's Turl, for example, is born the year the stars fell, 1833, marked as a portent in the McCaslin family ledgers.[9] He is raised by foster parents, since his mother and grandmother both lose their lives, one as a suicide that is a portent of his true parentage and the other in the act of bearing him. His grandmother and mother are both slaves, both children of Lucius Quintus McCaslin's old age, and Turl's mother, Tomasina, is L. Q. C. McCaslin's daughter.[10] Ike is born after long continence to an unlikely and very old couple, and both his name and rumors of his betrayal by Cass, among other things, identify him with the biblical hero. Roth Edmonds, whose mother also dies in childbirth, is born the year of an epochal flood and raised at least in part by the successful black sharecroppers Mollie and

Lucas Beauchamp. Ike's cousin Cass Edmonds seems to have had two foster fathers himself, the odd couple Theophilus and Amodeus McCaslin,
Ike's father and uncle. And because Ike's father dies when the boy is very
young, Cass becomes "rather his brother than cousin, and rather his father
than either, out of the old time, the old days." Sam Fathers, Ike's spiritual
father, receives his surname from the Chickasaw "Had-Two-Fathers"
because he is sired by a native American king but given to someone of
humbler station to raise because his mother belongs to a subject people.
Heroes are thus predicated many times in *Go Down, Moses*, including in
the name Samuel applied in the final story, "Go Down, Moses," to the
child who has been banished from the farm and executed for the murder
of a "high" authority. Although the only thing named Moses in Faulkner's
novel is a hunting dog that, in an allegory of slave-master relations, lives in
the same room as a caged fox that escapes frequently, provoking great
commotion but nothing else, the schema that predicate a hero are legion.

Janisse Ray's book predicates a hero, too, and in a fashion cognate with
Faulkner's allusions to myths of the hero's birth, biblical and otherwise.
Ray's parents are humble people and do not simply own a junkyard, they
live within its confines, where they tend a flock of sheep who keep the
grass clipped and snakes at bay. They tell Janisse a straight-faced story
about how she comes into their lives on Candlemas, a mid-winter festival
of light that the Celts associated with fertility and the Catholic Church
with the Virgin and the blessing of candles. Ray narrates the story this way:

> On this day, Candlemas, with winter half undone, a tormented wind bore down
> from the north and brought with it a bitter wet cold that cut through my par-
> ents' sweaters and coats and sliced through thin socks. . . . It was dark by six, for
> the days lengthened only by minutes, and my father had gone early to shut up
> the sheep. Nights he penned them in one end of his shop, a wide tin-roofed
> building that smelled both acrid and sweet, a mixture of dry dung, gasoline, hay,
> and grease. That night when he counted them, one of the ewes was missing. He
> had bought the sheep to keep weeds and snakes down in the junkyard, so peo-
> ple could get to parts they needed; now he knew all the animals by name and
> knew also their personalities. Maude was close to her time.
>
> In the hour they had been walking, the temperature had fallen steadily. It
> would soon be dark. Out of the grayness Mama heard a bleating cry.
>
> "Listen," she said, touching Daddy's big arm and stopping so suddenly that
> shoulder-length curls of dark hair swung across her heart-shaped face. Her eyes
> were a deep rich brown, and she cut a fine figure, slim and strong, easy in her
> body. Her husband was over six feet tall, handsome, his forehead wide and
> smart, his hair thick and wiry as horsetail.
>
> Again came the cry. It sounded more human than sheep, coming from a
> clump of palmettos beneath a pine. The sharp-needled fronds of the palmettos
> stood out emerald against the gray of winter, and the pine needles, so richly

brown when first dropped, had faded to dull sienna. Daddy slid his hands—big, rough hands—past the bayonet-tipped palmetto fronds, their fans rattling urgently with his movements, him careful not to rake against saw-blade stems. The weird crying had not stopped. He peered in.

It was a baby. Pine needles cradled a long-limbed newborn child with a duff of dark hair, its face red and puckered. And that was me, his second-born. (5–6)

The man's strength, the mother's heart-shaped loving face and easy body, the garden and snakes, a manger, and the foundling in the piney woods equivalent of bulrushes: certainly if myth and the Bible are any guide, this passage creates the same kinds of expectations as the title "Go Down, Moses" or the name Isaac in Faulkner's book. Eden, Joseph and the Virgin, and even Moses and Oedipus are evoked. Ike's case is in fact different only in circumstantial detail. Specific biblical references in Faulkner's novel include Abraham's attempted sacrifice of Isaac, the fate of Noah's son Ham, God's charge to Moses, and an imitation of Christ, and more. Other Old Testament allusions, sprinkled about like those enumerated in the folkloric version of Janisse Ray's birth, serve as templates behind Ike's story and even provide an unexpected gloss on his biblical name: when God tells Sarah and Abraham that they will finally have a natural child, they laugh not only at their own elderly state but more tellingly at the elderly state of their sexual partner. In a bit of slapstick, Abraham falls on his face twice when God gives him the news, and the second time he also laughs (Genesis 17:3; 17:17), saying in his heart, "Shall a child be born to him that is an hundred years old?" Sarah laughs twice, saying within herself, "After I am waxed old shall I have pleasure, my lord being old also?" (18:12). And in another slapstick exchange, God rebukes her laughter, and she claims "I laughed not," but God replies, "Nay; but thou didst laugh." And so the child is named Isaac, which means "laughter," a word, even including its cognates, that appears in the novel frequently but always as humorless expression. Laughter, however, is never applied to Ike, and never comes from him.[11]

The prelude to Ike's birth portrayed in "Was" resembles the Bible story of Sarah and Abraham in that it too is comedic. The topsy-turvy courtship of Buck and Sophonsiba in "Was" is indeed slapstick, though the poker table negotiations over the two slave lovers and the bartered bride are cruel. When Ike is old enough to perceive that the comedy of "Was" expresses his father's desire to evade marriage to a faded and ridiculous coquette, he will also be old enough to see no comedy likewise in the commissary ledger entries about his father's purchase of one Percival Brownlee, a feckless slave clearly identified as gay, an "anomaly" bought by a man who, with his twin, was said to have wanted only to rid himself of the slaves acquired by their father.[12]

The racial polarities of the landscapes where Ike comes of age express not only the heritage of slave plantations in Mississippi, but also ancient biblical divisions between slave and free. The two kinds of male enterprise that are contrasted in *Go Down, Moses* represent a real and also biblical and mythic dichotomy, too. By this I mean the contrast between a settled agricultural people and those who follow the nomadic life of herders or hunters. Cain and Abel, Jacob and Esau, Isaac and Ishmael again are invoked, and the debate between hunting in the woods or taking care of the farm becomes a pervasive trope for the *Go Down, Moses* cycle, where every story contains some form of hunt. Ike is actually not the only person who leaves the farm for a life in town or elsewhere: Sam Fathers repeats the biblical "let me go" so he can prepare himself to initiate Ike as a spiritual hunter; though he rents a sharecropper cabin on the McCaslin farm, the lumber crew leader Rider in "Pantaloon in Black" becomes an entrepreneur with a cash income and tries to stop the exploitation of his fellow workers; Samuel Worsham Beauchamp, one of Mollie and Lucas's grandchildren, is banished for breaking into the commissary where his family's records are kept alongside those of their McCaslin and Edmonds kinsmen; even Lucas experiments with a metal detector and neglects his crops, dreaming of gold and retirement. But Ike is the only one whose reasons are a preference for a "natural" life in the woods and shame about the materialist, and sexual, arrogance of his predecessors.

Yet Ike's first encounter with the primal forest may predict his failure to assume responsibility for improving the farm and the lives of those people, black and white, who depend upon it or, like Rider, who regard it as a safe haven. On his first hunt as a boy just coming of age, he sees the "wilderness through a slow drizzle of November rain just above the ice point as it seemed to him later he always saw it or at least remembered it—the tall and endless wall of dense November woods under the dissolving afternoon and the year's death, somber, impenetrable . . . the surrey moving through the skeleton stalks of cotton and corn in the last of open country, the last trace of man's puny gnawing at the immemorial flank" (195). The mood of his approach to the big woods is as melancholy as the opening of Poe's "The Fall of the House of Usher." Compare Ray's evocation of the weather and landscape of south Georgia as she comes to appreciate it:

> The creation ends in south Georgia, at the very edge of the sweet Earth. . . . By day the sun, close in a paper sky, laps moisture from the land, then gives it back, always an exchange. Even in drought, when each dawn a parched sun cracks against the horizon's griddle, the air is thick with water.
>
> It is a land of few surprises. It is a land of routine, of cycle, and of constancy. . . . Everything that comes you see coming." (3–4)

Ike, however, has an Old Testament apocalyptic bent even as a child, and later Boon Hogganbeck will accuse him of being parsimonious and pleasureless, still owning the first dollar he ever got. The opening paragraph of *Go Down, Moses,* reflecting Ike's stream of consciousness, concludes by identifying him as "a widower now and uncle to half a county and father to no one," and in "The Old People" the bond sealed between Ike and Sam Fathers at the killing of Ike's first deer provokes a passage in which Ike reflects upon Sam's existence "now drawing toward the end of its alien and irrevocable course, barren, since Sam Fathers had no children" (165). Ike repeatedly focuses on the ends of things—"as if the boy had already divined what his senses and intellect had not encompassed yet: that doomed wilderness . . . through which ran . . . an anachronism . . . out of an old dead time, a phantom" (193). Rationalizing his retreat from responsibility for the farm, he even portrays himself as the end of history: messianic, the last link in God's strange plan for the South. He takes no other action.

As in Ike's tale, in Janisse Ray's there are ironies, mistakes, revelations about the impact of the past upon the present, but instead of seeing herself as a messianic loner, paralyzed by shame, Ray deflates her own myth. "My sister," Ray writes, concluding the family tall tale about her birth, "had been found in a big cabbage in the garden; a year after me, my brother was discovered under the grapevine, and a year after that, my little brother appeared beside a huckleberry bush." As "early as I could question," she writes, "I was told this creation story," but she has a better idea: "If they'd said they'd found me in the trunk of a '52 Ford, it would have been more believable. I was raised on a junkyard on the outskirts of a town called Baxley, the county seat of Appling, in rural south Georgia" (6–7).

What follows this ironic version of an heroic birth, one that accepts the detritus of the junkyard as her point of origin, are fifteen chapters about Ray's life within and getting away from this place, and alternating with these chapters about herself, her parents, and her grandparents are fifteen chapters about the longleaf pine forests and the rich but untidy ecology of interdependent grasses, reptiles, animals, humans, and randomly seeded trees that these vast woodlands once nurtured. The titles of the life chapters give an idea of what they are about and chart a quest: Child of Pine, Shame, Iron Man, Junkyard, Native Genius, Heaven on Earth, How the Heart Opens, Light, Leaving, Promised Land. As in Ike's story, the reader learns about a history of trouble in Ray's family—madness and marital difficulty in previous generations that recur in the life of her stern father and dedicated mother. Because of the strict morality her father enforces, the family experiences social exclusion within their small Georgia community, and one interlude describes their experiences as the only white members of an African American Pentecostal church where the children are baptized after her father is converted by a distant radio evangelist.

Janisse Ray's conversion into an ecologist, however, bears more similarity to Ike McCaslin's initiation as a hunter in the big woods than to her father's religious experience. After a childhood playing with her siblings amid the wrecks of cars and hulks of useless machinery, she finishes high school and goes as far from her south Georgia home as one can go and remain in the same state. At North Georgia College in Dahlonega, a mountain town, she throws off the restraints her father's ways have imposed on her. Her liberated existence creates an increasingly deep separation from her parents, but it gradually brings her into a deeper awareness of her self and an understanding of the place from which she has come.

Her initiation into the woods comes in as strange a way as Ike's does. When Ike enters the woods out of curiosity to see the bear for the first time, his process seems accidental. Failing to find the bear, he first puts aside the gun that represents violence against nature and then the watch and compass that represent modern orientation in space and time. When he enters the timeless wilderness as a guest, not a hunter, immediately he is lost, and all the woods lore that Sam Fathers has taught him is without success. Failing to find even his own trail, he sits down to wait for someone to find him, and the legendary bear Old Ben comes to see *him*. The meaning of this encounter should be plain to Ike. It represents a far deeper initiation than what occurs when he kills his first deer, though that event—a shot he cannot remember—was followed later by a mystical encounter with the animal he believed he had killed. When the bear fades back into the forest, Ike sees the watch and compass on the bush where he left them before he got lost, another sign to Ike of a relationship to the bear and the grace that is to be obtained by hunting the bear. This is a promise of annual renewal that has religious implications, one expressed, for example, in the hymn "Amazing Grace": "I once was lost, but now am found, was blind, but now I see."

In Janisse Ray's story, a similar experience occurs this way: "When I was eighteen and away from my town," she writes, "I dived recklessly and surely into the world, not because it was a form of rebellion, as people might think, but as a form of healing and survival." The campus crowd into which she fell represented "the liquor drinkers and risk takers" (258), a group that sounds not too different from the hunters in the camps where young Ike first listens and learns while whiskey flows, tales are told, and dangerous game is hunted. The dangerous game for Ray is an invitation to go night rappelling down a steep mountainside. Easing sightlessly into the void she finds that the "danger, the excitement, the darkness, the thrill" were what she "had been missing." This descent into the underworld is followed, appropriately for a mythic quest, by an episode of skydiving, potentially even more dangerous. As she writes, "I dived recklessly and surely into the world."

As with the rappelling, to leap out of an airplane Ray has to give up knowledge and control: "I let go, tumbling out and away from the plane . . . flipping slow-motion through the heavens, then I heard a loud snap, and with an enormous rush of air, a billow of cloth flowered from my back . . . the chute checked my descent and I looked up. Triangles of red, blue, and yellow covered me like the wings of a beautiful angel. I was safe. Finally I could fly" (260). As she descends, "floating above the hubbub of the world," she is off target, a quarter mile from the airport, plummeting instead into a forest, but "straight toward a pine . . . that reached out its arms and caught me" (260). Here, still without quite understanding, she comes full circle back to the pines, though her native landscape is still a whole state away.

One semester following these experiences, she takes a botany course and meets "a mountain woman who smoked, toted a gun, and more or less did as she damn well pleased" (260), a feminine alternative to Ike McCaslin's Sam Fathers. In a self-created curriculum of courses that now apply to her life, Ray "slept under the stars and ventured out alone to hunt" rare flora. "It was as if my spirit had suddenly been let free. Nature was the other world. It claimed me" (262). What she realizes is that the mountain woods and the strange place in the old longleaf forest belt where she grew up are one and the same, and all places authentically known are similar: "A junkyard is a wilderness," she writes.

> Both are devotees of decay. The nature of both is random order, the odd occurrence and juxtaposition of miscellany, backed by a semblance of method. Walk through a junkyard and you'll see some of the schemes a wilderness takes—Fords in one section, Dodges in another, or older models farthest from the house—so a brief logic of ecology can be found.
>
> In the same way, an ecosystem makes sense: the canebrakes, the cypress domes. Pine trees regenerate in an indeterminate fashion, randomly here and there where seeds have fallen, but also with some predictability. Sunlight and moisture must be sufficient for germination, as where a fallen tree has made a hole in the canopy, after a rain. This, too, is order. . . .
>
> In junkyard as in wilderness there is danger: shards of glass, leaning jacks, weak chains; or rattlesnakes, avalanches, polar bears. In one as in the other you expect the creativity of the random, how the twisted metal protrudes like limbs, the cars dumped at acute, right, and obtuse angles, how the driveways are creeks and rivers. (268–69)

Ray has begun her education in ecology, and by the end of her narrative, differences with her parents are reconciled because she brings them a new child, her son. The book concludes with a dream that what she wants to do "might take a lifetime, one spent undoing. It might require even my son's lifetime" (268). For Ray this is all right; she does not pretend, like Ike, to be the messiah or the end of history, and when in her book she invokes the word "God"—as in "God doesn't like a clearcut" (123)—her theology is deliberately vague.

Faulkner's Old Testament sources, as it happens, record ample instances of the unpredictable ecology of human regeneration that Ray says is as characteristic of junkyards as of old forests. We know from the text of *Go Down, Moses*, in fact, that Isaac receives some training in the Bible and that, upon his twenty-first birthday when he delivers his winding and evasive rationale for repudiating the farm, his cousin McCaslin Edmonds parries Ike's biblical rationalizations with a barrage of ironic comments about events in Genesis, including Abraham's sacrifice of Isaac. McCaslin's sense of irony reflects that his knowledge of life gives context to the stories in the Bible. He has been like a father to Isaac, but he is no Abraham to Isaac, no Jacob to Esau. He is simply a man who has made the best of the worst circumstances in order to pass his young cousin's rightful heritage along to him when Ike reaches twenty-one. Ike's initiation into the skills, responsibilities, and mysteries of hunting is accomplished by an aged man who has held on to the old ways of his people, despite a brutal and shameful personal history. Seeing something in Ike worth nurturing, Sam sacrifices his own peace in order to do this, so that his "Let me go" (167) is not a plea for absolute freedom, but freedom to transmit a positive tradition to Ike.

From all this splendid nurture what has Ike gained? "The Bear" and "Delta Autumn" reveal that he has not learned how to live with responsibility in either of his two realms. He does not, as Sam Fathers has expected, repeat with Old Ben the rifle shot that results in his vision of the mystical and apparently immortal luminous buck. He does not take charge of the farm that McCaslin has struggled to make better than when he began to care for it. He does not commit to his marriage with an act of love that produces offspring and heirs. No fire burns on his hearth that signals the vitality—and risk—of a marriage. He does not even break through the shibboleth of race and incest that sets him on his false path in life.

Why can't Ike bring his transforming experience in the woods back to the requirements of everyday life? Why can't he see that renewal entails the loss of self-consciousness? Isn't this why he cannot remember the gunshot that felled the first buck? Though both Ike and Roth see Lucas Beauchamp as having a face "which had heired and now reproduced with absolute and shocking fidelity the old ancestor's entire generation and thought . . . *heir and prototype simultaneously of all the geography and*

*climate and biology which sired old Carothers and all the rest of us and
our kind"* (114), this is not something Lucas himself thinks about. He feels
no conflict within himself. "He didn't even need to strive with" his
McCaslin blood (101). That geography and climate and biology mix to sire
a family and a people remains an empty insight for Ike. He wants to correct a wrong that the heirs of that wrong have all found other ways to overcome and get on with their lives.

The many arguments between characters, and within characters, in *Go
Down, Moses* seem to confirm the impromptu character of the book's
composition. This does not mean that it was not hard work to construct
the novel, but clearly Faulkner found what he was writing about only after
he had begun to assemble a very different book. As he revised and
reassembled as many as a dozen pieces that he had sawed and planed for
the commercial magazine market, Faulkner reinvented a very minor character named Ike McCaslin and then found behind his existence a more
complex story. Ike's life and fate are the most newly constructed elements
of what became *Go Down, Moses.* A look at the concordance of the book
reveals sixteen occurrences of the name Ike and forty of the name Isaac,
but 298 occurrences of the name Lucas. This seems to corroborate that as
Faulkner first began to reassemble various materials to make this book, he
first thought it would be mostly about Lucas Beauchamp. But that a character named Isaac began to take a key role reminds us that when Faulkner
began this novel he was coming off the long-delayed completion of a book
begun under the title "Father Abraham," published in 1940 as *The Hamlet,*
a novel about the economic rise of the Snopes family, whose patriarch is
called "Ab." The Abraham analogy applied to the Snopes clan does not
merely reflect that the biblical Abraham was the father of a great multi-
tude through the child of his old age, Isaac, but that like the sharecropping
Ab Snopes in Faulkner's novel, Abraham of old traveled great distances—
from Babylon to Egypt and back toward Canaan—but like Flem Snopes he
enriched himself by trading on the attractiveness of his wife.

Though transforming "Father Abraham" may have put Isaac once again
on Faulkner's mind, Ike McCaslin is a recycled character. In "A Bear
Hunt" from 1934, we meet an "Uncle Ike" as an elderly hunter, and in
"Lion" from 1935, a story that lies behind elements of "The Bear," an Ike
McCaslin has a grandson named Theophilus (and this Theophilus will get
an identifiable twin in the 1938 novel *The Unvanquished* but a different
father). In the 1936 short story "Fool about a Horse," an Uncle Ike owns
two hardware stores in Jefferson and Theophilus McCaslin is an old city
resident. In the 1939 short story version of "The Old People" Ike McCaslin
is identified as an old hunter, and the first-person narrator is a boy who
sounds very much like a young Quentin Compson. In the three stories

about Lucas Beauchamp that become "The Fire and the Hearth" chapter of *Go Down, Moses* no McCaslins are mentioned. In the 1940 short story version of "Pantaloon in Black" Rider and Mannie are renting from "the local white landowner," and there is no mention of McCaslin property. In *The Hamlet*, also 1940, Ike McCaslin is identified as a farmer in the far part of the county who has allowed Ab Snopes and his family to winter on his farm. In the 1940 story version of "Delta Autumn" the wife and children of the old hunter are mentioned, without a family name, and in the short story version of "Was," entitled "Almost," the boy companion to Uncle Buck is Bayard, apparently the young Bayard Sartoris of *The Unvanquished* (1938) where the anti-slave principles of Buck and Buddy are first elaborated.

So Faulkner took a vaguely realized character, his name perhaps merely homage to the old hunter Ike Roberts of Oxford, and the author found over time opportunities to draw that character more and more specifically—add wife, children, name a child, then make the named child the named father (Theophilus), adding the named twin Amodeus, and then putting both of them, but mostly Theophilus (known as Buck), into an account of the Civil War and Reconstruction (*The Unvanquished*), but with no mention of a child named Isaac, before finding for Ike the crucial role in *Go Down, Moses*. No wonder so many writers envy Faulkner's power of invention.

The Ike of *Go Down, Moses* has his peculiar life assigned by the events and characters with which the author found him aligned or had to link him. "Was" and "Delta Autumn," the first and last episodes in the two main movements of novel—one trilogy about the farm, one trilogy about the big woods—both lay a heavy burden on Ike. So might "Pantaloon in Black" and the novel's seventh episode and coda, "Go Down, Moses," but Ike is absent from those stories. In fact, McCaslin, Edmonds, and Beauchamp males are all conspicuous by their absences in both of these grim stories about the deaths of young black men who might have been heroes, instead of victims, in a world Ike could have made better.

"The Fire and the Hearth" and "The Bear" are cognate multi-part accounts of coming of age: first Lucas Beauchamp and then Ike McCaslin. Comparing these two characters only, we glimpse Ike's failed marriage in high relief, and we also come to understand why Lucas is not a part of the hunting tradition: his brother James goes on the hunt as a servant called "Tennie's Jim" and eventually is another person who abandons the farm, running away to the North, apparently, for perfectly understandable reasons. Lucas remains, but renames himself and refuses to be anyone's servant or to act like a sharecropper. He succeeds, even without ownership, on the family farm as the best agriculturalist and as half of a legendary long marriage.

Against this backdrop, Isaac fails in many ways, though he seems still to be the exemplary hunter. However, unlike Lucas, and at the moment of his most crucial test, he does not pull the trigger of his weapon, and thus he owns no talismanic bullet that reminds him of his risk and his assertion of complete manhood. Instead, as his first entrance into the woods hinted, his heritage in the woods will be to venerate not life but death—the graves of Lion and Sam.

Janisse Ray concludes her book with a dream that she can gradually restore the ecology of the longleaf pine, which in turn is the ecology of the herbs, trees, wild things, and even such unlikely people as her grandfather or father who have thrived there at different times. They are "crackers," and *cracker*, she has explained, is a word by which her small-town Southerners were negatively defined: "a slow, dumb, redneck hick, a hayseed, inbred and racist, come from poverty, condemned to poverty: descendant of Oglethorpe's debtor prisoners. Descendant of people who pulled from the Union, fought their patria, and lost."(30) But the ecology of a cracker childhood has produced from a junkyard a writer, a conservationist, and an artist who concludes her book with an afterword entitled "Promised Land," a concept that someone named Isaac who holds up the Bible to justify himself should understand.

Janisse Ray does not make responsibility for the life of a place seem easy. "When we consider what is happening to our forests—and to the birds, reptiles, and insects that live there—we must think also of ourselves," Janisse Ray writes. "Culture springs from the actions of people in a landscape, and what we, especially Southerners, are watching is a daily erosion of unique folkways as our native ecosystems and all their inhabitants disappear. Our culture is tied to the longleaf pine forest," she writes, speaking of herself and her region. But culture is also tied to all the places where life has "sheltered us, that we occupy." The loss of place, she argues, is the loss "of health, of culture, of heritage, of beauty, of the infinite hopefulness . . . where time stalls." Thus one cannot, like Ike McCaslin, claim innocence and retreat from responsibility, because, as Ray writes, "All of our names are written on the deed to rapacity. When we log and destroy and cut and pave and replace and kill, we steal from each other and from ourselves" (271–72).

My students have affirmed that Janisse Ray's mythic memoir and the nature writing in *Ecology of a Cracker Childhood* help a reader of *Go Down, Moses* see the plight of nature in terms of the plight of an individual but also see the plight of culture in terms of the plight of nature. In other words, Ray helps us unpack from *Go Down, Moses* drama that encompasses ecologies of family, farm, community, and region, not merely the ecology of the hunter's woods. Nature and the individual are not separate issues, farmland and wilderness are not separate issues. The individual, the family, the farm, and the hunting grounds all are touched by the same influences of mentoring, husbandry, heritage, preservation, renewal, and love. That so much has gone wrong in Ike's world by the last of the hunting episodes, "Delta Autumn," is matched by what is wrong in the entire Western world. Driving to the now distant woods, the younger hunters speak of Hitler and America's potential drift into the hands of a similar racist tyrant, and it is Roth who sees clearly that self-congratulatory but empty jingoism is no way to resist such an evil. But because Ike fails in his responsibilities to local issues—to family, farm, and wilderness—his distant cousin Roth has no family, is miserably angry as a farmer, and a bad hunter. Roth illegally kills a doe instead of a buck and throws the antlerless head into the bayou to hide his crime. Roth's greatest misery, however, is also his revenge, for though he cannot return the farm to Ike, he leaves to Ike the repetition of those events in the family history Ike's misplaced messianism set out to mend. Ike must pay off and banish Roth's unacceptable mistress and their child, a woman who even in the peculiar false genetics of the racist South is, like Lucas Beauchamp, more McCaslin, and white, than anything else. "Go Down, Moses," the final episode of the novel, underscores the harsh results of banishment from the farm. This episode also demonstrates for the last time in the novel how the women of the South—without participation in the rites of renewal represented by the hunt—honor memory regardless of race and preserve and restore the ecology of family, an ecology that the Kentucky poet, novelist, and agricultural essayist Wendell Berry discusses in his collection *Home Economics*:

> People cannot live apart from nature; that is the first principle of the conservationists. And yet, people cannot live in nature without changing it. But this is true of *all* creatures; they depend upon nature, and they change it. What we call nature is, in a sense, the sum of the changes made by all the various creatures and natural forces in their intricate actions and influences upon each other and upon their places. . . . And so it can hardly be expected that humans would not change nature. Humans, like all other creatures, must make a difference; otherwise, they cannot live. But unlike other creatures, humans must make a choice as to the kind and scale of the difference they make. If they choose to make too small a difference, they diminish their humanity. If they choose to make too great a difference, they diminish nature, and narrow their subsequent choices; ultimately, they diminish or destroy themselves. Nature, then, is not only our source but also our limit and measure. (7–8)

Berry comes to a conclusion that is compatible with William Faulkner's exploration of farm and wilderness in *Go Down, Moses* and with Janisse

Ray's juxtaposition of longleaf pine with family history. The probability is, he writes, "that nature and human culture, wildness and domesticity, are not opposed but are interdependent. Authentic experience of either will reveal the need of one for the other. In fact, examples from both past and present prove that a human economy and wildness can exist together not only in compatibility but to their mutual benefit" (13). Janisse Ray's story demonstrates this.

But this, in brief, is the message that Ike missed. Faulkner and Janisse Ray did not.

NOTES

1. Olga Vickery, *The Novels of William Faulkner* (Baton Rouge: Louisiana State University Press, 1959), 127, 132.

2. Cleanth Brooks, *William Faulkner: The Yoknapatawpha Country* (New Haven: Yale University Press, 1963), 273.

3. Michael Millgate, *The Achievement of William Faulkner* (New York: Random House, 1966), 210, 211.

4. R. W. B. Lewis, *The American Adam: Innocence, Tragedy, and Tradition in the Nineteenth Century* (Chicago: University of Chicago Press, 1955), 194; Lewis Simpson, "Isaac McCaslin and Temple Drake: The Fall of New World Man," *Nine Essays in Modern Literature*, ed. Donald Stanford (Baton Rouge: Louisiana State University Press, 1965), 88–106.

5. *The Illustrated Walden*, ed. J. Lyndon Shanley (Princeton: Princeton University Press, 1973), 5.

6. T. S. Eliot, "The Dry Salvages," *The Four Quartets* (New York: Harcourt, Brace, 1943), 24.

7. Janisse Ray, *The Ecology of a Cracker Childhood* (Minneapolis: Milkweed Editions, 1999), 3–4.

8. *Mississippi: A Guide to the Magnolia State* (Jackson: Mississippi Advertising Commission, 1938).

9. William Faulkner, *Go Down, Moses* (1942; New York: Vintage International, 1990), 257.

10. This incest, horrific in Ike McCaslin's eyes, repeats a biblical story too, for after Lot's wife dies as they leave the wicked cities on the plan that God is destroying, he takes his two daughters into the wilderness to live, and there, despairing of being claimed by a husband, they make their father drunk and lie with him "that they may preserve the seed of their father," each bearing a son who becomes the founder of a people who remain long in the land (Genesis 19: 34–38).

11. *"Go Down, Moses": A Concordance to the Novel*, ed. Jack L. Capps (West Point: Faulkner Concordance Advisory Board, 1977), 825, 827.

12. Richard Godden and Noel Polk have published a detailed analysis of the ledger entries, suggesting that Buck and Buddy are not only brothers but jealous lovers, whose relationship is threatened by the purchase of Brownlee. "Reading the Ledgers," *Mississippi Quarterly* 55 (Summer 2002): 301–59.

Visceral Faulkner:
Fiction and the Tug of the Organic World

Scott Slovic

In Spring 2003, we were having an unusual spell of humidity in normally bone-dry northern Nevada, the high desert. A tropical squall in Mexico had pushed hot, humid air up into Arizona and all the way up through the northern part of the Great Basin Desert, where I live. I thought about turning on a fan in my study, in order to write in comfort, and then I thought, "No, a bit of sweat will help get me in the mood to think about Faulkner, the South, and the physical senses." I worked without a fan, sweat trickling onto my keyboard. In a way, that's what my essay is about— the physical senses and literature, and why I think it's important to explore the intersections between how we perceive the world and how we read literary texts. For me, certain kinds of literary texts—not necessarily all texts—function as elaborate ways of saying, "Hey, look at that—pay attention! Would you listen to that! And while you're at it, feel this, too. And then think about the implications of your own presence in a vibrant, physical world, in a community of interacting objects, forces, and organisms."

Sweat. When I think about the South, especially in summer (the time of the annual Faulkner and Yoknapatawpha Conference), I think of the experience of sweating. For me that's the ultimate physical evocation of the climate of this particular part of the world, just as squinting in the gleaming sunlight of the High Sierra is the quintessential physical experience in my usual stomping ground. An alternative title for this essay, in fact, is "Sweat, Tangle, Rot: A Sensory Ecology, through Literature, of the American South"—in a sense, this title describes what I actually plan to do here. However, I'm calling these remarks instead, "Visceral Faulkner: Fiction and the Tug of the Organic World." This title alludes to a statement that I take to be a beautiful explanation of one of the main branches of "environmental literature"—and perhaps of literature and art more generally. Indiana nature writer Scott Russell Sanders has written, "For most of us, most of the time, nature appears framed in a window or a video screen or inside the borders of a photograph. We do not feel the organic web passing through our guts, as it truly does." Sanders made this statement in his 1987 essay "Speaking a Word for Nature." His comment criticizes the pathology of contemporary literature—fiction in particu-lar—for its tendency to ignore or downplay the relationship between humans and the more-than-human world, to overlook the fact that we are, as he puts it, "animals, two-legged sacks of meat and blood and bone dependent on the whole living planet for our survival." "Our outbreath-ings," continues Sanders, "still flow through the pores of trees, our food still grows in dirt, our bodies decay."[1] Sanders articulates a state of mind I would describe as "sensory ecology"—a sensibility attuned to the self's embeddedness within the physical world, a state of mind sensitive to the emotional and intellectual implications of connection. Implicit is the notion that literature can somehow help writers and readers to "feel the organic web passing through our guts." The phrase "visceral Faulkner" refers to the success or failure of literature to help readers feel this gut-level sense of physical connectedness to the world. My subtitle evokes Edward Hoagland's essay "Dogs, and the Tug of Life," which suggests that the rea-son people like walking their dogs is to feel that sense of connectedness to something beyond themselves—to feel the tug of another life at the end of the leash. Hoagland extends this to the idea of feeling a fish tugging at the end of a line, suggesting that the tug itself and not the captured fish is often the crucial goal.[2] The "tug" implies connection.

I'll offer some comments on Faulkner here, but mainly as a jumping off point for my remarks on more recent authors. In certain ways, contempo-rary environmental writers are responding to, even reacting against, some of the tendencies of modernist authors, so it's useful to look at earlier aes-thetic and intellectual movements in order to understand what's happen-ing today. Let me say a word about my early approaches to reading Faulkner as a build-up to what I do now, as a so-called ecocritic. I vividly recall my own first encounters with Faulkner, sitting on the back deck at my family's home in Eugene, Oregon, fifteen or sixteen years old, poking my way through *As I Lay Dying* during the summer in preparation for a high school English class in the fall. It was hard for me to appreciate the nuances of Faulkner's language, the subtleties of culture and place in his representation of a part of the country that seemed so distant from my own experience. The name "Mississippi" evoked for me, at that time, the stories of Goodman, Chaney, and Schwerner and James Meredith and other icons of the civil rights struggle in the South—emotions of fear and pride located in a distant place.

I next found myself thinking about Faulkner when I was a senior at Stanford, attending a lecture course on Faulkner and Conrad, taught by Albert Guerard and Tom Moser. Almost as odd a context for thinking about Faulkner—the eucalypts and brown foothills of Palo Alto—as was Oregon. Professor Guerard, as I recall, usually got the call to talk about

Faulkner's novels, and he managed admirably to explain the novelist's aesthetic achievements in the context of high modernism. I worked hard—twenty years ago—to lose myself in the storyteller's intellectual world and to understand *The Sound and the Fury* in the tradition of modernist experiments in literary psychology. As I flew to the Memphis in July 2003 to attend the Faulkner and Yoknapatawpha Conference, I opened my copy of *Light in August* and found an old handout from Professor Guerard called "The Faulknerian Voice," emphasizing the author's use of such techniques as poetic voice, Joycean wordplay, oxymorons, and narration by conjecture. It didn't occur to me, when I studied Faulkner as an undergraduate, to think about the natural world—or the relationship between people and nature—as represented and explored in Faulkner's work.

I graduated from Stanford in 1983, having just completed the Faulkner course and three other English classes in a mad rush to stop paying that hefty tuition. A year later, I began graduate school at Brown and found myself missing the climate and landscape of the American West as I tried to make a home for myself in hot, humid, urban Providence, Rhode Island. As I've often explained to people, it was the sense of exile from the familiar landscape of the West, nearly two decades ago now, that drove me to begin paying specific attention to how authors render their experience of place and nature, nature being a particularly crucial aspect of any place (even urban places). I stumbled across a new collection of John Muir's wilderness essays in the Rockefeller Library at Brown back in 1984, and ever since then I've been fascinated—even obsessed—with the literature of nature. In the early 1990s, a group of us began using the term *ecocriticism* (derived from a 1978 article by William Rueckert) to describe our approaches to reading explicitly nature-centered literature or exploring the environmental implications of texts that don't foreground nature.[3] I guess you could say I'm now pretty much a full-time ecocritic.

The community of ecocritics is a rather supportive and friendly one for the most part. We tend to share the same general political views, and many of us like to hike . . . or kayak, rock-climb, sometimes even hunt. We like to be outside as much as we enjoy sitting in libraries. Sometimes we carry our laptops or at least our paper notebooks out on the trail with us.

An interesting controversy that impinges on the idea I'm floating here of a "sensory ecology" revealed through literature has exploded among the ranks of ecocritics since the publication of Dana Phillips's inflammatory Oxford University Press volume titled *The Truth of Ecology: Nature, Culture, and Literature in America*.[4] In this new book, Phillips challenges many contemporary ecocritics and many nature writers, too—often in a sneering, *ad hominem* fashion. He expresses assorted pet peaves concerning the work of these critics and authors. His favorite target, though, is Harvard scholar Lawrence Buell—who spoke at the Faulkner and Yoknapatawpha Conference when it focused on Faulkner and nature in 1996. In particular, Phillips castigates Buell for his approach to Gerard Manley Hopkins's poem "Pied Beauty" in *The Environmental Imagination: Thoreau, Nature Writing, and the Formation of American Culture* (1995).[5] Here are the specific Hopkins lines in question:

> Glory be to God for dappled things,—
> For skies of couple-colour as a brindle cow;
> For rose-moles all in stipple upon trout that swim;
> Fresh-firecoal chestnut-falls; finches' wings;
> Landscape plotted and pieced—fold, fallow, and plough;
> And all trades, their gear, and tackle and trim. (Qtd in Phillips 167–68)

Buell, in his comments on "Pied Beauty," exalts in "how delicately responsive the poem is to the stimuli it registers! Who would have thought to see trout's 'rose-moles all in stipple'? In this way," says Buell, "aestheticism produces environmental bonding" (qtd in Phillips 168). In other words, for Buell, vivid rendering of nature in aestheticized language—in literary language—inspires in readers a sense of heightened attentiveness to the world and, thus, what he calls "environmental bonding." Phillips objects to Buell's methodology, writing, "It seems to me that if this commentary is intended as ecocriticism, then ecocriticism needs to be given a strong dose of formalism. Without this purgative, ecocriticism will lapse into the merely appreciative mode that both formalism and literary theory are meant to cure" (168). Phillips mocks what he takes to be Buell's claim that "the discrete details of 'Pied Beauty' have a one-to-one relationship to particular moments of an experience of the natural world, a one-to-one relationship to particular 'stimuli,' and it should be clear that an impression isn't the same thing as a stimulus" (170–71). He argues that Hopkins, in the passage above, is referring to trout generically, not specifically: "Hopkins is 'referring' not to one trout but to all trout: presumably, he means brown trout, though not a unique one, not 'that brown trout swimming in that pool right there,' imaginary or otherwise. And this is another reason one ought not assert that the poem registers stimuli" (168–69). He vigorously asserts that Buell misreads the Hopkins poem "and employs twists of logic because he wants his reader to accept the paradoxical idea that heightened verbal artifice can effect a heightened visual perception of the natural" (169).

Dana Phillips objects to the fact that neither ecocriticism nor nature writing is ecological science. They never claim to be science, nor do they claim to supersede or surmount science. However, Phillips fears that this new movement in literary studies and literary art seeks to overtake and supplant science in discerning and articulating "the truth of ecology" and yet does the work of science badly. Toward the end of his book, he bemoans the fact that "too much of what is called nature writing proves, on closer inspection, not to be writing about nature at all; it is, instead, writing about a response to nature" (210). Phillips's perception seems reasonable to me, but his lament seems misdirected. Ecocriticism and nature writing tend largely to explore human responses to the physical world, to nature. The literature itself and the scholarship that illuminates and explains the literature are concerned with how we understand our experience of the world, how we learn about things beyond ourselves, how we come to value these phenomena, and sometimes how we feel when we learn that our behavior has resulted in various forms of loss and degradation. It's no great revelation to claim that ecocriticism and nature writing concern themselves with feelings, values, the workings of the human mind. Is this not what literature does? Is this not the proper territory of the humanities?

It seems to me that what we call "environmental literature" seeks to explore several broad and basic questions: What is the meaning of a human life? How are we, and the rest of our species, linked to other beings that inhabit the earth? What does it mean to live responsibly—consciously and conscientiously—in a particular place on the planet? These are questions that exist at the core of literary expression, regardless of nationality and regardless of thematic focus. Perhaps such questions seem so fundamental and obvious as to be trivial, so private as to be hopelessly specific, so universal as to be insolubly vague. However, Henry David Thoreau remarked in *Walden* that humans need to be prodded like oxen to stay awake, to keep moving—he says we need to be "goaded."[6] (Perhaps this is what Dana Phillips aims to do in *The Truth of Ecology*.) I find myself wondering how literature might function as a prod, a springboard, a guide—a stimulus designed to accentuate readers' engagement with the world, to make us conscious of our individual presence in the world. We begin to understand the world and our place in it through specific sensory experiences, not through factum upon factum of abstract information. Surprisingly, human beings are often not very good at deploying physical senses as a means of living fully and freshly, participating vigorously in daily life. Wallace Stegner, in his essay "The Sense of Place," refers to Wendell Berry's formula: "If you don't know where you are, . . . you don't know *who* you are."[7] I would take this statement back one step further and suggest that if you don't know how to trust or activate your senses, you can't know where you are. Mitchell Thomashow, in his book *Bringing the Biosphere Home: Learning to Perceive Global Environmental Change*, refers to the process used by the senses to take in vast, subtle planetary systems as "place-based perceptual ecology."[8] Thomashow makes an effective argument that ecological understanding even on a global scale begins with perception, with paying attention. My own simple claim is that literature can play an essential role in prompting our attentiveness to the world and thus, ultimately, in enhancing our apprehension of "the truth of ecology," to use Dana Phillips's grand phrase.

My focus is on the role of literature to help readers use their sensory faculties and thus achieve a greater awareness of their animal selves and their presence in particular places on earth. Some texts clearly function as sensory stimuli—or actually study how the senses operate—while other literary works serve different purposes, sometimes largely cerebral ones, sometimes even abstracting the physical world, distancing readers from their own surroundings. Diane Ackerman devotes her 1990 book, *A Natural History of the Senses*, to celebrating "how sense-luscious the world is."[9] "We like to think that we are finely evolved creatures, in suit-and-tie or pantyhose-and-chemise, who live many millennia and mental detours away from the cave," she writes, "but that's not something our bodies are convinced of. . . . We still create works of art to enhance our senses and add even more sensations to the brimming world, so that we can utterly luxuriate in the spectacles of life. We still ache fiercely with love, lust, loyalty, and passion. And we still perceive the world, in all its gushing beauty and terror, right on our pulses. There is no other way" (xviii–xix). Reappreciating the unabating vigor of the physical senses is an important function of the arts in general, but in the field of environmental literature, the understanding and activation of the senses takes on a moral and political valence—a purpose inclusive of and exceeding luxuriation. "The world," says Ackerman, "is a construct the brain builds based on the sensory information it's given" (304). Still, to suggest that nature writers and ecocritics are concerned only with the brain—or the mind— is to miss the ubiquitous, energetic efforts of these writers and scholars to discern the border between truth and illusion, reality and fantasy. From *Walden* to *Desert Solitaire*, one encounters this process of checking firm, physical reality against mental constructs. For a witty recent example, see Robert Michael Pyle's essay "Reality Check: Blurring the Boundaries between Ersatz Nature and the Living, Breathing World" from the July/August 2003 *Orion* magazine.[10]

In the remainder of this essay, I will discuss some specific literary works in order to show how these works help readers use their sensory faculties and thus achieve a greater awareness of their animal selves and their presence in particular places on earth. I am intrigued by the literary representation of tactile (sweat), visual (tangle), and olfactory (rot) experiences in the American South. The South, one could argue, is a particularly suitable region to produce a vivid literature of physical sensation. Robert Taylor Ensign's 2003 study, *Lay Down Your Ear upon the Earth, and Listen: Thomas Wolfe's Greener Modernism*, explains some of the key tropes of modernist representation of nature in works by Wolfe, Faulkner, and other writers of that generation.[11] Before discussing several recent works, I'll gloss Ensign's study as a way of showing the tradition more recent authors are building on and reacting against. The subtle strands of sensuality in Faulkner's work—and that of other modernists—have become major foci of Southern writing during the last half century. I will focus my attention here on such authors as James Dickey, Larry Brown, Tom Franklin, and Janisse Ray, showing how they demonstrate the operation of the physical senses in various contexts, complicating—and sometimes illuminating and perhaps justifying—the representationalist tendencies that Dana Phillips condemns.

Robert Taylor Ensign examines the novels of North Carolina author Thomas Wolfe and finds them to be anomalies in the canon of modernist fiction for the way in which they perpetuate romantic fascination with individual consciousness, defying certain literary conventions of the early twentieth century. For literature to serve as a useful means of prompting readers' attentiveness to ecological phenomena, the use of neoromantic narrators and personae is often crucial, enabling authors to draw readers into vivid, vicarious experiences of nature, experiences that may inspire readers to engage themselves directly with the world once they've closed the pages they're reading. Although most modernist authors were concerned with the creation of credible textual worlds, Thomas Wolfe may have anticipated contemporary interest in the physical experience of the actual world. As Ensign states, "Most modernist fiction writers tended, in principle, to distrust narrators who seemed either 'too' subjective or 'too' emotional. The government's hypocritical prosecution of World War One in the media had dramatized for them the deceitful possibilities of language and, combined with their desire to overturn the genteel writing and temperament which still dominated American letters in the early part of the twentieth century, they responded by pledging to write 'objectively,' to write 'true'" (15). Wolfe seems to anticipate the highlighting of sensory experience, sensory contact with nature, that would become a major subcurrent and later almost a dominant tendency in American writing at the end of the twentieth century. Ensign notes the prominence of the sensory experience of nature in Wolfe's work following the publication of *Look Homeward, Angel* in 1929, despite the fact that many of his narratives occur in city settings: Wolfe "not only brings nature 'into' these ostensibly inorganic environments," argues Ensign, "but also creates the impression

that nature is as much an overarching presence there as it is in rural settings" (69). Ensign follows Arnold Goldsmith's line of argument in *The
Modern American Urban Novel: Nature as "Interior Structure"* (1981),
where Goldsmith observes that American city novelists have represented
nature as "neither [a] principal character nor mere backdrop, but an inte-
gral part of the setting, language, symbolism, and even characterization"
in their work.[12] Ensign uses the following passage from *The Web and the
Rock* (1939) to illustrate the possibility of intense sensory engagement
with nature even in an urban context. Wolfe's character George Webber
makes this observation:

> In New York there are certain wonderful seasons in which this feeling grows to
> lyrical intensity. One of these are those first tender days of Spring when lovely
> girls and women seem suddenly to burst out of the pavements like flowers. . . .
> Another season is early Autumn, in October, when the city begins to take on a
> magnificent flash and sparkle: there are swift whippings of bright wind, a flare
> of bitter leaves, the smell of frost and harvest in the air; after the enervation of
> Summer, the place awakens to an electric vitality. . . . Finally, there is a won-
> derful, secret thrill of some impending ecstasy on a frozen winter's night. On
> one of these nights of frozen silence when the cold is so intense that it numbs
> one's flesh . . . the whole city . . . becomes a proud, passionate, Northern place.[13]

The surprising, almost transgressive emphasis on the vividness of nature
in a supposedly denaturalized environment is, in a sense, precisely what
accentuates the sensory encounter described in Wolfe's novel. As Ensign
puts it, "this 'seasonalizing' of the city not only adds greater vibrancy to the
urban landscape, but greater piquancy to seasonal images as well. While
there is magic in the greening of the once-brown earth, there is an especial
magic in the greening of gray pavement, gray faces, and gray spirits" (70).
A moment of sensitive engagement with flowers, trees, birds, butterflies,
chilly wind, or sunny warmth on a walk through Tokyo, New York, or
London can almost be more compelling and memorable for its unexpect-
edness than similar encounters in rural or wilderness environments.

Wolfe's contemporary William Faulkner is the most widely known and
thoroughly studied of Southern writers. Ensign offers an intriguing comparison of Wolfe (who actually left the South and spent time in New York
City) and Faulkner, focusing on their subtly different approaches to showing their fictional characters' sensory experience of nature. Ensign
observes that "not only is Faulkner's fiction typically Southern in featuring
the compelling presence of nature, but many of his descriptions of the
organic world are equally as romantic and poetic as Wolfe's" (110).
Faulkner's use of the first-person perspective, claims Ensign, makes the
subjectivity of his characters' sensations sometimes seem even more

pronounced than in Wolfe's third-person descriptions. Ensign provides the following passage as an example, showing how Faulkner crafts Quentin's memories in *The Sound and the Fury* (1929): "I could smell the curves of the river beyond the dusk and I saw the last light supine and tranquil upon tideflats like pieces of broken mirror, then beyond them lights began in the pale clear air, trembling a little like butterflies hovering a long way off."[14] Faulkner was able to get away with highly subjectivized descriptions of sensory experience even during an aesthetic era—modernism—when such subjectivity was considered regressive and unsophisticated because he was, as Ensign states, "*recognized* as a modernist and, as such, his romantic passages were seen as studied efforts to fractionate his rhetoric as well as his structure" (110). On the other hand, Wolfe was not recognized as legitimately modern and has traditionally been denigrated by critics as a writer who never surmounted obsolete representation of subjective experience. According to Ensign, "While their similarities are great, what most differentiates them is the relative loudness of the emotional voices they use to vocalize their romantic, rich, and sensual descriptions of nature: while Wolfe's rhetoric is typically set at a high volume, Faulkner's descriptions come across as more soft-spoken, devotional musings. In addition," he continues, "given that Faulkner's typical characters are not aesthetes, as Wolfe's are, they are not as well equipped, linguistically, to appreciate nature's beauty and, accordingly, they generally don't apprehend nature in romantic terms; rather, this is left to the narrator" (110).

Ensign singles out a passage from the conclusion of *Absalom, Absalom!* (1936) as a typical example of Faulkner's tendency to superimpose highly subjective—"romantic"—sensations upon characters' experience rather than crafting characters who seek out or make meaning out such sensations. Faulkner's character Quentin, who is a student at Harvard and feels "the chill pure weight of the snow-breathed New England air on his face," relies upon memory to "taste and feel the dust of that breathless (rather, furnace-breathed) Mississippi September night." Faulkner itemizes Quentin's remembered perceptions: "He could smell the horse; he could hear the dry plaint of the light wheels in the weightless permeant dust and he seemed to feel the dust itself move sluggish and dry across his sweating flesh just as he seemed to hear the single profound suspiration of the parched earth's agony rising toward the imponderable and aloof stars."[15] Ensign italicizes the word *seemed* to emphasize Faulkner's tendency to layer subjective experience upon his character rather than indicating that the character was fully enmeshed in the experience itself. It could also be that Faulkner's use of the word *seemed* twice in this sentence—"seemed to feel," "seemed to hear"—underscores the possibility of reconstructing powerful sensory experience through the imaginative act of memory. At issue in this discussion of how major twentieth-century Southern novelists convey sensory experience of nature, of place, is the particular role of *emotion* in accenting—deepening—the significance of sensory experience. There is, even in the intense, climactic chapter of *Absalom, Absalom!*, a sense of dispassionate detachment—Quentin seems to be watching himself watching the world, watching and analyzing. As Quentin remembers returning to the house he had known as a boy, Faulkner writes:

> [T]hey reached it at last. It loomed, bulked, square and enormous, with jagged half-toppled chimneys, its roofline sagging a little: for an instant as they moved, hurried, toward it Quentin saw completely through it a ragged segment of sky with three hot stars in it as if the house were of one dimension, painted on a canvas curtain in which there was a tear; now, almost beneath it, the dead furnace-breath of air in which they moved seemed to reek in slow and protracted violence with a smell of desolation and decay as if the wood of which it was build were flesh. (366)

The fullness or flatness of the remembered house, its uncertain shape and substance in Quentin's remembering mind, raises doubts about the firmness of memory and the solidity of sensory experience. The house, in memory, becomes as artificial, as illusory, as a painting on a canvas curtain—a curtain that reveals through it a more substantial reality, that of sky, stars, the firmament of nature, although even the heat of the stars is a projection of the human viewer's imagination. Down on earth, in the human realm, sensation is not celebrated as engagement with reality itself; rather, the reeking, super-heated air emanates with the ultimate meaning of the flesh, which can be nothing but desolation and decay. Faulkner's physical realm of experience is often a realm of disappointment, a realm to be downplayed, overcome. Ensign notes that "while Faulkner's characters notice the natural world, they rarely do so or are described as doing so with any great passion." In his effort to launch a reevaluation of Thomas Wolfe's importance as a protoecological author, Ensign asserts that Wolfe's singular use of emotion and subjective perspective exemplifies "a methodology that draws on both nature's capacity to evoke feelings and humankind's capacity to be emotionally receptive to non-human phenomena" (111).

Despite Thomas Wolfe's contrarian, antimodernist persistence in reinforcing the emotional aspect of sensory contact with nature, it was not until the 1960s and 1970s that Southern writers began consistently to overcome the coldness and detachment of modernist tendencies to symbolize and aestheticize the physical senses. A splendid example of this assertion of the primacy of sensation is James Dickey's novel *Deliverance* (1970),[16] a major literary landmark in the celebration of engagement with physical reality—the celebration of "sensory ecology."

Dickey's narrator, Ed Gentry, highlights his own sensory experiences throughout the narrative. The first-person perspective makes Ed's transformation from ennui (from despair and vague boredom) to entranced engagement vividly noticeable. In the novel's opening chapter, "Before," Ed notices a series of women in nearby cars as he drives to his office at the ad agency: "The women were almost all secretaries and file clerks, young and semi-young and middle-aged, and their hair styles, piled and shellacked and swirled and horned, and almost every one stiff, filled me with desolation" (15). The sense of lifeless artificiality symbolized by the women's hairstyles inspires Ed's sense of emotional desolation—the women's hair is artificial but his emotion is real. The desolation is a build up to the drained paralysis Ed feels as he sits at his desk in the office:

> Before I made a move, though, I sat for maybe twenty seconds, failing to feel my heart beat, though at that moment I wanted to. The feeling of the inconsequence of whatever I would do, of anything I would pick up or think about or turn to see was at that moment being set in the very bone marrow. How does one get through this? I asked myself. By doing something that is at hand to be done was the best answer I could give; that and not saying anything about the feeling to anyone. It was the old mortal, helpless, time-terrified human feeling, just the same. I had had a touch or two before, though it was more likely to come with my family, for I could find ways to keep busy at the studio, or at least to seem busy, which was harder, in some cases, than doing real work. But I was really frightened, this time. It had me for sure, and I knew that if I managed to get up, through the enormous weight of lassitude, I would still move to the water cooler, or speak to Jack Waskow or Thad, with a sense of being someone else, some poor fool who lives as unobserved and impotent as a ghost, going through the only motions it has. (18)

In his ghostlike lassitude, his sense of unreal separation from himself (his "sense of being someone else"), Ed cannot "feel [his] heart beat." He vaguely desires to feel something passionately ("at that moment I wanted to," he says), but there's little chance of this as he goes through the motions of his workaday life, struggling merely to "get through" daily responsibilities. Dickey is here describing what he takes to be the essential malaise of modern life—life that's characterized by comfort, routine, and unutterable boredom, boredom bordering upon a pulseless condition of numbness.

So, what the novelist sets out to explore in this narrative is the possibility that contact with nature—and people who live close to nature—might stimulate blasé suburbanites into a condition of *feeling*. The question is whether it's enough for the novel's four men from the city simply to enjoy a casual, recreational visit to the river or whether they must be placed in a situation of life-or-death survival. Lewis, in particular, desires to experience the most basic of struggles, the better to strip off the restraints of civilization: "Life is so fucked-up now, and so complicated," he says, "that I wouldn't mind if it came down, right quick, to the bare survival of who was ready to survive" (43). This abstract hope becomes a prophesy of what the four will experience on the river. The contrast between fantasy and reality is a prominent theme in the narrative, both before the four friends make their way to the Cahulawassee and after they get to the river. In this sense, the Faulknerian theme of mediating physical reality by memory and imagination emerges in *Deliverance* as well, but in Dickey's novel the characters seem well aware of the limitations of the mind and seek to couple fantasy with physical reality. "[Fantasy is] all anybody has got," says Lewis. "It depends on how strong your fantasy is, and whether you really—*really*—in your own mind, fit into your own fantasy, whether you measure up to what you've fantasized" (49). In recounting an earlier fishing trip, Lewis tells Ed about the experience of falling down a thirty-foot cliff and breaking his ankle on the rocks. "And now you're going back?" queries Ed. "You better believe it. But you know something, Ed? That intensity; well, that's something special. That was a great trip, broken ankle and all," Lewis explains (51).

The word "intensity" describes precisely what's missing in the suburban lives of the novel's characters. As soon as they leave the confines of greater Atlanta en route to the put-in location up in the mountains, Ed begins to notice the world around him—his senses begin to awaken, to inch toward special intensity. "I looked off at the blue forms of the mountains, growing less transparent and cloudlike, shifting their positions, rolling from side to side off the road, coming back and centering in our path, and then sliding off the road again, but strengthening all the time," Ed comments in describing the drive toward the mountain town of Oree (52). The mountains are not yet firm, or real, but he is observing them intently during the drive—and the image is "strengthening." A few paragraphs later, his vision and hearing are becoming so heightened as to be interchangeable in his description: "We were among trees now, lots of them. I could have told you with my eyes closed; I could hear them whish, then open to space and then close with another whish. I was surprised at how much color there was in them. I had thought that the pine tree was about the only tree in the state, but that wasn't the case, as I saw. I had no notion what the trees were, but they were beautiful, flaming and turning color almost as I looked at them. They were just beginning to turn, and the flame was not hot yet. But it was there, beginning to come on" (53). Although Ed's botanical knowledge is limited—he can't identify the deciduous trees that are changing color in autumn—he has already greatly expanded his knowledge of Georgia ecology simply by engaging his senses and realizing that trees other than pines abound in the state. The intensifying color of the changing trees serve also as codes for Ed's intensifying awareness of the physical world and the potency of sensation. He is quickly recovering from his suburban ennui, even as he and his friends enter an unanticipated realm of wildness.

As the novel proceeds, the language dances with sensory imagery—with emphasis on touch, sight, sound, and smell. Sweat, tangle, rot. Ed narrates the story by way of sensory details. In a sense, he creates a secondary narrative—there is the story of the canoe trip down the river, including dangerous encounters with violent backwoodsmen and equally risky rapids, but there is also the story of Ed's sensory intensification, his integration of his body and the physical world and his intellectual and emotional acceptance of himself as a sensing organism. Just before the four men put their boats into the Cahulawassee, they've been driving their canoe-laden cars deeper and deeper into the riverside underbrush:

> "Hold on," Lewis said, and tipped the car over forward. Rhododendron and laurel bushes closed in on us with a soft limber rush. A branch of something jumped in the window and stayed, lying across my chest.
>
> We had stopped, and I sat with the pressure of the woods against me; when I looked down I saw that one leaf was shaking with my heart. (68)

By contrast with his sense of disconnection from his own living self while sitting in the office a few days earlier, Ed is able to observe the pulsing of his heart through tactile contact with the lush underbrush. This is a rather vivid demonstration of what Robert Ensign describes as "nature's capacity to evoke feelings and humankind's capacity to be emotionally receptive to non-human phenomena" (111). In this particular example from Dickey's novel, the emotional receptiveness is characterized by the physical shaking of the leaf. As the novel progresses, Ed, in particular, collects more and more instances of sensory contact, sliding down the river bank and "feeling dirt on [his] hands for the first time in years" (69), observing that the river is "gray-green, very clear and yet with a certain milkiness, too" (70), stepping into the water to feel the "complicated urgency of the current, like a thing made of many threads being pulled" (73), hitting his paddle on bottom-rocks, which "put an odd, dissonant, intimate feeling into [his] hands" (73–74), and so forth. As the foursome moves deeper into the backwoods experience, Ed's sensory entrancement—his feeling of connection—deepens. "Loading the canoe, I had not really been aware of the water," he recalls, "But now I was. It felt profound, its motion built into it by the composition of the earth for hundreds of miles upstream and down, and by the composition of the earth for hundreds of miles upstream and down, and by thousands of years. The standing there was so good, so fresh and various and continuous, so vital and uncaring around my genitals, that I hated to leave it" (75). The frigid river is fresh and vital and makes Ed feel linked by way of the water's motion to the very composition of the earth, an ample span of land and time. Even unsavory phenomena become beautiful. "Cow dung," writes Dickey, "shone in the late heat, and there was a small, misty glimmering of insects wherever it had fallen" (75). This is not to say that Ed—or any other Dickey character—has achieved an enlightened sense of environmental stewardship. Nature, in this narrative, despite the imminent construction of the dam that has occasioned this final trip on the wild river, appears indomitable, indestructible. Ed notices a farm that "seemed to be battling the woods for existence"; he consumes a beer in "one long, unhurried epical swallow" and then holds "the wavering color of the can under water until it filled enough to sink, and let it go, down and on past my ballooning nylon legs" (75). One senses that the woods and the river are large and powerful enough ultimately to contain all that humanity can do to them. However, the impoverishment caused by human-wrought environmental changes (such as the damming of wild rivers) will make it harder and harder for people to achieve elemental contact with something other than themselves—and for Dickey this seems to be the great danger of such change.

Ed, Lewis, and their friends Drew and Bobby are everymen, ordinary in almost every way—ordinary jobs, ordinary families, living in ordinary places. Although the novel is written by a male author and focuses on male characters, it seems reasonable that most readers could identify with the characters, particularly with the first-person narrator, building—intensifying—our own emotional and sensory engagement with the physical world through empathy with Dickey's imagined characters. Other contemporary authors, currently or formerly associated with the American South, write of various locales—city situations, farm life, and remote natural settings—and seem bent specifically on heightening readers' sensory attunement to their own places in the world. I'll organize these according to my three core Southern sensory tropes—sweat, tangle, and rot.

First, sweat. I was turned on to Larry Brown's novel *Joe* (1991) by nature writer Rick Bass, who told me in a letter that he'd just finished reading it and it was an amazing work.[17] The novel is full of "visceral," physical sensations—varieties of pain (getting shot, beaten, bitten by a dog, rejected by one's children) and small, often tainted pleasures (a taxi ride on a hot day, beer bought with stolen money, one-night stands). In this passage Joe's watching his gang in the summer heat. His sleepiness in the heat mimics the death of the forest he's helping to subdue. This particular passage doesn't mention sweat *per se*, but it depicts a place in which heat—the cause of sweat—is a preponderant force:

> The other hands rose in a group like a herd of cows or trained dogs in a circus act when they saw the bossman stand up. They picked up their implements and

thumped their cigarettes away. The whole party moved off into the deep shade with their poison guns over their shoulders, the merciless sun beating down and the gnats hovering in parabolic ballets on the still and steaming air. The heat stood in a vapor over the land, shimmering waves of it rising up from the valleys to cook the horizon into a quaking mass that stood far off in the distance with mountains of green painted below the blue and cloudless sky. Joe stood in the bladed road with his hands on his hips and watched them go. He surveyed his domain and the dominion he held over them not lightly, his eyes half-lidded and sleepy under the dying forest. He didn't feel good about being the one to kill it. He guessed it never occurred to any of them what they were doing. But it had occurred to him. (202–3)

The unavoidable reality of sweaty heat in the summertime South seems an appropriate condition in which to apprehend the unavoidable reality— the consequences—of one's actions—in this case, making a living by destroying the place where the character lives. I see no particular paradox in using Larry Brown's eloquent passage to prompt my own—our own— efforts to perceive the world and the implications of our role in the world.

Tangle. Tom Franklin's short story "Shubuta," from his 1999 collection *Poachers*, is about a guy in Shubuta, Mississippi, who's lost his girlfriend but is still obsessed with her and with death and with the miasmic misery of life and love.[18] Everything in this story is in a state of decay or has already died. The first-person narrator reflects again and again about Willie Howe, a black watermelon farmer from Shubuta, who taped reading glasses to thirty watermelons and shot each through the left lens, then went in his house and shot himself through the right lens. This happened when Willie's wife left him—his brother-in-law was an optometrist. The narrator thinks of this as death with honor, with flair—as death with a "creative twist" (45). People, stories, emotions, and the physical landscape itself are complicated and entangled in this narrative. Three sections of the story begin with references to kudzu, that great symbol of perceptual and ecological entanglement in the South. Take section four, in which Franklin's narrator is aimlessly motoring around Shubuta, entrapped by his memories and fantasies. His earthbound existence is presented in sharp contrast to a buzzard floating high above (reminiscent of Edward Abbey's frequent references to buzzards in his fiction and nonfiction):

In the van, its rear end weighted down with melons, I dig in the cooler and find a beer. The landscape passes, two skinny silhouettes fighting with sling blades. My clothes and hair are damp from sweat, the four o'clock sun in my eyes. I come to a rest area and rumble off the road. Not a fancy place like on the inter-state, this one just pine trees and a few rotten picnic tables, a garbage can. Kudzu climbs the trees, scales power poles, goes wire to wire.

My cigarette package, empty, flutters to the ground. A far-off buzzard doing wide, slow turns above the tree line is the only thing moving. Uncle Dock calls them country airplanes, the way they glide. He says your average buzzard can see for miles. I suppose that old fellow up there can see me clear as day, though he's just a speck from here. (53)

Unlike the narrator's own occluded self-perception, his hampered view of who he is, who he's become since losing his girl, the buzzard "can see for miles," can see the narrator "clear as day." The land-bound kudzu, icon of entanglement, climbs and "goes wire to wire," seeking a buzzardlike vantage. Even the entangling vine seeks disencumberment. The human narrator yearns for the same, but resigns himself to less. Tangle joins sweat and rot in the passage to suggest not only metaphors for the character's mental state, but a sort of physical, environmental determinism. In this landscape of complexity, struggle, and decay, love is always pointing toward loss, life toward death. Perception of the physical place suggests these interpretations.

Rot. When is rot not a bad thing, a sorrowful indication of what once was? Ecologists and gardeners recognize rot, the decay of organic matter, as an essential, natural process. New life springs from old. Vegetables and flowers spring from compost. Georgia author Janisse Ray, the author of *Ecology of a Cracker Childhood* and of the 2003 assemblage of nonfiction titled *Wild Card Quilt: Taking a Chance on Home*, takes a fresh, upbeat, playful, muscular approach to ecological themes that pervade Southern literature. There's plenty of sweat and tangle in her work, plenty of blood and madness, but when she refers to "rot," she's thinking compost, not waste and misery. Her essay called "A Natural Almanac" from *Wild Card Quilt*[19] cuts a striking contrast with the other examples of recent Southern writing I've been talking about. It begins with admonitions to notice physical things. "To pay attention to the world," she writes, "where forests bend according to the wind's direction, rivers bring baskets of granite down from the mountains, and cranes perform their long, evolutionary dances, is a kind of religious practice. To acknowledge the workings of the world is to fasten ourselves in it. To attend to creation—our wild and dear universe—is to gain admission to life. One can live at the bone. This I wish to do." And she continues: "Details define the farm: the arrival and departure of birds, wildflower blooms, habits of animals, ripening of fruit, passing of cold fronts. The more attention we pay a certain place, the more details we see, and the more attached we become to it" (160). I would argue that all of the authors I've been discussing are, in one way or another, seeking to inspire attachment through attentiveness. When Ray talks about rot, it sounds like she's talking about love, nourishment, drama, and incipient growth. "Late summer I spend all day in the yard," she begins, "bending and toting and turning and pushing. I dig the garlic, harvesting some but replanting most, adding sheep manure, then matted pecan leaves. Even the dirt smells like garlic. I clip three wheelbarrow loads of overgrown vegetation, azaleas from around the walk, an errant crepe myrtle that hides oncoming traffic at the end of the driveway, dead limbs off the catalpa. I pile mountains of pine straw in flower beds and around the bases of the ancient pine trees" (166). The narrator of this essay does not perceive the world passively and muse about its contingent meanings. She interacts with her plants, her place, becomes part of the ecological system with the intention both of shaping her home to suit her own desires and needs and nurturing the elements of the landscape, such as the "ancient pine trees," that preceded her there. This particular example of the literature of sensory ecology models for readers a form of wholesome engagement that is rooted in paying attention.

This idea of a "sensory ecology"—a feeling for how the world works and how we fit into the world, derived from the reading of literature that helps us to be conscious of physical sensation—is not a phenomenon unique to the American South by any means.[20] I single out a handful of authors and texts merely to suggest that this is a potent motif in a particular branch of American writing, one that could be discussed more extensively on a national—and indeed, an *international*—scale as well. In the passage from Scott Russell Sanders's "Speaking a Word for Nature" with which I began this essay, he argues, "The gospel of ecology has become an *intellectual* commonplace. But it is not yet an *emotional* one" (226). Making ecological understanding an emotional, visceral facet of our common experience is the goal of this literature of sensory ecology—not only in fiction and nonfiction, but also in poetry and drama.

NOTES

1. Scott Russell Sanders, "Speaking a Word for Nature," in *Secrets of the Universe* (Boston: Beacon, 1987), 226.

2. Edward Hoagland, "Dogs, and the Tug of Life," in *Red Wolves and Black Bears* (New York: Penguin, 1972).

3. William Rueckert, "Literature and Ecology: An Experiment in Ecocriticism," in *The Ecocriticism Reader: Landmarks in Literary Ecology*, ed. Cheryl Glotfelty and Harold Fromm (Athens: University of Georgia Press, 1996).

4. Dana Phillips, *The Truth of Ecology: Nature, Culture, and Literature in America* (New York: Oxford University Press, 2003).

5. Lawrence Buell, *The Environmental Imagination: Thoreau, Nature Writing, and the Formation of American Culture* (Cambridge: Harvard University Press, 1995).

6. Henry David Thoreau, *Walden* (1854) and *Resistance to Civil Government* (1849), Norton Critical Edition (2nd edition). Ed. William Rossi (New York: Norton, 1992), 73.

7. Wallace Stegner, "The Sense of Place," in *Where the Bluebird Sings to the Lemonade Springs: Living and Writing in the West* (New York: Penguin, 1993), 199.

8. Mitchell Thomashow, *Bringing the Biosphere Home: Learning to Perceive Global Environmental Change* (Cambridge: MIT Press, 2002), 5.

9. Diane Ackerman, *A Natural History of the Senses* (New York: Random House, 1990), xv.

10. Robert Micael Pyle, "Reality Check: Blurring the Boundaries between Ersatz Nature and the Living, Breathing World," *Orion* 22.4 (July/August 2003): 70–71.

11. Robert Taylor Ensign, *Lean Down Your Ear upon the Earth, and Listen: Thomas Wolfe's Greener Modernism* (Columbia: University of South Carolina Press, 2003).

12. Arnold L. Goldsmith, *The Modern American Urban Novel: Nature as "Interior Structure"* (Detroit: Wayne State University Press, 1991), 10.

13. Thomas Wolfe, *The Web and the Rock* (1939; New York: Perennial Library, 1973), 221.

14. William Faulkner, *The Sound and the Fury* (1929; New York: Vintage, 1936), 195.

15. William Faulkner, *Absalom, Absalom!* (1936; New York: Vintage, 1972), 362.

16. James Dickey, *Deliverance* (1970; New York: Delta, 1994).

17. Larry Brown, *Joe* (New York: Warner, 1991).

18. Tom Franklin, *Poachers* (New York: HarperCollins, 1999).

19. Janisse Ray, *Wild Card Quilt: Taking a Chance on Home* (Minneapolis: Milkweed Editions, 2003).

20. See, for instance, David Mas Masumoto, *Four Seasons in Five Senses: Things Worth Savoring* (New York: Norton, 2003). This book consists of fifty-one brief essays about life on the author's farm outside of Fresno, California, with a focus on sensory experience.

McCrady's La-FAY-ette County

JEANNE DE LA HOUSSAYE

Much of a country's image is the result of its creative thinkers. We know more completely, and therefore enjoy these places because of these men, who have shown us a richness that we might never have seen.

These are the words of John McCrady, who sought inspiration from, and set much of his work in Oxford, Mississippi, and the surrounding countryside, places that served the same purpose for William Faulkner. Faulkner was fourteen when McCrady was born in Canton, Mississippi; sixteen years later, McCrady's family moved to Oxford. By then Faulkner was thirty. Their paths rarely crossed—although they did cross, and I'll get to that later. What links the two artists are their Mississippi roots: the Yoknapatawpha County described by Faulkner and the La-FAY-ette County depicted by McCrady. When I spell La-FAY-ette, I spell it as McCrady did—hyphenated, with the stress on the middle syllable. I'm a New Orleans girl, and most of the people who knew of McCrady while he was creating his second series of Oxford paintings were New Orleans people. We're quite familiar with Lafayette Square, Lafayette Cemetery, and the town of Lafayette, Louisiana, but La-FAY-ette? That's another world, McCrady's world, and he wanted us to pronounce it properly—the way the people of northern Mississippi say it.

John McCrady taught me design and painting, and not a day goes by that I don't apply his teaching to some project or other. My perspective is that of a McCrady student, as a teacher in his school, and as his friend and protégée. Some of what I'll share with you is personal reminiscence that can't possibly be documented. But, we'll see Faulkner's world through McCrady's eyes. In McCrady's paintings you'll find farms, towns, and countryside. What you won't find are the big houses. To my knowledge, he didn't paint a single one, so you won't find any evocations of the Compson House or the Old Frenchman's place. Let's take a look.

Reproductions courtesy the New Orleans Museum of Art.

1: *Political Rally*

But above all the courthouse: The center, the focus, the hub; sitting looming in the center of the county's circumference like a single cloud in its ring of horizon, laying its vast shadow to the uttermost rim of horizon; musing, brooding, symbolic and ponderable, tall as cloud, solid as rock, dominating all: protector of the weak, judiciate and curb of the passions and lusts, repository and guardian of the aspirations and the hopes: rising course by brick course during that first summer simply square, simplest Georgian Colonial.

—Requiem for a Nun

See the guy in the hat with the pipe? Behind him is McCrady himself and his future wife, Mary. The demagogue is Bilbo, or someone speaking for him. This painting is from 1935, when McCrady was only twenty-four years old. That year, he was included in a show at Boyer Galleries in Philadelphia, *Thirty-Five Painters of the Deep South*. The following year he had a one-man show at the same gallery.

2: *Swing Low, Sweet Chariot*

In 1937, McCrady completed the painting *Swing Low, Sweet Chariot* for a one-man show at the Boyer Galleries in New York. A lithograph was completed at the same time. From the twisting, almost palpable sky—a McCrady signature—emerges the heavenly chariot, manned by black angels, comin' for to carry home an old woman who is dying. The doctor's Model A has left tracks in the soft muddy road. In the thirties, all the roads in the rural South were narrow and rutted, making distances long.

That year, *Time* magazine called McCrady "a star risen from the bayous" who would do for painting in the South what Faulkner was doing for literature. Also in 1937, *Life* magazine published a five-page spread of the artist's work, and Stark Young praised McCrady's work in the *New Republic*. McCrady was young, but already he was being compared to William Faulkner.

I told you that McCrady's path rarely crossed Faulkner's, but they actually did meet, on the University of Mississippi campus. McCrady was just out of high school, Faulkner was fourteen years older, and they were both attending Ole Miss and working on one of the college publications. McCrady was a writer, Faulkner was an artist. I am glad they finally got *that* straightened out!

3: *Judgment Day*

In 1938, McCrady painted *Judgment Day*, in which his black angels once more appear in a painting that combines one of the great religious themes of the Renaissance with the spirituality of the black South. The following year he was awarded a Guggenheim fellowship to paint the life and faith of the Southern Negro. Robert Penn Warren also received a fellowship that year.

4: *Amory, Mississippi, 1888*

Oxford on the Hill, the painting used on the 2003 Faulkner and Yoknapatawpha Conference materials, was completed in 1939 along with a mural for the post office in Amory, Mississippi. Of *Oxford on the Hill*, McCrady wrote: "This land that I paint radiates for miles around the Court House at Oxford that stands high on a hill. Near it are trees that stand strong like our bones, supporting their masses. In their shadows are the people who are reflections of their environment: and I have recreated them."

5: *Heaven Bound*

I saw this painting many times in McCrady's studio. It's about four feet square. The mat was also McCrady's creation, carved into a layer of gesso. Look at the details beneath the figures: the rutted road between eroded banks, the murdered woman's body lying in a square of light outside her cabin, and the perpetrator being pursued by dogs from above and lightening from above.

6: *Hush, Someone's Calling My Name*

The stark countryside overwhelms the figure in this affirmation of McCrady's faith. McCrady was deeply religious all his life, as was his entire family. Which brings me to another connection. His father was the rector at St. Peter's—the very same priest who refused to marry William and Estelle, sending them out to College Hill Presbyterian for their wedding.

7: *Our Daily Bread*

The title of this 1941 painting refers less to the giving of daily bread than to the earning of it. Remember the church in "Shingles for the Lord"? How it was built with an ax, a froe, a wedge, and a maul? McCrady drew the kind of buildings that were made that way. To the right of the house, a tree's just been felled—probably for lumber. There's a fishpond in the midground with a lowhead dam that draws the overflow into a larger stream and might, with a little effort, be used to power a pump or a mill. This picture is about living off the land, about the balance between human life and the earth that supports it—about ecology. And notice the soil erosion in most of McCrady's pastorals. That's why we got kudzu, which worked only too well.

8: *Emporium*

. . . a section of rich river-bottom country lying 20 miles southeast of Jefferson. Hill-cradled and remote, definite yet without boundaries. . . .
                                                                    —*The Hamlet*

The title of this work is *Emporium* but it might be any tiny settlement here-abouts, including Frenchman's Bend. McCrady was on a roll in 1946. He completed a mural at Delmonico's Restaurant in New Orleans. A major exhibition of his work opened at Associated American Artists Gallery in New York.

9: *Retired*

Retired was painted in 1946, probably from the same sketch he used for the doctor's car in *Swing Low*. Mississippi was still one of McCrady's favorite subjects, but it had been many years since he had lived there. Like Faulkner, he had sought the creative atmosphere of the French Quarter, but unlike Faulkner, he had stayed, and therein lies one more connection between Faulkner and McCrady, not in Mississippi, but in the French Quarter. Running between St. Peter Street and the Cathedral is Exchange Passage, less than a block long. At the Cathedral end of the passage was Faulkner's apartment, now the site of Faulkner House Books. On the St. Peter Street end was the interior design shop of Marc Antony, and above it some unused rooms where writers met to talk. My source for this information was only five or six at the time, so please forgive her for remembering only three of the writers who met there: William Faulkner, John dos Passos, and Hamilton Basso. She was Basso's baby sister, and he often took her along to give their mother some time to herself. Many years later she married John McCrady.

10: *Repatriated*

Also painted in 1946, the scene in *Repatriated* was repeated nationwide as the soldiers came home from the war. McCrady depicts an African American reunion scene. That same year *Time* reproduced *Swing Low* in an article on Marian Anderson and traditional spirituals.

And then something terrible happened that brought McCrady's La-FAY-ette County and his black angels crashing down on him. A critic at the *Daily Worker* denounced McCrady and his work at the Associated show in New York as "a flagrant example of racial chauvinism." He was devastated, and his La-FAY-ette County paintings came to an end. It would be fifteen years before McCrady once more returned to his Mississippi roots for inspiration.

He never talked about it—I know what I know from Mary McCrady. He wasn't idle during this hiatus—he worked on a series of commissions for Standard Oil, did some New Orleans paintings, and opened a school in a building on Bourbon Street owned by Mary's family. In 1956, he painted a mural on the altar wall of Grace Episcopal Church in New Orleans. But the Mississippi countryside was absent from his work save for an occasion backdrop to a still life. His passion for La-FAY-ette/Yoknapatawpha was gone.

Why? Why would a comment from a left-wing critic wound him to such a degree? I think I know, but this is my opinion, and mine alone. I think he realized that the critic was right. His Southern blacks, even his angels, are caricatures, cavorting and carefree as children. Even the returning patriot walks with a comic gait. In McCrady's defense, this was the face that blacks showed to whites—it was safer that way. And I think that McCrady, a kind and gentle man, was distressed to think that he might have brought ridicule and pain to people for whom he had a genuine affection. This is my opinion—but I knew McCrady the man, and I think I'm right.

What follows are my own memories of John McCrady and his Mississippi Renaissance. I started school at McCrady's in early 1962. James Meredith started school, too, and so did Ruby Bridges. Things changed, including John McCrady's mind. When his school was closed for the month of August 1962, he returned to Oxford for a month of sketching—he never EVER used a camera. That sketch trip was to provide him with material he would use the rest of his life, and he returned to New Orleans to begin work on a new series of La-FAY-ette County paintings, the last great project of his life.

11: *Mr. Gulliver of Lafayette County*

The first painting—*Mr. Gulliver of Lafayette County*—appeared in 1963. He began the practice of bringing his paintings to the school in various stages of development to show students the progress of his intricate multi-stage technique. The painting is McCrady's interpretation of what would have happened had Mr. Gulliver landed in La-FAY-ette instead of Lilliput. Gulliver is a dead-on doppelganger of John McCrady, and the enterprising Mississippians are charging admission to see him. On the platform by his head, people are encouraged to get married and have a wedding photograph made with Mr. G. John McCrady—who always *did* want to be a cartoonist—was using humor to ease himself back into La-FAY-ette County.

12: *Dogtrot Parthenon*

"a passage showed, running through the house, right through the middle of it."

—Eudora Welty, *Losing Battles*

Eudora Welty was familiar with the dogtrot house, a mainstay of Southern architecture. The dogtrot house has an open passage down the center to keep it dry but ventilated—a good choice for this climate. This is the sort of house that small farmers occupied in La-FAY-ette—and in Yoknapatawpha—counties.

McCrady writes:

I found an old house high on a bluff in the country near Oxford. It was August, and it was a warm and dry day. I was impressed by this building as a good example of a style of architecture that is typical of this country. There the home stood, high and majestic like the Parthenon stands above Athens. The Dog-Trot architecture received its name from the people in this country who must have loved it, as it was so well represented throughout La-FAY-ette County. The depth of its inspiration compared with that prime image of universal art found on the Acropolis is perhaps shallow, but for some reason or other its popularity must be deserved.

13: *Golden Rule*

The site of this work is the Oxford Courthouse Square, near Square Books. The Golden Rule is gone—Ann Abadie says it's been yuppied up. McCrady—even in 1963—realized that Oxford was changing and wanted to get it all down as he both saw and remembered it. And please note that the African Americans in this and the subsequent paintings are portraits, not caricatures.

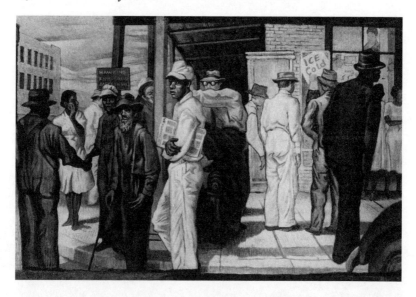

14: *Rural Symposium*

Although McCrady called this painting *Rural Symposium*, I would call it *Two Right Arms*. When he brought it to class, as he customarily did, one of the students pointed out that the central figure had two right arms—the one that remains, with the hand hugging the left elbow, and the other, which was stretched out to prop its owner against the post. Evidence of its removal is in the patch on the second post. McCrady presumed that each of the people in this painting was a subscriber to the *Oxford Eagle*. He writes:

> Saturday is a favorite day to gather and discuss many subjects and to collect opinions. Of what they talk is somewhat reflected in the *Eagle*, where letters are published from unsophisticated correspondents who represent the people throughout the surrounding hills. These letters are of news and obituaries, written by people who are quite philosophical and abundantly endowed with compassion.

15: *A.M.*

*It's a good thing the Lord did something for this country; the folks that
live on it never have. Friday afternoon, and from right here I could see
three miles of land that hadn't even been broken.*
                                                    —The Sound and the Fury

Look at the upper corner of this painting—unbroken land, sure enough.
A.M. is one of the earliest of McCrady's carbon/acrylic paintings, in which
a charcoal drawing is mounted on a gesso panel under layers of acrylic
varnish and then glazed and painted. It combines the best of drawing and
painting.

About his rural scenes, McCrady said:

> When I return to one of my favorite regions and become intoxicated with its
> sounds and silence, its smell and humidity, and ponder over the effect of it all,
> the thoughts of the mind seem to sing loudest when one is in the quiet presence
> of the fields; not only are they loud and clear, but I find that they give me inspi-
> ration for what I wish to paint and write.

This was McCrady's daughter Tucker's favorite painting. It could have
been mine—my mother wanted to buy it for me. It was only $400 since
McCrady was just beginning his comeback. And my father said, "Marion,
that's ridiculous, the child's an artist herself, she can paint her own."
Daddy, Daddy, Daddy.

16: *To the Glory of God*

This painting was completed in 1964 from a sketch made in 1939 when John and Mary McCrady were traveling the South making sketches for the Guggenheim project. His chiaroscuro composition is particularly strong here and the undulating countryside is echoed in the sky.

17: *Repetition with Variation*

McCrady named this painting for his favorite design principle, repetition with variation. See how the subtle changes in angle and shadows from one log to the next bring about a combination of variety and unity. The scene was often repeated in the South of the sixties: the abandoned share-cropper's cabin, a victim of mechanized farming. Faulkner, you will remember, was caught in the same situation when he started up a mule farm just as tractors took over.

IT'S PHENOMENAL · LA-FAY-ETTE COUNTY   John McCrady

18: *It's Phenomenal*

This small carbon/acrylic painting from 1965 shows better than most the drawing beneath the painting. Note McCrady's spelling at the bottom of the page—and also the sensitive portrayal of the child. In 1968, McCrady completed a mural of local scenes for the Bank of Oxford. That same year he painted *The Citadel*, another rendering of the La-FAY-ette County courthouse that is still, I think, in the collection of the Duvall family of Oxford.

He still had several books of sketches from August 1962, and planned to continue his La-FAY-ette paintings, but the Sweet Chariot was close behind him. He died in December of 1968, following cancer surgery. The rest of the paintings were left undone, and both were gone, Faulkner and McCrady. Now, when you read one, I hope you'll remember the other, and let the two artists enrich each other.

Collecting Faulkner

SETH BERNER

So . . . you fell in love with William Faulkner in tenth grade, you think you finally understand what his books are about, and you are going to reward yourself by buying yourself a collection of Faulkner. Fortunately, the first piece of advice for one setting out to collect Faulkner is easier to understand than the texts themselves. Unfortunately, that advice is: don't bother. Unless you have almost unlimited funds and unlimited storage space, trying to collect Faulkner will only cause you nightmares.

For instance, take *The Sound and the Fury*. Actually, I should say to *try* to take it. To be collectible a book should have the original paper wrapper (the "dust jacket") that covered it when the book was first published. A collectible copy of *The Sound and the Fury* in the most decrepit dust jacket you can imagine will cost you $5,000. Improve the quality somewhat and the price doubles. One that might be described as attractive will ring up at the register at $20,000; and a copy in as-new condition could easily go for $30,000–$50,000. Faulkner's most magnificent failure will be your most magnificent bankruptcy. *The Sound and the Fury* is not the only title in this price range;[1] and while most other "collectible" editions of Faulkner books will be cheap by comparison, many will still be measured in the thousands of dollars. Buying Faulkner is not for the faint of wallet.

Faulkner was prolific. He wrote many books; those books went through many printings in many languages and in many countries. His writing appeared in magazines and on movie screens. More has been written about Faulkner than any writer other than Shakespeare. Storing all the materials that might fit within the parameters of a Faulkner collection would take hundreds and hundreds of feet of shelving.

Of course, this does not mean that you should forget about collecting Faulkner. It means that you should think seriously about *why* you want to collect Faulkner. What are you looking for, what are you hoping to accomplish? Just as it is both possible and necessary to draw up a blueprint before trying to assemble a house, it makes a great deal of sense to get an idea before you start of what you hope to have when you have a "Faulkner collection." A big mistake most novice collectors make is not knowing what their focus is, resulting in a collection that has no discernable form and no way of deciding if something should or should not be added to the collection.

And in the case of Faulkner it can result in investing large amounts of time and money only to find that you cannot afford to go forward and can no longer go back. My real advice to one starting out to collect Faulkner is to decide, before beginning, why you are collecting and to make realistic assessments of how much time, space, and money are available for the pursuit.

There are two basic motivations for collecting anything, and they both apply to Faulkner. Collecting Faulkner as an investment is not a bad idea. Faulkner prices have done very well compared with other commodities over the last thirty years, or even the last five. Buy Faulkner selectively and you might realize a nice profit. I will not give specific investment advice here, I will give only some basic guidelines. If you are interested in buying Faulkner to make a profit you should study the book market as you would the stock market; you might be well advised to hire a Faulkner broker, as you might a stock broker. Your paramount concern should be with condition. You need to buy the best preserved copies available, for in the long run they are more likely to increase in value than inferior copies. Scarcity is a great equalizer; damaged products that are almost nonexistent in perfect condition may still be fine investments. And demand plays a big part in the Faulkner market. *The Sound and the Fury* and *Light in August* and *Absalom, Absalom!* are experiencing extraordinary market appreciation. But buying for investment is always a risk, and you should not start unless you are prepared to accept losses.

The other reason for collecting is emotional, which can cover almost anything other than money. An investor could just as easily be buying plumbing supplies, but an emotional collector wants something in particular, and nothing else will do. This paper is aimed at those who want Faulkner in their lives.

There is no such thing as a "proper" collection for an emotional collector. A collection can consist of anything a person would like it to. The owner can define a collection, just as Faulkner defined his county, by saying both what is and is not in it. A collection need not include *everything*, and it need not include expensive things. The rule for investors—buy the best that money can buy—can be modified for emotional collectors: buy the best that can reasonably be afforded. If you are serious about collecting, I would advise against always settling for the least expensive copy available—there is not necessarily virtue or happiness in being miserly. But neither will there be happiness in putting yourself into debt for something you do not need.

I meant to scare you with my introductory warning about cost. Hardback first editions[2] can be quite expensive. But a collection does not need to include first editions. It might not even need to include hardbound books. Here are some examples.

Most Faulkner stories appeared in magazines before appearing in book form, which is to say that the true first edition of a story is often a magazine. There are some that are extremely difficult to find,[3] but for the most part a collection of magazines with Faulkner appearances will satisfy the three rules an ordinary collector should keep in mind: the collection has a definition, it is affordable, and it will occupy a finite space.

Faulkner paperbacks often have much more attractive cover art than the Faulkner hardcovers and are considerably less expensive. I would love to see a reasonably complete collection of Faulkner paperbacks. If you think American editions are too easy to find, you can try British (challenge for advanced collectors: while paperbacks almost never have dust jackets the first British edition of *Soldiers' Pay*, published by Penguin Books, did). Or you can see if a second copy of the Burmese edition of *The Bear* exists.

Faulkner wrote for the movies; the movies wrote for Faulkner. You can collect posters, scripts, photos, and so forth pertaining to movies Faulkner wrote or that are based on Faulkner novels or stories. You'll get beautiful graphics that will impress friends who think Faulkner depressing and unreadable.[4]

Faulkner's Nobel Prize Speech is his best known nonfiction and one of his most recognized writings of any kind. There are people who think it masterful, and those who think it the height of insincerity—it is writing that affects people. It was published in pamphlet form, on posters, in anthologies, in magazines, and in these formats in many countries all over the world. There might be 300 distinct items containing that speech in whole or in excerpt. Most of them will be affordable, not just in Faulkner terms but by any collecting standards. When assembled, they will fit on a small number of shelf units, so you will not need to banish your kids to the garage to make room for the collection. If you need further incentive, consider that to the best of my knowledge no one has attempted a complete collection of the Nobel Prize Speech. This means that when you have succeeded to a great degree you will be able to write a bibliography of your collection that other collectors will thank you for and want to read.

These are just some examples of collections within the reach of an average person. As a collector you can carve out any other territory that appeals to you.

What appeals to most people—even after having been told about other options—is American "first editions."[5] My warning notwithstanding, it is possible to collect Faulkner first editions. You can assemble a satisfying collection without *The Sound and the Fury* or the other titles you cannot reasonably afford. Even in this day of escalating prices for Faulkner, several titles can be found in adequate first edition condition for under $100 each.[6] This is good news! The bad news is that collecting "first editions" is not trivial. There are details you need to learn, understand, and remember. And if you are new at this, you may be surprised to find that *collecting* Faulkner can be as challenging as reading him.

If you are going to collect "first editions" you need to know that "edition" and "printing" are two different concepts. An "edition" is, essentially, text. It is the words that are in the book, the kind and size of the typeface used to put the words on the pages, the width of the lines on a page, the number of lines on a page, the illustrations, if any. An edition in nontechnical terms is internal appearance. While external appearance—the binding—can also define an edition, it is the internal features that are most important.

As a general rule the text cannot change within an edition, except to correct printing errors. Correction of a word incorrectly inserted by the publisher or the correction of a flaw in the printing process is permissible, but anything resembling a textual rewrite creates a new edition, as does a new arrangement of the text on the page. Within an edition all texts should look and read alike.

A "printing" is an occasion when the printing press was put to use. A publisher will specify a number of copies to be printed the first time a book is being produced. Modern best sellers might be produced in quantities of hundreds of thousands of copies at a time; Faulkner's titles were generally produced in quantities of less than three thousand. When the copies sell out, the publisher needs to produce more. If the same text setup is used, what is being created is a subsequent printing. An edition can, and often does, go through many printings. Thus, one can have a first edition, first printing; a first edition, second printing; a first edition, third printing; and so on. And the same applies to a second, third, or later edition. The publication pedigree of most books includes both an edition number and a printing number. To be collectible a book generally must be the first printing of the first edition.

In common usage the correct description "first edition, first printing" has been shortened to simply "first edition." Reputable sellers using the simple term "first edition" should be describing a first printing of that edition. Not all sellers are reputable, or sufficiently knowledgeable. It is essential that collectors keep in mind that a "first edition, ninth printing" can be accurately described as a "first edition" because such a book is, in fact, a first edition copy. But it is not a *collectible* first edition copy. If there is any doubt about whether a book meets your needs, you must investigate further.

One further detail is important. Sometimes a change in production occurs not just between one printing and the next, which is typically when production errors are corrected, but in the course of the production of a particular printing. The most famous instance of this in the world of Faulkner is *As I Lay Dying*. Through an error the first capital letter on page 11 of the first printing of the first edition was not even with the rest of the line of type. The difference is not microscopic; it is quite noticeable. And someone did notice it. After about 200 copies had been printed the press was stopped, the capital "I" was knocked back into line, and the printing continued, with the remaining 1,000 copies or so produced with the "I" properly lined up. The difference in appearance is called a "state"—the dropped "I" is the first state, the correctly lined up "I" is the second state. A collector prefers the first edition, first printing, first state.

There are few instances of different states within the first edition, first printing in Faulkner. The other best known examples are *The Town* and *Go Down, Moses*. The first state of *The Town* has gray paper for the pastedowns and free end pages;[7] the second state has white pages. There are also some binding differences. The binding of *Go Down, Moses* is available in nine different colors—black is the first state, the other colors are tied for second. Otherwise, you do not need to worry about the "state" of a Faulkner book.[8]

Identifying "edition" is generally not difficult. First step is to make sure that a copy in consideration is published by the publisher that had been responsible for the first edition of that book.[9] For instance, the first publisher of *Mosquitoes* was the firm Boni and Liveright. This means that a copy published by Horace Liveright, or Liveright Publishing Company, is not what you want.[10] Also, the book first came out in 1927; so if you see a much later date you likely do not have a first edition, whatever else the copyright page might say.

Identifying printing is much less easy. There is *no* uniform rule for identifying the printing of a book. Each publisher gets to decide for itself whether or not to include this information in a book, and if so how. Practices vary widely from publisher to publisher, and publishers can change practices over time. The only firm rule is that if there is an explicit reference to a second or later printing the book is not a first printing.

While this is not true for all books by all authors, for Faulkner the general guideline is that printing number can be determined from the copyright page.[11] A first printing of a Faulkner first edition almost always says "first edition" or "first printing" on the copyright page. Almost, but not always. There is no statement at all in the first printing of *Soldiers' Pay*, *Mosquitoes*, *Sartoris*, *A Green Bough*, *Doctor Martino*, *Absalom, Absalom!*, *Knight's Gambit*, and *Requiem for a Nun*. The first printing of these books is identified by the absence of a statement of a later printing.

What I have given here is the general guideline for books published during Faulkner's lifetime. More recent publications have variations on these rules. As a more complete overview on identifying printings I recommend a recent edition of *First Editions: A Guide to Identification* edited by Edward Zempel; or the *Faulkner Author Price Guide* or *Collected Books: The Guide* to *Values* 2002, both by Allen and Patricia Ahearn. All of these are currently in print. Do not be embarrassed about consulting a guide—even experienced dealers use them constantly.

As with all good rules there are exceptions. The first is that book club copies do not count. Books distributed by book clubs are almost never collectible, even if the book appears to be a first printing. During Faulkner's lifetime, copies distributed by the major book clubs were so designated by a small, clearly defined indentation on the lower right corner of the back cover of the book. The indentation might take different shapes—square, circle, or a decorative figure were used. What matters is that it has the appearance of being intentional. Look closely, for sometimes it is small. If you see an intentional indentation you should assume that the book is a book club copy and so not collectible. It is true that an emotional collector can follow the common sense of his or her budget, but a book club copy is not acceptable as a first edition. It is good only for reading.[12]

While one might think that Faulkner was too "difficult" for the mass consumption of book clubs several titles were distributed that way. Book club copies of *The Reivers* are frequently offered as first editions because the copyright page has the statement, but the little dot on the back cover is the determining factor. You must also look for a book club mark on *Collected Stories, The Faulkner Reader, A Fable, The Wishing Tree,* and *Requiem For a Nun.*[13]

The exception to the no-book-club rule is if a book has importance and was not produced outside a book club. The best example of this in Faulkner is *Miss Zilphia Gant,* published by the Book Club of Texas in 1932. This was the first publication of this story, and in fact the only publication until it was included in *The Uncollected Stories* forty-six years later. The book is considered an essential part of a Faulkner collection, notwithstanding its book club origin, and frequently sells for over $1,500.

The normal practice is represented by the three hardbound volume set in a slipcase of the Snopes trilogy. This was never sold commercially, it had the limited distribution of the book club, and is a very attractive set; but because these are not first printings of anything and the material is all readily available elsewhere, the book club origin is a kiss of death. The set is not considered collectible and has no value except as copies to be read.

The other principal exception to the "first edition, first printing" rule is a copy discarded by a library. An ex-library copy will do only if nothing else is within reach. Faulkner prices being what they are, you might find that you can not afford any but ex-library copies. Unlike book club copies, which are never acceptable, ex-library copies will do until fortune smiles more sweetly. Just be aware that you are compromising greatly, and should consider getting a "better" copy if and when possible.

Thus far I have permitted the assumption that a first edition will be a hardcover book. Most often this is correct, but in fact a first edition need not always be a hardback. Some books get published *only* as a paperback. *A Rose For Emily and Other Stories*, published by Armed Services Editions, was published only in softcover form. Sometimes a softcover edition comes before the hardbound. Although I do not think this ever happened with Faulkner, Richard Ford's *The Sportswriter* is an example of this—the softcover predated the hardback by many years. A true collection of first editions may include softcovers as well as hardcovers. Printing and state matter with softcovers just as they do with hardcovers.

To be collectible a book that originally came with a dust jacket should still have its jacket. From about 1920 on, most hardbound books and some rare softbound books have been published in jackets. The same considerations concerning desirability of some printings over others applies to dust jackets. Jackets are modified more frequently than books. Sometimes changes are subtle. Perhaps only a single digit changes somewhere on the jacket. Sometimes an entire block of text or an illustration is replaced. Sometimes the jacket is redesigned altogether. Differences between jackets are designated as states, not editions or printings.

Generally, a particular state of a jacket went with a particular printing. Sometimes a particular state of a jacket went with several printings of the book. The book might have gone through several printings before any changes were made to the jacket. And sometimes the jacket changed even during the course of a single printing. A collector needs to know which jackets went with which printings of which editions. If a particular printing of a book was originally available in two different jacket states, a collectible copy is acceptable in either of those jackets. The earlier state of the jacket is the more desirable. *But*, a jacket that was not originally packaged with a particular printing cannot be put with that printing later. If a first printing was only produced in a first state jacket, a copy in a second state jacket is not in acceptable collectible condition.

The guides to editions are of almost no use in identifying jackets. There are some obvious details a collector can look for. If a dust jacket mentions a book that had not yet been published when the book in question was published, the jacket is a later state. The presence of reviews of the book itself generally signals a later state dust jacket, as the first state jacket would have been prepared before reviews had been written. If the price on the jacket is higher than books were generally selling for at the time of first publication the jacket is likely a later state. (And if the dust jacket has no printed price at all it may well be from a book club copy, and so not acceptable for that reason.) Beyond the obvious, though, it is sad but true that in this realm there is no substitute for experience; and even general experience in book selling might not be enough. Mistakes with dust jackets are distressingly common, even by reputable honest dealers.

First printings of only three Faulkner books were available in either first or second state dust jackets: *The Sound and the Fury* (price change for *Humanity Uprising*, a book listed on the back panel), *The Hamlet* (reviews added to the back panel), and *The Town* (numerals removed from the bottom of the front flap). For all other books only one dust jacket is correct for the first printing. Any jacket but the first state is an incorrect jacket.[14]

Most of the value of a first edition in a dust jacket is in the jacket. A book in a correct jacket is typically worth ten times or more a book without a jacket. I mentioned in a note above that *Soldiers' Pay* in dust jacket sells in five digits; the book without jacket sells for about $700, and a copy in the wrong jacket will not sell for much more. Be very careful when spending a premium for a first edition in a dust jacket, for if you get a wrong jacket you might have thrown away a large amount of money, even if the book itself is a correct first edition.

Condition matters in collecting, but how to evaluate it is largely a personal decision. The ideal is a book looking as it did when it was first published, with no flaws from use or misuse. Most changes from this original condition will be negatives, as the book shows signs of longevity. The fewer flaws the better is the unfailing motto. Some rare events are positives: an authentic Faulkner signature, or a copy once belonging to someone important—these add value. How bad is a particular flaw? How good is a particular plus? How to evaluate a combination of pluses and minuses? Book plates, owners' signatures, tears in the dust jacket, tape inside the jacket—all of these are details you need to notice and weigh. There is no mathematical formula for balancing the pros and cons. Decide for yourself what bothers you to what degree, compromising on condition as necessary to remain true to the primary principle of spending no more than can reasonably be afforded.

I will make two suggestions. First, a book without a dust jacket will likely be less satisfying in the long run than one with a jacket, even a flawed jacket. While jacketless books will be found for considerably less money than jacketed ones, I think it wiser to buy one book in jacket than ten without. Not so much for the sake of financial appreciation, though that may likely be the case, but because the book is more *complete* in its jacket.

Second, a rebinding is always an undesirable change from the original. Edition is defined by text, but a first edition is an entire package. I would rather have the original covers in poor condition than exquisite leather replacing those covers. This does not mean that a book rebound in fine leather has no value, just that the value will be in the binding, not as a Faulkner first edition.[15]

More exciting than first editions are materials signed or personally created by Faulkner. Some authors signed anything put in front of them, and signed materials from them are relatively common. Not so with Faulkner. He signed very rarely and very reluctantly. I state categorically that he never signed a book plate, likely never signed an index card, and might not have signed more than a dozen "slips of paper" in his entire lifetime. The overwhelming majority of the materials on the market purportedly signed by Faulkner are forgeries. One considering the purchase of signed Faulkner materials should assume that such materials are forgeries until proven authentic and should not pay any more for such an item than would be paid for a novelty or curiosity unless and until legitimacy is established beyond serious doubt.

The safest signed materials you can purchase are copies from the seventeen books that were produced by a publisher in a "signed limited edition." These copies were signed by Faulkner personally, in quantities as stated in the limitation for each book, ranging from a low of 100 for *Go Down, Moses* to a high of 1,000 for *A Fable*. All together around 12,000 official, signed copies were issued by publishers. These represent the only signed Faulkner materials offering little risk of forgery. If the book appears to be genuine the signature is almost certainly authentic.[16]

Faulkner did sign some materials outside the official limited editions, for friends, relatives, and people who actually did him favors. These authentically signed books are quite special and make splendid additions to a collection. I recommend looking only at books with additional information written in by Faulkner, preferably the name of the person getting the book, the date and/or the location. These biographical details likely will not be known to a forger and often can be verified through research into Faulkner's life. Also, the additional writing gives more opportunity to authenticate what is written than does just a signature. Handwritten letters are particularly rare but they do exist. Examine the entire body of the letter, and make sure that every character is in Faulkner's style.

Letters that are typed leave us with the problem of just a signature to authenticate. Faulkner's original book typescripts have been published, as have some letters.[17] Compare the typing in those published volumes with the typing in the letter to see if the typist appears to be the same. Identify the recipient. Was this a person who was likely to have received the letter in question? Authenticating a Faulkner typed letter involves detective work.

While it is true that emotional collectors need not be as concerned with value as investment collectors, spending thousands or even hundreds of dollars on materials that are not what is expected will be neither financially nor emotionally satisfying. There is little risk of serious injury in reading classic Faulkner "incorrectly"; there is considerable risk in buying those books incorrectly. I therefore urge anyone tempted to buy expensive Faulkner materials to take specific precautions.

If you want to do the buying yourself, treat the challenge as you would any difficult and potentially risky undertaking. Take seriously the acquisition of knowledge. Go into used book stores and libraries and look at the books on the shelves. If there are multiple copies of a title, compare them. Remember what you see and learn.[18] When you meet a dealer specializing in Faulkner, ask questions.

Bibliographies have been published of several major Faulkner collections. The best is *Catalog 48: The Carl Peterson Collection* published by Serendipity Books. Although nominally a catalog of materials for sale, it offers the most comprehensive, organized discussion of what was published when and what things should look like. This catalog is still available from the store.[19] The Serendipity catalog is an updated version of Carl Peterson's original *A Faulkner Collector's Notebook*, which is now out of print. Peterson was one of the two leading Faulkner collectors. The other, Louis Daniel Brodsky, has also published a bibliography of his collection: *Faulkner: A Comprehensive Guide to the Brodsky Collection; Volume 1: The Bibliography* (available from University Press of Mississippi). Until the publication of these volumes *William Faulkner: Man Working 1919–1962*, compiled by Linton Massey for the University Press of Virginia, was *the* reference for Faulkneriana (this, too, is out of print). All of these offer a wealth of information on what an edition should look like, or should not look like. Some offer guidance on dust jackets. They are indispensable reference for anyone wanting to build a collection. No one collecting should be without a good reference library. Anyone who is serious should have *all* of them! There are other, smaller bibliographies as well. Reading bibliographies might be rather dull, but consider collecting Faulkner a course and a good bibliography the text. You might pass the course without doing the reading, but the highest grades ultimately will go to those who put in the most effort. And a lower grade might mean thousands of wasted dollars!

Collecting Faulkner is a discipline within the broader field of book collecting generally, and so you need to know not just the details pertaining particularly to Faulkner collecting but also terms and concepts that arise in book collecting at large. Book collecting has specialized language and operating principles. There are many good guides available on the details of collecting. *ABC for Book Collectors* by John Carter and Nicholas Barker is available in a 2000 edition and is quite helpful.

As you learn the "whats" you should also be learning the "how muches." This is no laughing matter in the context of goods changing hands for four or five digits. Knowing whether a book is a first edition is important; so too is knowing whether it is a good value. You need not be obsessed with value to appreciate knowing that a book offered at $1,000 can frequently be found for half that. This is information you will not have until you have spent some time in the field.

Which is why I suggest an initial period during which you will only study without purchasing. A year might be good idea, at least six months should be the minimum during which you will put no money at risk while you get a better familiarity with the concepts and specifics. The restraint you show today will likely spare you preventable mistakes. And while it might be agonizing to turn down that bargain in front of you, it might take a few months of studying the market to learn whether it really was a bargain.

Safer than trying to do it yourself is to hire the services of a dealer who specializes in Faulkner. This does not eliminate the need to become better informed yourself. You will still need to be able to discuss materials intelligently with your guide, and that means learning at least general book collecting terminology and some basics of Faulkner collecting and pricing. Working with a dealer will reduce the amount you will need to do yourself and, more importantly, will greatly reduce the risk of uncorrectable mistakes. It will cost you money in fees charged by the dealer but it can be money well spent. Do not yourself buy materials costing more than minimal amounts that you have any uncertainty about; instead, let the dealer make the purchases for you. The dealer will screen out materials that are not as they should be; and if the dealer makes a mistake (s)he will accept returns and issue refunds.

Some serious collectors wish to remain anonymous, preferring that their wealth, assets, or spending not become common knowledge. If that is a concern for you, working through a dealer will help keep your collecting private.

Whether you work with a dealer or build your collection yourself there is little harm and much excitement in looking for materials. There has never been a better time to look for books. The internet has put at our fingertips books that as little as ten years ago may as well have been on another planet since we had so little chance of ever learning of their existence. Now, a few keyboard strokes and mouse clicks will put before us materials from sellers from across the globe, or even on the next block. The internet is the best way to learn more with less effort.

The big internet auction is e-Bay (www.ebay.com). It has also become one of the best ways to build a Faulkner (or any other kind of) collection. Typically a search for "William Faulkner" in e-Bay will result in a list of 900 items. Most likely will be of no interest; some might cause an increased heart rate. The common, the less common, and the breathtakingly rare have been offered for sale at e-Bay auction.[20] There is no reason to think that the future won't hold more of the same.

There are other online auctions as well. Yahoo and Amazon are two that have survived against e-Bay's almost complete control of the market. As time permits, you might find it worthwhile to check those auctions as well.[21]

An auction is a competitive buying environment, in which potential buyers compete and the person offering to pay the most wins.[22] It is nerve wracking and uncertain. Less anxiety inducing is buying for set prices. There are several online databases in which member dealers can list items for sale at specified prices, as in conventional catalogs. The biggest, my favorite, is ABE Books (www.abebooks.com). Search for particular titles or do a general search for Faulkner and you will be given a list of every book in the database meeting your search criteria. For one title there might be hundreds of copies; for "Faulkner" there might be tens of thousands.

The internet has altered the pricing landscape in very complicated ways. In summary, the prices of "common" things have come down, while the prices of truly rare items have gone up. But new collectors typically get carried away and overpay. And as dealers see higher prices they start raising their set prices, which often don't get met, because they are unreasonable. ABE lets you sort search results by price, from lowest to highest. The range of prices for seemingly identical things seems explainable only by dealer greed. Assuming that two sellers have comparable reliability there is generally little reason to buy an expensive copy when a less expensive one in the same condition is there for the taking.

There are also great "real world" markets for books. Visit all the used book stores you can get to. Frequently. You never know what will be on the shelf, or might be brought out from behind the counter if you ask. Let the dealer know your interest, even if you see nothing of interest today you might get a call in the future if something you want comes in. Even a dealer who specializes in something not of interest might run across books he does not want for his own use and would be willing to let you get them for a reasonable "finder's fee." It never hurts to make friends with someone buying and selling anything.

Some dealers still issue catalogs on paper. See if getting on the mailing list makes sense for you. This is often a way to "see" the stock of dealers who do not have shops you can walk into.

There are real world auction houses. Christies and Sothebys sell all manner of goods, as long as they are the finest in the world. Their several branches handle only the most expensive items, so unless you are affluent you might find the experience frustrating. Swann's Galleries in New York City is the biggest book-specialty auction company. Other book specialty auction companies include Pacific Book Auctions in California; Waverly in Washington, D.C.; and Baltimore Book Company. Not all sales will include Faulkner, or literature at all. Contact the companies for a schedule and description. All of the companies I have mentioned maintain high professional standards. You can be confident that books are as described, and that purchases should go smoothly. Most companies will let you submit bids through the mail or over the internet or bid live over the telephone if you can not attend in person.

Collecting is an expression of a passion, and any author or book or poem you feel passionate about can be a fit subject for a collection. Some collections will go down in value. I collect one author other than Faulkner, and much of what I have bought by her is worth less today than when I bought it. Don't worry about it. Buy it because it makes you happy, and it will make you happy. If you are going to fill your life with "stuff," why not make a lot of that stuff books? As long as your collecting does not become an obsession or addiction it can express itself in as many ways as your life will permit.

NOTES

1. Faulkner's first book, *The Marble Faun*, sells for $5,000 without any jacket and with its pages falling out. Maybe even with some pages missing. Add a decrepit jacket and add $15,000. The signed, limited edition of *Go Down, Moses* is now trading at around $20,000. *Soldiers' Pay* in the rare dust jacket sold at auction in 2000 for $32,000. This turned out to have been a bargain, for the next year a copy brought $50,000.

2. "First edition" is one of the most important terms in book collecting. It actually has a very precise meaning. Unless you already have a good working understanding of the term "first edition," do not assume that you know it. I will be defining the term later in this paper.

3. Faulkner contributed to several University of Mississippi publications in the teens and twenties. All of those school journals are virtually impossible to find. Your ability as a collector will be judged by whether you find the August 6, 1919 issue of the *New Republic* containing "L'Apres Midi d'un Faune" (Faulkner's first commercially published piece); the three issues of the *Double Dealer* containing the material later collected in *New Orleans Sketches*; the April 1930 issue of *Forum* with "A Rose For Emily"; and, perhaps the most elusive of the theoretically obtainable Faulkner periodicals, *College Life*, Winter 1936 issue, with "Two Dollar Wife."

4. The Holy Grail of Faulkner movie materials is anything original from *The Story of Temple Drake*, the 1933 film version of *Sanctuary*.

5. Because Faulkner is an American author, "first edition" in his context implies first *American* edition. There is no reason why this should be so, for a book will have a "first edition" in every country in which it was published. In some cases a foreign edition preceded the first American—for instance, *New Orleans Sketches* was published in Japan before it was published here. *Faulkner at Nagano*, an important collection of speeches, was published *only* in Japan. In this paper I will follow convention and use the phrase "first edition" to mean first U.S. edition. The principles of collecting apply equally to foreign editions; papers could be devoted to the specifics of foreign editions.

6. *Requiem For a Nun, A Fable, The Town, The Mansion,* and *The Reivers* can regularly be found for less than $100. Most posthumous works other than limited editions should be under $100 as well.

7. Hold a hardbound book in your hands. Open the cover. The paper pasted to the inside of the cover is the pastedown. That paper should actually be twice as wide as the cover, so that the part to the right of the cover looks like a blank first page in the book. The continuation of the pastedown is called the free end page, or fly page. There are front and rear pastedowns and free end pages, for the front and rear of the book.

8. How important is state? It depends. With *As I Lay Dying* the value difference between the first and second state is about $800. With *The Town* the difference is less than $50. With *Go Down, Moses* the value difference varies from dealer to dealer and variant binding to variant binding.

9. *The Marble Faun*—Four Seas Co, 1924
    Soldiers' Pay—Boni and Liveright, 1926
    Mosquitoes—Boni and Liveright, 1927
    Sartoris—Harcourt, Brace and Company, 1929
    The Sound and the Fury—Cape and Smith, 1929
    As I Lay Dying—Cape and Smith, 1930
    Sanctuary—Cape and Smith, 1931
    These Thirteen—Cape and Smith, 1931
    Light in August—Smith and Haas, 1932
    A Green Bough—Smith and Haas, 1933
    Doctor Martino—Smith and Haas, 1934
    Pylon—Smith and Haas, 1935
    Absalom, Absalom!—Random House, 1936
    The Unvanquished—Random House, 1938
    The Wild Palms—Random House, 1939
    The Hamlet—Random House, 1940
    Go Down, Moses—Random House, 1942
    Intruder in the Dust—Random House, 1948
    Knight's Gambit—Random House, 1949
    Collected Stories—Random House, 1950
    Requiem for a Nun—Random House, 1951
    A Fable—Random House, 1954
    Big Woods—Random House, 1955
    The Town—Random House, 1957
    New Orleans Sketches—Rutgers University Press, 1958
    The Mansion—Random House, 1959
    The Reivers—Random House, 1962

This list includes only American editions of books published during Faulkner's lifetime, excluding limited editions which had only one printing. A complete list would include books published posthumously and foreign editions, especially English.

10. Sticklers for accuracy will point out that this is not true—a successor firm could acquire the original plates and continue printing, replacing only the publisher's name, thereby continuing with the same edition. It is safe to say that the successor firm will be creating later printings. Since the purpose of this paper is to help the inexperienced in identifying "first edition, first printing," my simplistic explanation in the text provides a procedure that will give the desired result.

11. The "copyright page" is the page containing the copyright information for the book. This page is almost always on the back of the title page. If you do not see it there look through the pages before and after the text until you find it somewhere.

12. The term "reading copy" is used in a pejorative way by dealers and collectors to indicate a copy that has no collectible value and is good for nothing but reading. Later printings, ex-library, book club, damaged copies, and paperbacks fall into this category. While there is some merit in distinguishing "collectible" copies from "noncollectible" copies, I mean no insult to books from the wrong side of the tracks or people who own them. Works of fiction are written to be read, and I hope that all collectors will have copies that they can risk getting dirty or torn in order to remind themselves why they are collecting in the first place.

13. In recent years book clubs have stopped putting an indentation on the back cover. Sometimes a statement appears on the copyright page. Often there is no visible sign at all. Only experience will tell you whether a particular book was issued by a book club or not. None of the mass-produced Faulkner books of the last twenty years have any significant value in any edition, so whether a copy is book club or not makes little monetary difference.

14. This is not technically accurate. The dust jacket for *Mosquitoes* first featured a design known as the Yachting Party, before the Mosquito design was settled on. Virtually all first printing copies of *Mosquitoes* were wrapped in the Mosquito design jacket. The Yachting Party design was used for later editions by later publishers, but only one Yachting Party jacket—literally one—from Boni and Liveright is known to exist. So while the Mosquito design is technically the second state of the first printing dust jacket the phenomenal scarcity of the first state jacket directs my advice to not even think about it.

15. There is a third reason for collecting Faulkner, besides investment and emotion—for research. Scholars working on Faulkner need first editions for proper citations. Because the only concern is the text and because the text remains essentially the same for all printings of an edition, a scholar can work with a later printing of a first edition; might not care if a copy is ex-library, book club, unattractive or rebound; and might not need a dust jacket at all. Scholars can save a considerable amount of money by working with "noncollectable" first edition copies. Keep in mind that textual typographic errors do sometimes get corrected in later printings. Whether the proper citation should be the first printing incorrect version or the later-printing corrected version will come from the rules of scholarship.

16. The Faulkner signed limited editions were published without dust jackets. Most were published instead in plain glassine wrappers. The absence of the original wrapper is not considered a defect; the presence of a genuine wrapper is considered a bonus. Two of these—*Pylon* and *A Fable*—were issued in cardboard slipcases. The latter should always have the case present; the former is difficult though not impossible to find with the case.

17. Garland Publishing issued at least forty-four over-sized volumes of photocopies of Faulkner typescripts. Reproductions of typed Faulkner letters can be seen in *Faulkner: A Comprehensive Guide to the Brodsky Collection, Volume 2: The Letters* (Jackson: University Press of Mississippi, 1989).

18. Libraries are good places to see editions that are no longer in print. Public libraries sometimes replace original bindings with sturdier generic bindings. Learn to recognize original from replacement bindings.

19. 1201 University Avenue, Berkeley, CA 94702.

20. In spring of 2003 e-Bay was the venue for a copy of the second printing of *Soldiers' Pay* in dust jacket. While the normal rule is that only a first printing is collectible, this second state dust jacket is not owned by any of the big collections. Based on current information this may be the only copy of this jacket to have survived.

21. Internet auctions have their own rules, tactics, and etiquette. Outlining that information is beyond the scope of this paper. Be aware that you do need to learn how to swim in an internet auction before you jump in.

22. In theory—the widespread misuse of "reserves" (an undisclosed figure above the stated minimum acceptable bid) in internet auctions means this often is *not* the case, for when there is a reserve there will be no sale unless the reserve as well as the minimum is met. This is one of the things you need to learn about internet auctions.

Contributors

Eric Gary Anderson teaches American and American Indian literature at George Mason University. He is the author of *American Indian Literature and the Southwest: Contexts and Dispositions* as well as numerous essays in books such as *Speak to Me Words: Essays on Contemporary American Indian Poetry* and *South to a New Place: Region, Literature*. Currently he is working on two research projects, one on early Southern captivity narratives and one on William Faulkner's ecological imagination.

Seth Berner is a book dealer and collector living in Portland, Maine, specializing in William Faulkner. For years he has maintained the world's biggest online catalog of materials by, about, and pertaining to Faulkner, at www.bernerbooks.com.

Jeanne de la Houssaye is a nationally recognized illustrator. She studied painting and design with John McCrady and later earned a degree in communications from Loyola University. She lives and works in New Orleans, loves American authors, and paddles the sandy creeks of Louisiana and Mississippi in a knock-your-eye-out orange kayak.

Ann Fisher-Wirth is professor of English at the University of Mississippi, where she teaches courses in poetry and environmental literature. She is the author of *William Carlos Williams and Autobiography: The Woods of His Own Nature* and of many articles on American writers; she has also published a book of poems, *Blue Window*; a chapbook, *The Trinket Poems*; and many poems in national journals. She has had Fulbrights in Switzerland and Sweden. In 2005 she will become vice president, and in 2006 president, of ASLE: Association for the Study of Literature and Environment.

Thomas L. McHaney is Kenneth M. England Professor of Southern Literature at Georgia State University in Atlanta. His most recent books are a trilogy in the Gale Group's Guides to Great Literature series, published in 2000: a biography of Faulkner, a study of *The Sound and the Fury*, and a history of the Southern Renaissance.

François Pitavy, professor emeritus at the University of Burgundy, is a specialist of Southern literature and particularly of William Faulkner. His latest book is a monograph on *The Sound and the Fury: Le bruit et la fureur de William Faulkner*. He is coeditor of Faulkner's novels in Gallimard Pléiade series, currently at work on volume four, for which he is retranslating *A Fable* and *Requiem for a Nun*.

Scott Slovic is professor of literature and environment and chair of the graduate program in literature and environment at the University of Nevada, Reno. He is the author, editor, or coeditor of twelve books, and since 1995 he has edited the journal *ISLE: Interdisciplinary Studies in Literature and Environment*.

Cecelia Tichi is the William R. Kenan Jr. Professor of English at Vanderbilt University. Among other books, she is the author of *Exposes and Excess: Muckraking in America, 1900–2000* and coeditor, with Amy Lang, of the forthcoming *What Democracy Looks Like: A New Critical Realism for the Post-Seattle World*.

Joseph R. Urgo is professor and chair of the Department of English at the University of Mississippi. He is the author of *Faulkner's Apocrypha: "A Fable," Snopes, and the Spirit of Human Rebellion*, among other books and essays on American literature and culture.

Michael Wainwright worked ten years as a computer programmer, first for the British Ministry of Defense and then with the solar energy division of British Petroleum, before completing a BA in literature and mathematics at the University of Kingston. He earned his MA and PhD from Royal Holloway (University of London), where he lectures in twentieth-century American literature. *Katabasis*, an original screenplay, is currently in preproduction for independent television in the U.K.

Philip Weinstein is the author of several books, the most recent being *Faulkner's Subject: A Cosmos No One Owns, What Else But Love?: The Ordeal of Race in Faulkner and Morrison*, and *Unknowing: The Work of Modernist Fiction*. Past president of the William Faulkner Society (2000–2003), he also edited *The Cambridge Companion to Faulkner*.

Index